Athletic Director's SURVIVAL GUIDE

MIKE KOEHLER & NANCY GIEBEL

PRENTICE HALL
Englewood Cliffs, New Jersey 07632

Library of Congress Cataloging-in-Publication Data

Koehler, Mike
Athletic director's survival guide : ready-to-use techniques & materials for effective leadership / Mike Koehler, Nancy Giebel.
p. cm.
ISBN 0-13-531476-3
1. School sports—United States—Management. 2. Athletic directors—United States. 3. Sports administration—United States. I. Giebel, Nancy. II. Title.
GV346.K64 1997 96-52230
796'.06'9—dc21 CIP

Printed in the United States of America

10 9 8 7 6 5 4 3 2 1

ISBN 0-13-531476-3

PRENTICE HALL
Career & Personal Development
Englewood Cliffs, NJ 07632
A Simon & Schuster Company

On the World Wide Web at http://www.phdirect.com

Prentice Hall International (UK) Limited, *London*
Prentice Hall of Australia Pty. Limited, *Sydney*
Prentice Hall Canada Inc., *Toronto*
Prentice Hall Hispanoamericana, S.A., *Mexico*
Prentice Hall of India Private Limited, *New Delhi*
Prentice Hall of Japan, Inc., *Tokyo*
Simon & Schuster Asia Pte. Ltd., *Singapore*
Editora Prentice Hall do Brasil, Ltda., *Rio de Janeiro*

DEDICATION

We would like to dedicate this book, first of all, to our families for tolerating our incessant demands for more time, then to the many junior high school and high school coaches we have worked with over the years who never cease to amaze us with their commitment and selflessness. It's nice to know that, in spite of media claims to the contrary, our nation's young athletes really are in good hands. Finally, we would like to recognize the self-sacrifice of the hundreds of young athletes we have met over the years, young men and women who have learned the values of dedication and team membership and who assure us by their hard work that the promise of our nation is being fulfilled every day.

ABOUT MIKE

Mike Koehler played fullback for Marquette University and the University of Nebraska, coached high school football for thirty-one years, counseled high school students for twenty-five, and has been an adjunct professor of educational administration and supervision since 1974. Currently, he is devoting all his time to writing, teaching at the university level, speaking at conventions, and consulting with schools on teacher supervision and on the eligibility and recruitment of student athletes. Mike is the author of scores of articles for professional journals, a nationally syndicated radio show, a newspaper column, and the videotape, *The ABCs of Eligibility for the College-Bound Student Athlete*, which is being marketed by the College Board. It currently is in its second edition.

In addition to this book, Mike has written ten other books, the four most recent being *Advising Student Athletes Through the College Recruitment Process*, *Building the Total Athlete*, *Department Head's Survival Guide*, and *Football Coach's Survival Guide*, all with Prentice Hall. He currently is in the planning stages for two more books—one a biography of his grandfather, Jim Thorpe—and is involved in a variety of speaking engagements across the country.

Mike has been married to his wife Pat since 1962. He has three delightful daughters, Kathleen, Carrie, and Peggy; two fine sons-in-law, Bruce and Dwight; and he enjoys time spent with his two grandchildren, Eric Michael and Cassie Jean.

For additional information or to contact Mike for consultation or in-service presentations, write or call:

Mike Koehler
Ideation, Inc.
8246 Voss Rd.
Minocqua, WI 54548
715-358-8802

ABOUT NANCY

Nancy Giebel has been a teacher, coach, administrative assistant, assistant athletic director, and athletic director at Glenbrook South High School for over fifteen years. She was involved in athletics in high school and college, and has coached swimming and diving for over twenty years.

She graduated from Indiana University in 1981, and completed her master's degree in 1986. She is currently working towards completing her doctorate.

Nancy is a member of the National Interscholastic Athletic Administrators Association and is also involved with the Illinois Athletic Directors Association. She has held many conference positions, including program chairperson, and this year is the Illinois Conference Chair.

Ms. Giebel just completed her chairmanship as Diving All-America Chair for the National Interscholastic Swimming Coaches Association. This organization chooses the top diver in the United States for All-America consideration.

ABOUT THIS RESOURCE

The job of the athletic director is probably among the most misunderstood in any school building. Some teachers regard athletic directors as former coaches who are killing time between their last game and their first day of retirement. Many are characterized as likable but ineffective geezers who slap backs, make schedules, and tap the keg at the annual staff picnic. Other teachers see them as personable disciplinarians who know how to "ride herd" on perhaps the most headstrong group of people in the building—the coaching staff.

Unfortunately, each of these perceptions in some schools is true. That's what makes it so difficult for the rest of us to convince the educational community that athletic directors are among the most important people in the school system. Our problem is compounded further by the fact that athletic directors are generally "behind-the-scenes" forces that influence the behaviors of coaches but receive little recognition from others in the building.

The focus of *Athletic Director's Survival Guide*, therefore, is to argue that athletic directors—a significant number of whom are women—perform an essential task within the building, and to identify and discuss strategies and materials that increase both their visibility and their effectiveness. Fortunately, such tasks are relatively easy. Even the most inveterate academic in the building realizes that coaches have a powerful influence on youngsters. Veteran teachers often seek out coaches to help with misbehaving or uncommitted students in class.

Such teachers realize that coaches, perhaps more so than anyone else in the building, have a key to unlock powerful motivational influences in young athletes that can spill over from athletic competition into the classroom. Unlike their classroom counterparts, coaches work with youngsters who are well motivated on the field or court and who value most of the experiences they find in sports. As such, they are receptive to the expectations of their coaches.

It seems reasonable, then, to argue that athletic directors are important people in schools; they influence the coaches who influence the kids. This is a significant responsibility—one that is addressed comprehensively in this book. We look at the functions assigned to athletic directors, discuss successful strategies for achieving them, and provide a wide range of materials that practicing or potential athletic directors can use to make their jobs easier.

These materials consist of sample memos, letters, forms, charts, and other informational materials that can be duplicated and used to interact successfully with coaches, students, administrators, and parents. The book, then, provides insights into the behaviors that make athletic directors successful. It also offers materials that can be used immediately to give added dimension to the job.

Section One, for example, discusses the athletic director's work with student athletes, provides information on emphasizing the balance between academics and athletics and the importance of communicating eligibility standards, training rules, and athletic codes. Section Two discusses the challenging tasks of hiring, motivating, informing, supervising, and evaluating coaches.

Section Three discusses working with parents, using them as allies in the development and maintenance of successful programs. Sections Four and Five address the sometimes complicated and controversial tasks of developing schedules for practice and competition and administering the departmental budget. Each of these tasks requires a great deal of skill if coaches are to interact cooperatively.

Section Six looks at the athletic director as one of the school administrators, and provides strategies for working cooperatively with other departments in the building, for promoting school spirit, and for broadening the visibility and impact of athletics. Section Seven discusses strategies and provides materials for maintaining effective public relations and for establishing relationships with local and state organizations and others like the National Collegiate Athletic Association (NCAA), the National Association of Intercollegiate Athletics (NAIA), and the National Junior College Athletic Association (NJCAA).

Section Eight discusses a process for responding to immediate as well as unanticipated legal issues. This is, perhaps, one of the most critical aspects of the AD's job. Unfortunately, routine responsibilities can be so pressing that many athletic directors are unable to find the time to keep abreast of the many legal issues affecting their jobs. This section considers ways to address those issues.

Section Nine looks at ancillary issues such as working with cheerleaders and pompon squads, finding team physicians, working with commercial recruiters, dealing with booster clubs, and being involved in national organizations for athletic directors. Finally, Section Ten deals with the task of finding and working with support staff: announcers for contests, ticket takers, crowd control personnel, security guards, equipment managers, contest officials, and secretarial and custodial personnel.

Athletic Director's Survival Guide covers the full spectrum of the athletic director's responsibilities. It provides conversational discussions of proven strategies for working with coaches, young athletes, teachers, administrators, and parents; and it offers scores of field-tested materials for administering a complete program of athletics. It is a resource that you will keep within arm's reach; you will read it now and refer to it often in the future. It complements your natural ability to work with others, to coordinate time-consuming and sometimes perplexing tasks, and to overcome the demands of time.

Most important, *Athletic Director's Survival Guide* provides the processes and materials for maintaining a total sports program, for cultivating the competencies of coaches, and for enriching the educational and personal experiences of thousands of young athletes—the ultimate goal of any athletic department.

Mike Koehler

Nancy Giebel

CONTENTS

Pages listed in italics are reproducible pages.

SECTION TWO: WORKING WITH COACHES 33

SECTION THREE: WORKING WITH PARENTS 61

SECTION FOUR: SCHEDULING AND RELATED ORGANIZATIONAL DUTIES 97

SECTION FIVE: DEVELOPING THE BUDGET 125

SECTION SIX: THE ATHLETIC DIRECTOR AS A SCHOOL ADMINISTRATOR 159

SECTION SEVEN: MAINTAINING EFFECTIVE PUBLICITY 201

SECTION EIGHT: KEEPING ON TOP OF LEGAL ISSUES 229

SECTION NINE: CONSIDERING THE ANCILLARY ISSUES 259

SECTION ONE

Meeting All the Needs of Young Athletes

To paraphrase Will Rogers: "The world of sport ain't what it used to be—and never was!" The expected character-building aspects of athletic competition have surrendered, especially in professional sports, to taunting, bench-clearing brawls, gold chains, chest bumping, and trash talk. Recent university studies have revealed that secondary students involved in two or more sports use drugs and alcohol and engage in unprotected sex and violent behavior more than their nonathletic classmates.

As shocking as this may be, perhaps it isn't new. Drinking bouts among college and professional athletes at the turn of the century were legendary, and fighting was commonplace. Ty Cobb climbed into the stands more than once to silence hecklers; rough-housing in John McGraw's clubhouse often caused one or more Giants to miss baseball games; and Jim Thorpe's Oorang Indians, the smallest franchise in the NFL, were often frisked for guns and knives before being permitted by local sheriffs to disembark from trains to get to football games.

It may be that coaches and parents are operating under old-fashioned assumptions about the social and personal value of athletic competition. That parents and others in society put all their eggs in the sports basket for needed exposure to the developmental influence of athletic values may be disappointing. Certainly, sports participation still subjects youngsters to the caring but insistent hand of a coach and to the physical and emotional demands of team membership, but sports alone are no longer able to combat the social influences that result in shocking statistics.

If sports are simply a reflection of society and less the influence on adolescent behavior that we want them to be, we have a lot of work to do if we hope to combat the increased violence in our society, especially in our schools. Teenage homicide is at its highest point in our nation's history. Guns kill fifteen teenagers every day. In a recent ten-year period, teen-age homicide increased well over 200 percent, and schools across the country have reported alarming increases in violence, some indicating that up to 25 percent of all students have been victimized by schoolmates.

Jerry-Szpak and Brown recently reported in the *Journal of Child and Adolescent Substance Abuse* that only 14 percent of adolescent athletes in a recent survey described themselves as nondrinkers and that 21 percent of them reported drinking during the

..ey were surveyed. A couple of years earlier, Carr et al reported in the *Journal of Alcohol and Drug Education* that male athletes in their study drank alcohol significantly more than male nonathletes and that male athletes drank to intoxication significantly more often than female athletes.

Other statistics are almost as significant. Ten percent of teachers claim to be victims of violence, and potential problems are evident in the signs of emerging gang activity in even our most affluent suburbs. That such violence is also reflected in the behaviors of athletes, especially professional athletes, is disturbingly obvious. As a friend once said, "I went to watch a fight and a hockey game broke out!"

Once an isolated example of sports violence, hockey has been joined recently by other professional sports. In just two recent years, athletes in the National Basketball Association (NBA) were involved in twenty-one fights and thirty-six game suspensions. In only one recent year, baseball experienced seventeen brawls and twenty-nine suspensions. Fortunately, the league officials stepped in to develop sanctions for such behavior, but the problem remains.

Violence remains primarily in the attitudes of some professional athletes and coaches. Consider the quote from Earvin "Magic" Johnson, found in a recent copy of the Sunday magazine of the *Chicago Tribune*: "You have to have some dislike for your opponent if you're going to win a championship." George Allen was quoted in the same publication as having said: "Every time you win, you're reborn; when you lose, you die a little."

Such emphases on winning disregard more traditional notions of respect for one's opponent and the uncomplicated pleasures found in participation for its own sake. "Dislike of your opponent" and "dying a little every time you lose" transform athletic competition into a thoughtless disregard of traditional sports values and a stressful preoccupation with winning. Those of us who agree with such statements are a part of the problem. We all must be a part of the solution.

MEETING THE ATHLETIC NEEDS OF STUDENTS

Parents and school personnel must join forces to promote a common value system that develops the character in young athletes our society so desperately seeks. Coaches alone can't do it—not any more. Changing social patterns, modified value systems, and a mindless emphasis on winning at all costs affect so many of us that adult collaboration is now more important than ever if we want to steer our children in the right direction.

Parents, coaches, teachers, and school administrators must communicate their expectations with one another, then present a united front that expects of young athletes nothing less than acceptable personal and social behavior. If every adult who works with children and teenagers promoted a common core of values, student athletes would sense a high level of expectation in every corner of their lives.

These values are not religious in nature; coaches and other school personnel need not fear legal reprisals from those in our society who would keep God out of our schools. We share them with coaches, teachers, parents, and school administrators by distributing a Violation Policy Statement like the one in Figure 1-1. It can be distributed individually or during large- and small-group meetings with parents and school personnel to promote discussion and clarify program goals.

Figure 1-1
Drug, Alcohol, and Tobacco Violation Policy

First Offense
In Season—20% of season contests (drugs/alcohol)—10% for tobacco
Out of Season—warning & probation

2nd Offense
In Season—60% of season contests (drugs/alcohol)—30% for tobacco
Out of Season—Same as in season first offense for next season.

3rd Season
In or Out of Season—Suspension from all athletics for the remainder of the school year.

Invitationals, Tournaments, Multi-Day Events & Doubleheaders count as one contest.

An athlete may practice with the team during a suspension and may sit on the bench in street clothes during a contest. They may not dress for any contest during the suspension.

Any athlete who holds either an elected or appointed team captaincy may be required to relinquish his/her position upon violation of the guidelines.

First Offense in Season
(# of contests allowed/drug & alcohol suspension/tobacco suspension)

Fall		**Winter**		**Spring**	
B. CC	10/2/1	B. Basketball	21/4/2	Baseball	28/6/3
Football	10/2/1	B. Swimming	16/3/1	B. Gymnastics	13/3/1
B. Golf	17/3/1	Wrestling	17/3/1	B. Tennis	17/3/1
B. Soccer	18/4/2	G. Basketball	20/3/1	B. Track	17/3/1
G. CC	10/2/1	G. Gymnastics	13/3/1	B. Volleyball	21/4/2
G. Golf	16/3/2			Badminton	17/3/1
G. Swimming	14/3/2			G. Soccer	18/4/2
G. Tennis	15/3/2			Softball	23/5/3
G. Volleyball	20/4/2			G. Track	15/3/1

Second Offense in Season
(# of contests allowed/drug & alcohol suspension/tobacco suspension)

Fall		**Winter**		**Spring**	
B. CC	10/6/3	B. Basketball	21/13/7	Baseball	28/17/9
Football	10/6/3	B. Swimming	16/10/5	B. Gymnastics	13/8/4
B. Golf	17/10/5	Wrestling	17/10/5	B. Tennis	17/10/5
B. Soccer	18/10/5	G. Basketball	20/12/6	B. Track	17/10/5
G. CC	10/6/3	G. Gymnastics	13/8/4	B. Volleyball	21/12/6
G. Golf	16/10/5			Badminton	17/10/5
G. Swimming	14/8/4			G. Soccer	18/11/6
G. Tennis	15/9/5			Softball	23/14/7
G. Volleyball	20/12/6			G. Track	15/9/5

Printed with permission from Glenbrook South High School.

Such a discussion is essential if parents and school personnel are to achieve consensus regarding the goals and values of the athletic program. The discussion is most effective if the values are easily remembered and conceptually clear. That's why we like to encourage coaches, parents, and teachers to emphasize these "Five Cs:"

Cooperation

Imagine a highway crowded with nothing but cooperative drivers or businesses employing only cooperative employees. Unfortunately, anyone rooted in reality realizes that both are impossible. Pure cooperation in our society is as unlikely as universal abstinence, antiviolence among gang members, and the proverbial chicken in every pot. As unlikely as it may be, however, it is desirable—and worthy of our collective efforts to achieve it.

The positive synergy that results from such cooperation not only increases social and economic output but decreases the mutual antagonism that currently is alienating so many of us from one another and from our social institutions. Such specifics as quality circles and collaborative planning in the workplace and cooperative learning in the school demand students and adults who are capable of close cooperation. Athletic teams demand it—as should family interactions, behavior in the classroom, and involvement in the community. Promoting it is the responsibility of all adults.

Commitment

We have heard several coaches claim that many young athletes express interest in sports but seem unable or unwilling to commit to them. In fact, recent studies indicate that growing numbers of students, both boys and girls, avoid sports participation because it "just isn't fun." Their levels of commitment, therefore, are understandably related to the pleasures they derive from participation. When stress replaces fun, coaches everywhere can expect less student interest.

Expecting commitment from young athletes, therefore, must first acknowledge their primary motivations. Coaches can't assume that youngsters can be "motivated into" the self-sacrifice required of athletic competition. Young athletes commit to sports programs that justify occasional pain and self-sacrifice. Their developing values, therefore, result not from a blind acceptance of someone's need to win but from a commitment to relevant goals and activities that satisfy their own ego and social needs.

Coaches must understand these needs and seek to satisfy them on a daily basis if they hope to develop a sense of commitment in their athletes. To the extent that athletes fail to reflect such commitment, coaches must look in the nearest mirror to determine what they are doing wrong. Lack of commitment results more from a failure in the athletic program than from player resistance or apathy.

Coaches will never teach values like cooperation and commitment when they talk about team membership and dedication to goals but behave in ways that reflect only their desire to win. The same is true of the desire to emphasize self-control with young athletes.

Control

We believe that punishment is always a last resort—that it becomes only when student self-discipline breaks down. Self-discipline involves intern trols and functions well, as long as the needs that drive it are satisfied. Once a st dent's ego and social needs are no longer satisfied, self-discipline begins to break down, and external discipline is required to control behavior. The balance between self-discipline and needs satisfaction, therefore, is critical for every athlete and warrants the attention of coaches, parents, and teachers.

Discipline in every home, school, and sport must first emphasize self-discipline, the internal control that sustains a sense of balance in one's life. John Wooden, the legendary basketball coach at the University of California in Los Angeles (UCLA), demanded such balance from each of his players. Wooden asserted that it was as critical when guarding an opponent or taking a jump shot on the court as when finding time to study or avoiding a fight off the court.

Emotional equilibrium complements physical balance during athletic performance. It avoids excesses, promotes clear thinking, sustains focus, and assures consistency. That's why emotional balance is essential to any kind of success in life and is the foundation for the self-discipline that assures control in any kind of system, including schools and athletic programs.

Consistency

Emotional balance promotes a consistency in the lives of athletes that affects everything they do. It establishes a constancy of purpose and levels of reliability that reflect on the court or field, in the classroom, at home, and in the community. Everyone wins—especially the athletes, who move comfortably from one responsibility and relationship to another, benefiting themselves as well as their parents, teachers, and coaches.

Conscience

Their teammates and opponents benefit as well. Renowned educator Art Costa, a professor at the University of California in Sacramento and a leader in the study of intelligent behavior, indicated a few years ago that empathy is a characteristic of intelligent people, that it enables them to understand the needs and motivations of others and to establish mutually supportive relationships. Ours is a society sorely in need of more empathy.

Because sport reflects society and, to a lesser extent, influences it, coaches must promote intelligent behaviors in young athletes and encourage them to respect opponents as well as teammates. Magic Johnson's current notion that you somehow must dislike your opponent if you hope to win a championship must give way to the more traditional, if apparently outdated, idea that opponents must battle each other relentlessly but promote mutual respect on the playing field.

A relatively few years ago entire gymnasiums grew silent during an opponent's attempted free throw and football players helped "the enemy" off the ground after each play. Fans cheered an opponent's outstanding play, and coaches sympathized with each other when they lost key players to injury. Although some of these behaviors still exist, most of them have become fond memories of bygone eras in sport—moments of nostalgia for those of us who are old enough to remember them.

THE RESURGENCE OF VALUES IN THE NATION'S SCHOOLS

Such values represent a foundation for the development of consensus-building activities with coaches and parents. To the extent that each seeks and accepts nothing short of the "Five Cs," our communities, schools, and teams will begin to reverse the statistical trends that signal so many problems in our society. Athletics will find itself more a solution and less the victim of such problems. That we all work together, therefore, is the central focus of this first chapter—and, perhaps, the remainder of this book.

The responsibilities of the athletic director after such consensus among parents, coaches, and teachers is achieved are vital if students are to benefit from athletic participation. Primary among these responsibilities is the guarantee that the athletic program is doing all it can to promote the values by assuring that athletes and coaches behave in ways that are consistent with them.

When the self-discipline of young athletes breaks down and some form of external response is required, athletic directors and other school administrators must ally with coaches when sanctions are imposed, if such sanctions are reasonable and fall within the guidelines of the athletic department. Coaches across the country have been complaining for decades that when athletes break training rules or otherwise violate the school's athletic code, some administrators expect coaches to disregard or ameliorate punishment, particularly when parents intervene with school authorities.

Many administrators are more interested in serving the needs of the parent community, as diverse and contrary to the expectations of the athletic program as they may be, than in holding young athletes accountable for their misbehavior. When athletic directors become more responsive to the expectations of influential parents and less interested in promoting the values of athletic participation, the entire program suffers. At that point, sports remain more a reflection *of* and less an influence *on* society's problems.

That's why it's important to use the materials in Figures 1-1 and 1-2 to promote a dialogue among coaches and parents in order to achieve consensus on these very important issues. Figure 1-2, from Mike's *Building the Total Athlete*, outlines the behaviors that are expected of all athletes. If it's complemented with the reproducible codes provided in Figures 1-3 and 1-4, everyone involved in the program understands not only the rules of the athletic program but the consequences if such rules are violated.

If parents sign the form as well, the athletic department can reasonably expect them to encourage their children to abide by the rules and to accept the consequences should they violate them. Lawyers call this *substantive due process*; we call it common sense. If your athletes and their parents understand the rules of the athletic program and the consequences of violations, even have a hand in shaping them, they probably will help promote them and will be less inclined to seek special favors or to threaten legal action once sanctions are applied to violators.

Figure 1-2
The Athlete's Pledge

Individual and team success in sports results from commitment. The extent to which young athletes are able to make such commitments reflects their maturity as well as their dedication to family, friends, school, and team. Your coach already has made a similar kind of commitment. You will receive a copy of it. For these reasons, we ask you to read and agree to the following **Pledge:**

As an athlete in my school, I promise:

1. To be a worthy representative of my teammates and coaches, abiding by school and community expectations and reflecting my team's values of commitment and hard work.
2. To maintain my health and fitness levels by following the training rules as prescribed by the Athletic Department.
3. To reflect the knowledge that a commitment to victory is nothing without the commitment to hard work in practice.
4. To attend every practice unless excused by my coach.
5. To understand that my future as a responsible adult relates more to my academic than my athletic activities.
6. To find the time to satisfy my family relationships and responsibilities.
7. To accept the responsibilities of team membership: cooperation, support of my teammates, shared responsibilities, positive interaction, and mutual respect.
8. To reflect good breeding by expressing my feelings and ideas intelligently and appropriately.
9. To reflect my belief that true strength involves gentleness and that even the toughest athlete is sensitive to others.

I have read the above statements and promise to live up to them:

(Signature) ______________________________

Date: ______________________________

Figure 1-3
Code of Conduct

High School officials, coaches of athletic teams and sponsors of student activities believe that students who are selected for the **privilege** of membership on teams, squads, performing groups, clubs, and other school organizations should conduct themselves as responsible representatives of the school. In order to assure this conduct, coaches and sponsors enforce a Code of Conduct. Furthermore members of teams and organizations who fail to abide by the Code of Conduct are subject to disciplinary action. Members of teams and organizations must always serve as exemplary of high moral character and must demonstrate appropriate academic commitment which is expected from all students. As recognized representatives of their school, members are expected to exhibit appropriate behavior during the season (activity) or out of season, in uniform or out of uniform, on campus or off campus.

Section A—Extracurricular Activities and Education

1. The High School District has as its primary goal the academic education of all students. Therefore, each coach or sponsor has the obligation to encourage students to perform within reasonable academic expectations.
2. All student use of tobacco products, alcoholic beverages, or possession or use of non-prescribed controlled substances or paraphernalia for their use will not be tolerated, and the violator will be subject to disciplinary action.
3. We strongly disapprove of students staying home on school days to rest for events that day or night. The administration reserves the right to limit participation of students in cases of non-attendance at school.
4. Rule enforcement will be consistent and immediate. School officials are not expected to police off-campus, non-school activities unless the violation is brought to public attention, is sufficiently severe to bring discredit upon the organization, and is clearly proven.
5. Each coach or sponsor has the prerogative to establish additional rules pertaining to the activity supervised. These rules may include attendance at practices, contests, trips, etc. Rules set by the individual coach or sponsor must be in writing and approval by the Coordinator of Athletics or the Coordinator of Student Activities and communicated to the student participants *before* the activity begins.
6. Students suspended from school by the Dean's Office will not be allowed to participate in activities or athletics while they are on suspension.
7. The Dean's Office will be notified of all violations of the Code of Conduct and the consequences of the infraction. In addition to the penalties imposed by the Code of Conduct, such infractions will also be subject to appropriate Board of Education disciplinary policies.

Section B—Procedures

A student may be suspended from participation in any activity according to the following procedures:

1. All reports of violations of the Code of Conduct are to be made either to the Coordinator of Athletics or to the Coordinator of Student Activities.
2. The coordinator of the respective area contacts the student, the parents, the coach or sponsor to inform them of the violation and the procedures to be followed. If requested, a meeting is scheduled within three (3) school days. This meeting includes the coordinator of the area, the student, his or her parents, if they desire, and the student's coach or sponsor.
3. The coordinator and the coach or sponsor will determine the course of action. The student and his/her parents are notified of the decision immediately.
4. Any student who violates the guidelines and/or does not satisfactorily complete the season or activity may not be eligible for any awards or special recognition given for participation in the activity. Furthermore, a student who holds an elected or appointed office or position (i.e., peer leader, team captain, student organization officer) may be required to relinquish said position upon violation of the guidelines.
5. Penalties will be applied in every area of activity in which a student participates. Any offense constitutes a violation in all activities covered under the guidelines.

Section C—Guidelines for Action

Guidelines are for the school year and refer to infractions which occur in or out of season. Guidelines also apply during the entire calendar year when the student is actively engaged in a school-related activity on or off campus.

ATHLETICS

Consequences for infraction by athletes are determined by the following guidelines:

1st Offense

Out of Season—Minimum penalty—warning and probation
In Season—Suspension from at least one contest.

2nd Offense

Out of Season—Suspension from at least one contest. Penalty will begin with the initial contest of his/her next athletic season.
In Season—Suspension from at least one-half of the season.

3rd Offense

In or Out of Season—Suspension from all athletics for the remainder of the school year.

These suspensions may carry over from season to season during a single school year.

SCHOOL ACTIVITIES

Consequences for infractions by participants in school activities are determined by the following guidelines:

CLUBS AND ORGANIZATIONS

(Special interest clubs, student government, class boards, honorary societies)

1st Offense

Suspension from club meetings/activities for at least two weeks.

2nd Offense

Suspension from club meetings/activities for at least four weeks.

3rd Offense

Suspension from club meetings/activities for remainder of the school year.

The suspensions do not carry over from year to year.

STUDENT PERFORMANCE ORGANIZATIONS

(Music, speech, debate, swim, dance, sports-related activities)
Consequences for infractions by members of performing organizations are determined by the following guidelines:

1st Offense

When Not Participating—Minimum penalty—warning and probation.
During Participation—Minimum penalty—Students will not be permitted to participate in and/or audition for the next major performing event and/or four weeks of Saturday detentions.

2nd Offense

When Not Participating—Minimum penalty—Students will not be permitted to participate in and/or audition for the next major performing event and/or four weeks of Saturday detentions.
During Participation—Suspensions for at least the next two performances.

3rd Offense

At Any Time—Suspension from the remainder of the performing events for the entire school year.
These suspensions do not carry over from year to year.

Second D—Right of Appeal

A student and his or her parents may appeal a decision by writing a letter to the coordinator of the respective area with copies to the principal, within three (3) days following the meeting. This letter should request a hearing with the Administrative Council at the school.

Within five (5) school days after the letter is received, the coordinator of the area will notify the parents and the participant of the time and place of the appeal hearing. The school's Administrative Council will hear both sides of the case and will take action which they consider to be in the best interests of the student and the school. During the time between the original decision and the hearing, the principal has the authority to waive the action which has been taken.

Student signature: ______________________________

Parent signature: ______________________________

Printed with permission from Glenbrook South High School.

Figure 1-4
High School Athletic Code

Athlete's Name ______________________________ *Sport* _________________________

Year in School (Please Circle) *FR* *SO* *JR* *SR* *Date* _________________________

Athletics Philosophy

High School officials, coaches of athletic teams and sponsors of student activities believe that students who are selected for the privilege of membership on teams, squads, performing groups, clubs and other school organizations should conduct themselves as responsible representatives of the school. In order to assure this conduct, coaches and sponsors enforce a Code of Conduct. Furthermore, members of teams and organizations who fail to abide by the Code of Conduct are subject to disciplinary action. Members of teams and organizations must always serve as exemplars of high moral character and must demonstrate appropriate academic commitment which is expected from all students. As recognized representatives of their school, members are expected to exhibit appropriate behavior during the season (activity) or out of season, in uniform or out of uniform, on campus or off campus.

The High School District has as its primary goal the academic education of all students. Therefore, each coach or sponsor has the obligation to encourage students to perform within reasonable academic standards.

All students' use of tobacco products, alcoholic beverages, or possession or use of nonprescribed controlled substances or paraphernalia for their use will not be tolerated, and the violator will be subject to disciplinary action.

We strongly disapprove of students staying home on school days to rest for events that day or night. The administration reserves the right to limit participation of students in cases of nonattendance at school.

Rule enforcement will be consistent and immediate. School officials are not expected to police off-campus, nonschool activities unless the violation is brought to public attention, is sufficiently severe to bring discredit upon the organization, and is clearly proven.

Each coach or sponsor has the prerogative to establish additional rules pertaining to the activity supervised. These rules may include attendance at practices, curfew, dress, and general conduct of participants during practices, contests, trips, etc. Rules set by the individual coach or sponsor must be in writing and approved by the Coordinator of Athletics or the Coordinator of Student Activities and communicated to the student participants before the activity begins.

Students suspended from school by the Dean's Office will not be allowed to participate in activities or athletics while they are on suspension.

The Dean's Office will be notified of all violations of the Code of Conduct and the consequences of the infraction. In addition to the penalties imposed by the Code of Conduct, such infractions will also be subject to appropriate Board of Education disciplinary policies.

My signature acknowledges that I have attended the Code of Conduct meeting and I have heard the presentation regarding policies and procedures of the athletic department.

Signature of Parent ____________________ Signature of Student ______________________

Printed with permission from Glenbrook South High School.

Desirable behaviors become reality when everyone agrees with them, when athletes, parents, coaches, teachers, and administrators accept a common core of values and cooperate in a collective attempt to achieve them. That we all work together, therefore, is essential to the success of the program and to the individual accomplishments of the student athletes.

WHY "THE PROGRAM" MUST PREVAIL

Exactly what is the "athletic program?" What is the "football *program*," the "basketball *program*," or the "field hockey *program*"? "The program," whether a particular sport or a combination of all the sports in your school, is a body of people and procedures that seeks common goals. The goals involve winning, participation, teamwork, a sense of accomplishment, personal growth, and a range of individual needs that coaches and young athletes bring to school each day.

"The program" is all of them, and the success of the program is more important than any one of them. It is more important because the program is yesterday's, today's, and tomorrow's athletes, all of whom are or will be seeking the benefits that it can provide. No one individual, therefore—not even the most successful coach or athlete in the school's history—should receive treatment that compromises the benefits of the program.

Within the past thirty years, significant elements in our country have challenged bureaucratic impersonality and the tyranny of "city hall." Many of these challenges have been successful. They have reaffirmed the importance and the value of the individual in our society, an outcome that has rewarded the sacrifice of so many activists among us and the high cost they paid to achieve their goals.

As important as this success has been to all of us, it continues to exact a high cost, particularly within many of our social institutions. We have worked so hard to buy individual freedom that, as a society, we may have diminished individual responsibility. Crime is increasing daily on our streets and in our schools. Criminals are back among us before their prison terms are complete. Juries are being influenced by well-skilled lawyers capable of manipulating the truth. And, yes, students in many schools are relieved of the consequences of their misbehavior because "they're good kids" or because Mom and Dad threaten school authorities with legal action or reprisals within the community.

When schools are coerced into compliance with parental expectations, they fail to realize that "the program" suffers. So does the student, who is relieved of the consequences of his or her misbehavior but is suddenly burdened by a code of behavior that obscures adult responsibility and values dishonesty and a childish fear of punishment. Too many people in our society fear and avoid the consequences of their behavior. If we are to reverse such tendencies, schools will have to help lead the way.

We are not advocating a return to organizational impersonality when we underscore the importance of "the program." Rather, we are seeking a balance between a continuing acknowledgment of the individual and the need for reasonable consequences, an adherence to principles and rules of behavior that are in the best interests of athletes and coaches alike. When we achieve such consensus early in the school year, parents and school personnel find themselves working for common purposes and sharing the responsibility of promoting the athletic as well as the academic needs of young athletes.

Assuring the Academic Needs of Students

Coaches assume a broad responsibility when they agree to work with young athletes. Contrary to popular opinion across the country, the term "student athlete" is *not* an oxymoron, and coaches are instrumental in assuring that the term defines the responsibilities of every young person who commits to one or more sports programs. Their influence on young athletes is unquestioned in the minds of most teachers, and even of some university personnel.

Teachers have been requesting the help of coaches for decades when student athletes misbehave in the classroom, disregard homework assignments, or perform poorly on tests and quizzes. They reason that the influence of coaches on the field or court extends into the classroom or home and that a few well-chosen and appropriately delivered words from them can inspire even the most intransigent student. Generally, they're right.

Such confidence in the influence of coaches is also reflected in university studies. One in particular, conducted by Dr. Rick Turner at the University of Virginia, illustrates the point. Dr. Turner was convinced that high school coaches represented "God figures" to most junior high school and secondary students and that the involvement of coaches in the scheduling of courses and the actual classroom performance of student athletes would result in improved achievement.

His research confirmed his belief. Students who experienced the significant involvement of coaches signed up for more academic courses and achieved at a higher level than they had before being involved with coaches. We cite Dr. Turner's study not to suggest that schools add tutoring or counseling responsibilities to coaches' workloads, which are sizable already, but to acknowledge their influence in the lives of young athletes.

That's why, early in the school year, we like to hold a large-group meeting with all our athletes and their parents to emphasize the importance of academics and to detail the eligibility requirements of the NCAA's Bylaw 14.3. We engage coaches in the process because young athletes listen to them and carry their message home and into the classroom. We also invite an occasional speaker, usually a former coach, to share his or her unique message regarding the importance of academics as well as athletics in the lives of students.

Most important, we want students and parents to understand that our school and athletic programs value education and that we want to work closely with parents to assure an appropriate educational experience for each child who enters our doors. Our message, as illustrated in the reproducible in Figure 1-4, High School Athletic Code, is consistent with our school's mission statement and establishes our expectations for every student in the athletic program. Feel free to use it for distribution to your athletes and parents.

Encouraging Participation

This first meeting also represents an opportunity to invite uncommitted students to hear coaches, to learn more about certain sports, and to find answers to questions regarding time commitments and general expectations. We encourage you to anticipate this meeting by distributing the letter and the accompanying materials in Figure 1-5 to students expecting to enter your school in the fall.

Figure 1-5
Sample Letter to Parents of Incoming Freshmen

High School Athletic Department

Date

Dear Parents:

Freshman Orientation Night will be held Wednesday, March 13, at 7:30 P.M. Although the evening is planned to help you assist your son or daughter with high school planning, we encourage incoming freshmen to attend the orientation meeting with their parents.

There will be a general meeting in the auditorium at 7:30 P.M. The meeting will cover course registration procedures, an academic road map through high school, as well as a review of activities and athletic opportunities.

After the general session you may feel free to leave or to tour the building and explore the programs we offer. If you have questions about *academic placement* issues you must see the appropriate *Instructional Supervisor* in the Field House.

Ms. Darlene Colmar, your child's counselor, will also be available in the Field House if you think you need to discuss your child's schedule at this time. Counselors will be at the junior high schools twice in the next three weeks to explain registration procedures and then to meet individually with your child to review and approve the courses selected. Schedule adjustments can be made through May by contacting Ms. Colmar at 486-4534.

We look forward to seeing you.

Sincerely,

Assistant Principal
Pupil Personnel Services
Enclosures

Printed with permission from Glenbrook South High School.

Figure 1-5, continued
High School Athletic Department

From:

Date:

Re: Summer School Courses

Summer Baseball By invitation only Site: GBS	June 11–July 26 $100	M–F GBS only	4:30–8:30 P.M.
Summer Boys' Basketball Site: GBS	June 12–July 12 $80	M–F GBS only	8:00–10:30 A.M. V, S & F
Summer Girls' Basketball Site: GBS	June 11–July 12 $80	M–F	8:00–10:00 A.M. V & JV
	June 17–July 5 $50	M–F	10:00–11:30 A.M. FR
Summer Cross Country/Track Site: GBS	June 17–July 26 $55	M–TH GBS only	8:00–9:30 A.M.
Summer Football Site: GBS	June 24–July 26 $80	M–F GBS only	3:00–6:00 P.M.
Summer Boys' Gymnastics Site: GBS	June 18–July 26 $55	T,W,TH GBS only	6:00–8:00 P.M.
Summer Girls' Gymnastics Site: GBS	June 18–July 26 $55	T,W,TH GBS only	6:00–8:00 P.M.
Summer Boys' Soccer Site: GBS	June 17–July 26 $55	M,W T,TH GBS only	6:00–7:30 P.M. 7:30–8:30 A.M.
Summer Girls' Soccer Site: GBS	July 15–July 26 $55	M–F GBS only	5:00–8:00 P.M.
Summer Girls' Softball Site: TBA By invitation only	June 17–July 26 $85	M,W GBS only	4:00–8:00 P.M.
Summer Girls' Volleyball Site: GBS	July 15–July 26 $60	M–F GBS only	7:00–10:00 A.M. V, JV, F
Summer Boys' Volleyball Site: GBS	July 15–July 26 $60	M–F GBS only	7:00–10:00 A.M. V, JV, F

Figure 1-5, continued
High School Athletic Profile

NICKNAME: Titans
ENROLLMENT: 2182
COLORS: Navy and Gold
CONFERENCE: Central Suburban League, South Division
ATHLETIC COORDINATOR:
ASSISTANT ATHLETIC DIRECTOR:
ATHLETIC TRAINER:
INTRAMURAL DIRECTOR:
ATHLETIC SECRETARY:
PHONE:

Number of Athletes in Athletic Program 94–95	**Total** **1253**
Total Number of Names on Eligibility Lists	**Total** **1960**
Number of Athletic Contests 1994–95	**Total** **1296**

SPORTS OFFERED AND HEAD COACHES

FALL	WINTER	SPRING
Cross Country-Boys	Basketball-Boys	Badminton-Girls
Cross Country-Girls	Basketball-Girls	Baseball-Boys
Football-Boys	Gymnastics-Girls	Gymnastics-Boys
Golf-Boys	Swimming-Boys	Soccer-Girls
Golf-Girls	Wrestling-Boys	Softball-Girls
Soccer-Boys		Tennis-Boys
Swimming-Girls		Track-Boys
Tennis-Girls		Track-Girls
Volleyball-Girls		Volleyball-Boys

Total Number of Sports Offered:	**23**
Total Number of Teams:	**74**
Number of Coaching Positions:	**88**
Number of Coaches:	**67**

The materials may be distributed to elementary or junior high students, depending on whether you are in a junior high school or a senior high school. The important thing is that you share them sometime in the spring of the year to get the students and their parents thinking about your athletic program. Your willingness to return phone calls and to share additional information will also help sell the program.

PROMOTING AND ADHERING TO ELIGIBILITY REQUIREMENTS

The introduction to the NCAA's Bylaw 14.3 in the fall of the year is just the first step in promoting academic eligibility for all student athletes. Your school may have its own athletic eligibility requirements; your state certainly does. Students must also abide by them in order to participate in the athletic program. For that reason, such expectations should be distributed to students and parents, so all are aware of the additional requirements that affect them.

In addition, the eligibility of student athletes is necessarily an all-school responsibility. Meet at least once each school year with teachers to share information about eligibility requirements and to discuss their willingness to notify the athletic department about student athletes who fail to meet those requirements. The Agenda for Athletic Guidance Meeting in Figure 1-6 is helpful during such a meeting and can do much to involve teachers in the process—sometimes well before the ineligibility of certain students becomes an issue.

That's why it's advisable to have teachers notify the athletic department each week about student eligibility. The forms in Figures 1-7 and 1-8 work well and can be distributed each week to remind teachers to share information about the academic progress of students. Such reminders are important elements in the communication process between the athletic department and the other departments in the school. The reminder in Figure 1-8 not only requests information but reaffirms everyone's responsibilities to the young athletes in the school.

You are also encouraged to share the form in Figure 1-9 with the guidance department to promote adherence to eligibility requirements. Most counselors are preoccupied, especially early in the school year, with college and job applications, then find themselves involved in registration and scheduling issues. The subject of eligibility requirements for student athletes is often far down their list of priorities. Athletic directors make friends when they provide materials that make counselors' jobs easier.

Finally, it's also a good idea to provide such forms as those in Figures 1-10 and 1-11 to athletes and their parents to assure their continuing awareness of eligibility requirements. These forms are particularly helpful when parents meet with counselors to discuss registration for the next year's classes.

Figure 1-6
Agenda for Athletic Guidance Meeting

Agenda

I. Goal for Meeting

II. IHSA Requirements
   - A. Must be passing a minimum of four classes
   - B. Responsibility of notification of athletes
   - C. Semester ineligibility vs. weekly ineligibility

III. Material Sent to Instructors
   - A. Copies of information that instructors receive
   - B. Process from athletic office for individual athletes

IV. Exemption from Physical Education
   - A. Requirements
   - B. Process

V. School Roles
   - A. Guidance
   - B. Athletics
   - C. Instructors

VI. NCAA Rules
   - A. Clearinghouse
   - B. Clarification of Division I, II, and III

V. Discussion—Questions and Answers

Figure 1-7
Memo—Requirements for Participation in Athletics

ATHLETIC DEPARTMENT

TO: Faculty and Staff

FROM: Athletic Department

RE: Requirements for Participation in Athletics

DATE:

Attached you will find a copy of the athletes who are currently enrolled in your class. These athletes are currently eligible to participate in an athletic activity. If you note at anytime during the semester that one of your students is failing an activity, please notify the athletic office either in writing or by phone. The student will be removed from that activity until grades are at a passing status.

Next to each student's name is the sport that the student is participating in and the coach who is involved. If you have any specific questions regarding the student athlete, please do not hesitate to call the coach or athletic department.

Figure 1-8
Sample Athlete List for Faculty

ATHLETIC DEPARTMENT

The following individuals are enrolled in your class. Please notify the athletic department if a student athlete is failing your class at anytime. Thank you in advance for your assistance.

Name	*Grade*	*Course Title*	*Sport*	*Coach*
John Smith	09	World Civilization	Basketball	Weissenstein
Jenny Jones	10	World Civilization	Gymnastics	Osowski
David Brown	09	World Civilization	Wrestling	Cichowski
Chris Cross	12	Sociology	Basketball	Weissenstein
Jane Person	11	Sociology	Basketball	Romanek

Figure 1-9
NCAA Academic Eligibility Requirements

NCAA Academic Eligibility

The NCAA has established a central clearinghouse to certify athletic eligibility for competition at a Division I or II institution. The following is important information you will need to know to be eligible for financial aid, practice, and competition during your first year. If you have questions, please contact your coach, guidance counselor, athletic director, or the NCAA National Office at 913-339-1906.

To be certified by the Clearinghouse, you must:

1. **Graduate from high school.** You should apply for certification before graduation if you are sure you wish to participate in athletics at the college to which you will be admitted. The Clearinghouse will issue a preliminary certification report when you have had all your materials submitted. After you graduate, the Clearinghouse will review your final transcript to make a final certification decision according to NCAA standards.
2. **Earn a grade-point average of at least 2.00** (on a 4.00 scale) in a core curriculum of at least 13 academic courses which were successfully complete during grades 9 through 12. Only courses that satisfy the NCAA definition of a core course can be used to calculate your NCAA GPA. No special values are allowed for "+" or "-" grades. The chart below shows what your core courses must include at a minimum.

Core Units Required for NCAA Certification

	Division I	Division II
English Core	4 years	3 years
Math Core*	2 years*	2 years
Science Core	2 years	2 years
Social Science Core	2 years	2 years
From English, Math or Science (additional CO8 core)	1 year	2 years
Additional Core (English, Math, Science, Social Science Foreign Language, Computer Science Philosophy, Nondoctrinal Religion)	2 years	2 years
TOTAL CORE UNITS REQUIRED	**13**	**13**

***IMPORTANT NOTE:** For students enrolling as college freshmen during (academic year) ,Division I certification requires 2 years of math, including at least 1 year of algebra and 1 year of geometry (or a course for which geometry is a prerequisite.)

3. **Earn a composite score of at least 17 on the ACT or a combined score of at least 820 on the recentered SAT (or 700 on the nonrecentered SAT) on a national test date.** For Division I: The minimum grade-point average in the 13 core courses and required ACT or SAT score vary according to the Initial-Eligibility Index below. This index is scheduled to take effect for students enrolling as college freshmen during (academic year) who wish to participate in Division I athletics.

Core GPA	ACT	RC SAT	SAT
above 2.500	17	820	700
2.500	17	820	700
2.475	18	860	710
2.450	18	860	720
2.425	18	860	730
2.400	18	860	740
2.375	18	860	750
2.350	19	910	760
2.325	19	910	770
2.300	19	910	780
2.275	**19**	**910**	**790**
2.250	19	910	800
2.225	20	950	810
2.200	20	950	820
2.215	20	950	830
2.150	20	950	840
2.125	20	950	850
2.100	21	990	860
2.075	21	990	870
2.050	21	990	880
2.025	21	990	890
2.000	**21**	**990**	**900**

Printed with permission from Glenbrook North High School.

Figure 1-10
Eligibility Requirements for Intercollegiate Sports

DIRECTIONS: The following discussion contains very important information. You **MUST** abide by it if you plan to play a sport in college. THE BAD NEWS: If you fall short in any area, you will not be eligible to receive a scholarship, practice, or play in an NCAA Division I or II school during your first year. For that matter, you may **NEVER** play a sport in college if you are declared academically ineligible. THE GOOD NEWS: The rules are not hard to follow. If you maintain a decent college-prep program in high school and study to the best of your ability, you will have no problem with the following requirements.

Be sure to write them down as we go along, and ask questions at any time. We're here to make sure you understand the rules.

The NCAA's Bylaw 14.3 (Proposition 48)

1. Graduate from high school.

2. Maintain a grade point average of ____ on a 4.0 scale and earn a composite score of ____ on the ACT or a ____ on the SAT OR earn a lower grade point average but a higher ACT/SAT score. Ask your counselor or coach to see the NCAA "Sliding Scale." It shows the relationship between test scores and grade-point average.

3. Maintain a program of at least _____ academic units (full year courses), including the following:

   - English—4 years
   - Math—2 years
   - Social Studies—2 years
   - Science—2 years
   - Other: __________, __________, __________, __________, __________, __________, __________, __________.

NOTES:

Figure 1-11
NAIA Requirements

The requirements of the National Association of Intercollegiate Athletics (NAIA) are similar to those of the NCAA. The NAIA also awards athletic scholarships and requires its own set of eligibility requirements. Write them down as they are mentioned:

YOU MUST MEET ANY TWO OF THE FOLLOWING THREE REQUIREMENTS:

1. Graduate from the upper half of your high school class.
2. Earn a grade-point average of ____ on a 4.0 scale.
3. Receive a composite score of ____ on the ACT or a score of ____ on the SAT.

For further explanations of some of the specifics of test scores and academic program, see your coach and counselor. You may have a unique situation that requires special consideration. Talk to your coach and counselor anyway, if only to make sure that you are meeting the requirements of either organization.

NOTES:

THE WHY OF TRAINING RULES

Schools should promote the athletic department's training rules as guidelines for good health. They are not nutritional hurdles that the school places in front of kids to complicate their lives. The medical community has condemned alcohol and tobacco; fair-thinking parents prohibit drug use; and coaches and doctors nationwide forbid steroid use. Each has good reasons for such prohibitions. Alcohol and tobacco impair athletic performance and pose a variety of health problems. Other drugs, including steroids, may enhance aspects of athletic performance, but they affect kidneys, reproductive capability, the heart, and personal and social relationships.

Mike has discussed training rules, drug use, and nutrition extensively in his book, *Building the Total Athlete*, also published by Prentice Hall. For detailed explanations of proper nutrition and the harmful effects of alcohol, tobacco, and drugs, you may find it useful to purchase a copy for your school library. Three reproducibles from the book, Figures 1-12, 1-13, and 1-14, not only provide information but promote awareness on your part and that of your coaches and athletes regarding the effects and warning signs of tobacco and drug use.

This knowledge alone is often a sufficient deterrent for young athletes to avoid drugs. It is especially effective when such information is distributed to every athlete in the program to enable all of them to identify warning signs and to use their collective influence to curtail drug use among teammates and other students. The literature is full of examples of schools that use junior and senior high school athletes to influence their peers, particularly younger students, to avoid drugs. The more all students know, the more they avoid the destructive effects of tobacco and drugs.

Finally, training rules introduce young athletes to a fitness and dietary regimen that promotes lifelong health habits. Daily exercise during practice and competition can be complemented by sound nutrition and recognition of the life-shortening attributes of tobacco, alcohol, and other drugs. When discussing training rules with parents and athletes, therefore, use the reproducible in Figure 1-15 to explain their importance.

SHARING INFORMATION WITH STUDENTS AND PARENTS

To be effective, each of these pieces of information must be shared with students and parents in a setting that promotes clarification and discussion. Schools that simply make the forms available, or that distribute them randomly in the weight room or during team meetings, fail to impress on student athletes the significance of the information. They also do little to inform parents of the value of training rules or the importance of academic eligibility, or to gain their support of the athletic program.

Offer large-group meetings early each school year to introduce and discuss eligibility and participation requirements with students and parents. Such meetings should also promote academics for its own sake, highlighting the relative shortage of athletic scholarships and the unlikelihood of professional careers.

Figure 1-12
ALCOHOL AND TOBACCO
Something to Think About

DID YOU KNOW THAT:

- Adults who drink excessively can become alcoholics in 5 to 15 years.
- Teenagers who drink excessively can become alcoholics in 6 to 18 ***months***!
- Preteenagers who drink excessively can become alcoholics in only ***3*** months!
- Recent research claims that teenagers who smoke a pack or more of cigarettes a day are 45% more likely to use marijuana than nonsmokers.
- Over half the people killed in drunk driving accidents are teenagers, even though they account for only 20% of licensed drivers.
- The only age group in this country whose life expectancy is actually ***decreasing*** is teenagers!

Someone once said that alcohol is what put the "wreck" in *recreation.* All the statistics out there agree. We know, for example, that the greatest enemy of today's teenagers—is today's teenagers. They are killing each other in gang activity, each others cars, and at parties when they encourage each other to drink too much. We also know that teenagers are also their own best friends. Friends watch out for each other because they care. Let's find *good* friends, then, the kind that really care about us, and listen to them.

We only magnify our problems when we look at them through the bottom of a glass. We help resolve them when we see them through the eyes of a good friend. Alcohol and tobacco use violates training rules, but that's only one reason not to use them. The best reason is that they just aren't good for you, especially if you hope to develop the lung capacity so important for athletics and lifelong health.

REMEMBER:
Alcohol and tobacco are poisons;
treat them accordingly.

Figure 1-13
Taking a Closer Look at
MARIJUANA

DO YOU CARE ABOUT WHAT YOU PUT INTO YOUR BODY?

If so, think about these facts:

- Compared to 10 to 20 years ago, today's marijuana is ten to twenty times more poisonous to your system.
- Marijuana has become so acceptable to unsuspecting teenagers that a recent government study discovered that only half of the nation's 12- to 17-year-olds see any risk in using it.
- Some recent statistics have indicated that one joint can damage the lungs as much as 100 cigarettes.
- One joint contains as many as 421 different chemicals.
- When lit, that same joint can contain as many as 2,000 chemicals!
- Marijuana is fat soluble, which means that it can stay in your system for anywhere from 1 to 3 weeks.
- Such continuing toxicity can cause significant damage to your respiratory system.

Fortunately, growing numbers of people in our society are becoming very careful about what they put into their bodies. Even if you weren't an athlete, you certainly would be concerned about the poisons your body would absorb every time you smoked just one joint. Maybe that's why one study indicates that marijuana use has dropped off 35% to 40% among some college students.

For athletes, however, marijuana use is especially damaging because of what it does to your lungs. If you are serious about your sport and ***really do*** care about your health and fitness levels, you would have to search long and hard and still would be unable to find even one reason to justify smoking even one joint.

THINK ABOUT IT.

Figure 1-14
The Warning Signs of Drug Use

Coaches, parents, and students should all be aware of the warning signs of drug use. We must know them in order to recognize symptoms, then to help the drug user in whatever way we can. We all know that drugs, no matter how desirable they may seem to us, have the potential to kill. Parents, coaches, and ***real*** friends don't want teammates and close friends taking such chances with their lives. A friend who lacks the pride and self-confidence to avoid drugs needs our help. Please read this sheet very carefully so you will be in a better position to provide that help. Your coaches already are familiar with these signs.

NAME OF DRUG	WARNING SIGNS
Alcohol	Slurred speech, unsteady walk, slowed reflexes, relaxed inhibitions, glazed eyes.
Cocaine	Restlessness, increased excitement, glass vials, glass pipe, razor blades, syringes, needle marks.
Marijuana	Red eyes, dry mouth, excitement, laughter, increased hunger, rolling paper, pipes, odor of burnt hemp rope.
Hallucinogens	Focus on detail, anxiety, panic, nausea, capsules, tablets, blotter squares.
Inhalants	Nausea, dizziness, headaches, poor coordination, drowsiness, poor muscles control, smell of inhalant on clothing and breath.
Narcotics	Nausea, dizziness, drowsiness, inability to feel pain, pinpoint pupils, cold and moist skin, needle marks.
Stimulants	Alertness, talkativeness, loss of appetite, weight loss, irritability.
Depressants	Drowsiness, lack of coordination, capsules, confusion, slurred speech, needs more sleep.
Steroids	Significant weight gain, acne, altered moods, increased anger, puffiness in face, hair loss, deeper voice in girls.

Figure 1-15
Some Straight Talk About Training Rules

Do you know why so many states keep the drinking age over 21? They have learned from the medical community that our livers don't mature until we become young adults—at or beyond the age of 21! What that means is that teenagers have the potential to become alcoholics in a much shorter time than adults, in some instances, months for teenagers as compared to many years for adults. Our training rules also recognize similar problems. Smoking, drinking, and drug use can cause significant problems for all of us, but particularly for young adults, who tend to be more affected by them.

Consider these additional facts:

1. Nicotine is a poisonous alkaloid. Just a small amount in your blood stream can kill you in about an hour.
2. Smoking is as addictive as cocaine.
3. A recent university study found that adolescents who smoked marijuana ate irregularly and showed symptoms of nutritional deficiencies such as muscle weakness and fatigue.
4. Studies indicate that up to 10% of frequent marijuana smokers will become addicted.
5. Research also indicates that marijuana addiction leads to the use of stronger, more addictive drugs.
6. One of those stronger drugs is amphetamines, commonly called "speed." Recent research indicates that prolonged use can cause the significant damage of brain cells, resulting in serious physical and cognitive problems.
7. Steroid use has been linked to heart and brain damage.
8. Alcohol use is directly linked to thousands of teenage deaths every year.
9. Alcohol addiction is passed on to family members. The sons of alcoholic fathers, for example, are *four* times more likely to become alcoholics than the sons of nonalcoholics.
10. When compared to the tissues of the lungs, a piece of tissue paper looks like a sheet of iron. That's why smoking and drug use are so dangerous to the lungs.

These are just *some* of the reasons to follow your school's training rules!
BE SMART—STAY HEALTHY!

Students and parents who understand and accept the fact that only one in every one hundred high school seniors receives a scholarship to play for a major university begin to perceive the classroom as something other than a resting place between the breakfast table and the practice field. In addition, athletes and their parents must be helped to realize that only seven one-thousandths of one percent of high school senior football players and only four one-thousandths of one percent of high school senior basketball players ever play professionally.

Once these realities are shared with student athletes in settings that promote dialogue, schools may begin to reverse the significant statistical trends that describe the tragedy awaiting so many young athletes. The Center for the Study of Sport in Society, located at Northeastern University in Boston, recently released the results of a survey they conducted among high school athletes.

Among other things, they discovered that a full 40 percent of inner-city Africa-American high school athletes *expect* to play a professional sport at some time in the future. We emphasize the word "expect" because, when compared with the small percentage of high school athletes who eventually do play a professional sport, these students are setting themselves up for disappointment or potential tragedy.

If such information is shared appropriately, students participate in high school sports for the right reasons. They sense the excitement of teamwork and shared goals, and they realize the satisfaction of maximum effort. They play a sport, not for its future promises but for its immediate pleasures. And, most important, they learn to accept academic as well as athletic responsibilities and to prepare for futures that are reasonable and within their control.

We are not in the business of destroying dreams. Dreams can be inducements to action; they envision better futures. Experience has taught us, however, that the smaller the mind, the bigger the dream. When dreams begin to restrict the view of life's possibilities, therefore, we ask student athletes and their parents to expand their horizons and to envision and plan for alternative futures. Such a request requires ongoing dialogue.

These large-group meetings, therefore, serve to invite parents to meet with coaches, counselors, and athletic directors to discuss immediate problems and future plans. As indicated earlier in this section, few people influence students as effectively as coaches. Similarly, no one has more information than counselors regarding preparation for college or work after high school. Seeing that these two people work with athletes and their parents to influence the development of alternative futures is a primary responsibility of the athletic department.

THE WHAT AND THE HOW OF COALITIONS

Teachers, coaches, and counselors assume job responsibilities that promote uniform school goals but that often push them in different, sometimes contradictory directions. Their specialization can result in services for students and parents that are compromised by relative isolation. The special advice they share with families is valuable and appreciated but can be insufficient unless coordinated with the expertise of others in the building.

The combined expertise of coaches, counselors, athletic directors, and others like college and vocational consultants is necessary if student athletes and their parents are to make reasonable decisions regarding academics and athletics and how each affects the future. You must help develop such coalitions. Consider the following examples of "special knowledge" each person brings to the process.

The Coach

- The ability to compile statistics that provoke the interest of college recruiters.
- The knowledge of how to contact college coaches and initiate the recruiting process.
- An awareness of the competitiveness of college athletics and the ability to steer high school athletes and their parents toward college programs that are consistent with the athlete's playing ability.
- The resources to create and share films and tapes that document player performance.
- The ability to notify appropriate media sources to assure recognition for deserving athletes.
- The power to assure fair treatment from college coaches during the recruitment or selection processes.
- The knowledge of NCAA requirements regarding recruitment and financial aid.

These are just a few examples of the importance of coaches in the coalition. Certainly, they make their biggest contributions during the season, when they teach the fundamental skills and the strategic knowledge that is so important for every young athlete. College coaches *recruit* "blue chippers"; junior high school and senior high school coaches *make* them.

It is equally important to recognize that coaches have responsibilities to young athletes and their parents that extend well beyond fundamental skills and strategy. Their influence and input are critical if student athletes are to establish the academic as well as the athletic credentials that result in opportunities to play a sport in college. Guaranteeing such input is one of the major responsibilities of athletic directors.

The Counselor

- The resources to administer career inventories and to assist with each student's vocational development.
- A knowledge of how to help with the college selection process.
- An understanding of the relationship between course selection and the eligibility requirements of the NCAA and other regulatory organizations.
- The ability to help with college selection and admission processes.
- The resources to monitor the student athlete's academic progress through school.
- The ability to identify colleges that satisfy the educational as well as the athletic needs of student athletes.

Counselors also deal with the personal and social aspects of student behavior and invariably find themselves burdened with a volume of paperwork that rivals that of the federal government. They, too, have to be encouraged to help with the special needs of student athletes and to maintain a knowledge of rules and regulations that change almost yearly. This is not an easy task and requires of athletic directors a strong process orientation that results in frequent contact with significant people in the building and in the community.

Initially, it results in the kinds of large-group meetings we recommended earlier. Then it must result in follow-up meetings that respond to the specific needs of students and parents. It must include supervisory relationships with coaches that promote their professional growth and their continued willingness to work with student athletes and parents beyond their immediate seasons.

Your task must involve periodic updates of significant NCAA legislation; you can use the form in Figure 1-16. Similarly, it must involve a sharing of all information that is relevant to a wide range of coaching responsibilities. It must involve in-service programs that broaden the perspectives of coaches, promote their understanding of preadolescent and adolescent behavior, enhance their strategic knowledge, and increase their understanding of intercollegiate athletics and its relationship to their players.

Future sections of this book address each of these issues and more. The important point now is that only the combined expertise of coaches, counselors, parents, and athletes can result in good decisions—the kind that promote satisfying experiences now and in the future.

ENGAGING STUDENTS IN THE ORGANIZATION OF THE PROGRAM

The final element in meeting the needs of young athletes involves the degree of their input regarding the nature and scope of the athletic program. The current emphases on collaboration in much of the professional literature include the input of students and parents as well as that of teachers and other school professionals.

Students provide a unique perspective on the organization and operation of the program. As persons on the "receiving end" of program decisions, they are sensitive to the thinking of coaches and athletic directors. They are generally among the first to sense the need for change and to realize the inadequacy of certain policies and practices. Their input can be especially valuable in the following areas:

- The development and evaluation of program goals.
- The evaluation of training rules and the consequences of violations.
- The potential involvement of athletes in community activities.
- The promotion of fund-raising activities inside and outside the school.
- Requirements for awards and recognition.
- Possible involvement with booster club activities.
- Coordination of concessions and security for athletic contests.
- Public relations activities.

Figure 1-16
The NCAA and Other Groups

Following is some information you might find helpful as you work with one or more of our school's student athletes. It involves changes in NCAA legislation, as well as information regarding one or more of the other regulatory organizations. Call the Athletic Department if you should require clarification and/or additional information. Thanks.

Athletic directors should seek student input into program decisions not just to appease a segment of the student body but to tap a valuable organizational resource. Students provide a unique perspective on all aspects of the school system, especially the athletic program, a cocurricular activity that provides some of their most enjoyable school experiences and enduring memories. They represent much more than "clients" of the program; students *are* the program and can help create it as well as benefit from it.

The athletic director who treats students as colleagues regarding the organization and operation of aspects of the program encourages a sense of ownership among students and does as much to promote widespread participation as even the most popular coach. Student participation in the school's athletic program involves more than winning or the personal "charisma" of coaches. It involves a sense of community—even family—among everyone involved in the program. Such a feeling begins with *you*.

PAPERWORK AND THE NEEDS OF STUDENT ATHLETES

Let's conclude this section with a brief discussion of one of the least desirable responsibilities of the athletic director. Unfortunately, its inevitability suggests its importance, especially as it relates to the legal aspects of our jobs and to the special needs of athletes. Imagine an athletic department office composed of four bare walls, a couple of desks, and an occasional visitor. You can bet that not much is happening in it.

By contrast, most offices are knee-deep in memos, schedules, permission slips, injury reports, coaching records, press releases, athletic codes, inventory sheets, and enough loose-leaf notebooks to fill the Library of Congress. Desks are barely visible under the mounds of paper, and visitors come and go like bargain hunters at a fire sale. Something is definitely happening in these offices.

But is the activity purposeful? Does it accomplish what the athletic directors hope to accomplish? The odds are that it does. Most good athletic directors probably have a couple of walls of shelves, with each form in its designated slot and a secretary or a set of personal habits that can remember due dates, mailing schedules, coaches' birthdays, and the first name of every equipment salesperson.

LET'S WRAP IT UP

The athletic director has one of the most important jobs in the school. The influence of coaches in the lives of student athletes is well documented everywhere in the media. We need not argue the point here; we need only acknowledge that athletic directors influence the lives of the people who influence the athletes. Their influence is far-reaching, extending subtly but persistently into the lives of hundreds of students each year. When they model the values that are important to the athletic program, they invariably see them reflected in the behaviors of coaches and athletes.

Mike's recent experience demonstrates that point. A very close friend of the family, suffering for several years from cancer and recently returned to the hospital for additional radiation treatments, died quietly in the arms of her husband. Her courage had astonished even her closest friends and was evident in the dignified acceptance of her fate. In the process, she taught her friends and family an important lesson.

As educators, we have believed for years that the hope of our country depends on our young. Louise taught us, however, that it is found in the behavior of people, usually the adults among us, who live and die with dignity and courage. She taught us that every time someone proves to the rest of us that courage and dignity are possible, even in the face of pain and impending tragedy, we are all more capable of both. Hope, then, only *accompanies* the unpredictable futures of the young; it is *created* by courageous and dignified people every time they share their special message with us.

They teach us that dignity is possible; simple consideration is possible; and courage in the face of adversity is possible. Our personal and social horizons are broadened by their example, and the narrow range of negative behavior that characterizes so much of our society is no longer the only alternative available to the young. Such is the responsibility confronting everyone who works with young people, especially those of us who choose to lead.

SECTION TWO

Working with Coaches

First, a quick story:

We consulted once with an athletic director who was convinced that her coaching staff was unwilling to help seniors with their college planning, particularly as it related to continuing a sport in college. In fact, she described them as saying, "It ain't my job," and she asked us to meet with them for lunch one day to try to "steer them in the right direction." She even asked us to tell them what their responsibilities were regarding eligibility, recruitment, and college planning.

No thanks; that's not our style. We prefer to believe that most people want to do the right thing and—given the proper circumstances—would find the time to meet with seniors and their parents to help them find the appropriate college experience. We agreed to meet with her staff, but decided to take a different approach. We welcomed them to the meeting, introduced ourselves, addressed the topics of college planning and eligibility very generally, then asked the coaches if there was anything we could do to help them with these responsibilities.

Mike even asked a very specific question: "Do you even feel that this is a part of your responsibility as coaches?" An answer from a veteran on the staff, described earlier by the AD as one of the most resistant, was immediate:

"Of course we want to help. I, for one, just don't know what to do. The NCAA changes the rules so often that it's just about impossible to keep up with them. If these kids can commit to me for four years, I can certainly commit to them for four weeks."

Aside from a couple of coaches who responded very little during the meeting, most of the other coaches agreed with him. They worried about being out of touch with these kinds of topics, including updated knowledge regarding the current talent levels of today's college athletes. Given their concerns, we asked them what we might do to help.

The floodgates opened! When the waters calmed, we had decided to provide periodic NCAA updates to coaches, and even to counselors and teachers. We promised to intervene with the administration to get a phone in the coaches' area to promote communication with college coaches. We even decided to talk to the administration about relieving one or two coaches from their corridor, study hall, or lunch room supervision to meet with student athletes in the athletic department so that they could discuss their questions about eligibility and recruitment.

The meeting went well. As important, our friend learned something about her coaching staff. She admitted to us afterward that she had characterized them unfairly, and that she now recognized the need for more in-service training to keep them current on NCAA legislation, recruiting procedures, and the changing realities of college athletics. Like teachers, coaches need information—and the elimination of obstacles that inhibit its effective use.

To illustrate further, Mike worked with a prominent golf pro once to develop an instructional book and videotape, and was intrigued by his distinction between coaching and teaching. The pro believed that teaching involved inculcating values and goals in each student, in essence pushing them in certain directions. He believed, on the other hand, that coaching involved guiding, leading, encouraging, motivating, disciplining, and role modeling. It's an interesting distinction, if not completely valid.

We would be hard-pressed to find even one third-grade teacher who doesn't guide, lead, encourage, motivate, push, prod, and pull during the better part of every school day. In fact, he or she probably would tell you that instruction is exactly that. Instructing youngsters is virtually impossible without motivation and discipline. So we prefer not to make such a distinction, but we do believe the golf pro has a point about coaching.

WHAT IS A COACH?

Coaches are part parent, part drill sergeant. They provide one of the most important links in the evolutionary chain of dependency that is competitive sport. Student athletes make up most of the other links—their relationship with coaches forged by the heated and growing sophistication of competition. At one time independent of coaches, athletes are now involved in athletic programs that are to turn-of-the-century sports what Nintendo is to tick-tac-toe.

The sophistication of strategy, motivational technique, and team organization now requires adults who can lead youngsters through the developmental tangle of adolescence toward the personal fulfillment that comes with athletic and academic success. Once required only to show up for games, athletes now practice almost daily, during and after the season, and commit themselves to activities ranging from lifting weights to dropping pounds. Athletic competition is no longer a stroll down the common to "agitate a bag of wind," as an early university president once described football.

The athlete's commitment to sports in both high school and college now highlights his or her dependency on coaches for a knowledge of strategy and fundamentals and for their help not only to further but to finance a college education. College coaches now dangle scholarship offers, and high school coaches help young athletes reach for them.

The chain of dependency, therefore, is mutual. Athletes need coaches to compete successfully in sports requiring sophisticated strategy, and coaches need athletes if they are to field teams. Even a marginal disinterest within a student body for a particular sport depletes team numbers so insidiously that coaches soon find themselves struggling to maintain their programs.

Effective coaches acknowledge this mutual dependency by trying to win contests while making young athletes have fun and feel good about themselves. They do this during the season and long afterward if they hope to attract athletes to their programs and achieve winning records. The most successful do it because they like working with youngsters and enjoy watching them achieve both academically and athletically beyond high school.

Finally, coaches need athletic directors to help them achieve their goals as they work with young athletes, parents, and other school personnel. The conscientious coach who reaches out to young athletes and their parents to help the athletes learn a sport that probably is growing in sophistication each day, succeed in the classroom as well as on the field or court, and make the difficult transition from high school to college or work needs the moral and informational support of a good athletic director.

WRITING WORKABLE JOB DESCRIPTIONS

The primary personnel need within any athletic department is to find knowledgeable and, if possible, experienced coaches who enjoy working with students and are willing to extend themselves, beyond the season if necessary, to help their athletes achieve in the classroom, behave appropriately in school, and make the transition to college. Such involvement can't be legislated. Coaches must be naturally predisposed and appropriately supervised to assume such added responsibilities.

The actual supervision of coaches will be discussed later in this section. For now, let's simply acknowledge that both supervision and evaluation of coaches are meaningless if job descriptions are unavailable to provide standards of performance. *Substantive due process* is a legal requirement that relates to everyone who supervises and evaluates personnel. To meet this requirement, job descriptions must provide the substantive functions and tasks to be performed by coaches, which also serve as the criteria to be used during the evaluation and supervision processes.

Coaches require as many professional growth activities as anyone else in the school system. Their influence on the positive development of teenagers often extends well beyond that of classroom teachers. That they use this influence responsibly is critical in every school, and it requires ongoing professional growth experiences for coaches. Much of this professional growth begins with well-conceived job descriptions.

Figure 2-1 provides a reproducible form for athletic directors to use when developing job descriptions for coaches. Figure 2-2 provides a sample description for head coaches, but can also be used for assistant coaches. The descriptions outline key areas of responsibility that can be used to make hiring and evaluative decisions during the year. Notice that they include reference to the following general headings:

Professional Expertise

Coaches are, first of all, the most knowledgeable people in the building about the strategy and fundamentals of their particular sports. One of their primary tasks, therefore, is to provide their athletes and assistant coaches needed leadership in developing a sophisticated sports program, one that engages everyone in appropriate practice activities, the development of needed fundamental skills, and up-to-date strategy for contests. In addition, good coaches will provide periodic evidence of their efforts to maintain their professional expertise, and athletic directors will pledge their support as needed.

Personal Behavior

Unlike turn-of-the-century job descriptions for classroom teachers, those for today's school systems no longer require regular church attendance, curfews, and ankle-length skirts. Such expectations are as outdated as scrubbing the floors and stoking the potbelly stove, but many schools still expect teachers and coaches to model appropriate behavior in and out of school. Poor grooming, drunkenness in the community, swearing, and immoral behavior are still taboo and may not signal prompt dismissal, as they once did, but they can result in the eventual loss of a job or a coaching position.

School Relationships

Coaches are also expected to maintain positive relationships with school personnel, teachers, administrators, counselors, and others who complement their responsibilities. If the noun *coach* has anything to do with the verb *coach*, then, by definition, coaches "work together" with others in the building to promote collaborative activities that enhance the development of student athletes and the maintenance of successful athletic programs.

Community / Parent Relationships

The same is true of collaborative activities with parents and essential others in the community. Coaches are highly visible representatives of any school system. They are frequently invited to speak to community organizations, feeder schools, and fraternal groups. They are as important as anyone in establishing a supportive relationship between the school and the community. An element in their job description, therefore, emphasizes the additional time they will be expected to devote to community activities.

Figure 2-1
Job Descriptions for Coaches

Head Athletic Coach for ____.
(sport)

Qualifications: Please check appropriate line(s) below

______Valid ________________________________teaching license
(State)

______Employed in School District

______ACEP/NFICEP Certified

______Years of Coaching Sport

Head Coaching Duties and Responsibilities

Professional Expertise

Personal Behavior

School Relationships

Community/Parent Relationships

Fiscal Responsibilities

Figure 2-2
Sample Completed Job Description for Coaches

Head Athletic Coach for ______Swimming______.
(*sport*)

Qualifications: Please check appropriate line(s) below

__X__ Valid ______Illinois______ teaching license
(*State*)

__X__ Employed in School District

_____ ACEP/NFICEP Certified

__10__ Years of Coaching Sport

Head Coaching Duties and Responsibilities

Professional Expertise

1. Instructs athletes in fundamental skills, training, and strategies necessary to achieve success.
2. Has a knowledge of game rules and league regulations and implements these rules on a consistent basis.

Personal Behavior

1. Students will receive instruction and guidance that will lead to positive values, acceptable behavior, and self-discipline.
2. Coach will exhibit responsible conduct both in and out of the competitive arena.

School Relationships

1. Maintains records for sport such as physicals, insurance forms, parent consent forms, etc.
2. Promotes professional growth by encouraging staff attendance at clinics and conferences.
3. Assigns staff specific duties, supervises the assignments, and completes proper evaluation at end of season.

Community/Parent Relationships

1. Responsible for good public relations with media, booster clubs, parents, and officials.
2. Consistently releases positive information to media on a regular basis.
3. Promotes sport among parents, players, and fans at all times.

Fiscal Responsibilities

1. Responsible for submission of yearly budget to athletic director.
2. Responsible for all equipment collection and the cost of any misplaced equipment.

Other Responsibilities

1. Monitors athletic locker rooms before and after practice and contests.
2. Secures all doors and windows before leaving facility.
3. Develops in each athlete a respect for school property and its care.

Fiscal Responsibilities

An athletic director we know describes her budget as "a mathematical confirmation of her greatest fears." For others of us, it's little more than a set of checks and balances—the checks ultimately depleting the balance. The athletic budget is like the only pizza at a picnic; everybody wants a piece of it, but there's never enough to go around. To make matters worse, coaches vie among themselves to get the biggest piece. The budget constitutes one of the biggest responsibilities for athletic directors as well as coaches, because it always involves potential disagreement.

In total, these general areas constitute the "nonnegotiables" of the head coach's job responsibilities. They are required functions of head coaches and, in essence, constitute the core of what head coaches are expected to do. Additional functions and tasks may be added but usually involve some negotiation with the coaching staff.

CONSENSUS BUILDING WITHIN THE COACHING STAFF

Collaboration among coaches and athletic directors is extremely important during such negotiations. It generally leads to improved decisions and encourages coaches to *own* the decisions that are made in the group. To encourage effective collaboration, athletic directors should routinely seek consensus within their departments. This guarantees that all the coaches share a common perception of the value of athletic participation and of their responsibilities to student athletes. The Coach's Pledge in Figure 2-3 provides the starting point for a discussion of key responsibilities, some of which can provoke heated debate.

When the dust settles, however, athletic directors have in hand a document that represents the thinking of the entire department and can serve as a standard for all to reach. One or two of the elements within the pledge may change, based on the predispositions of the coaches and the athletic director's ability to influence their thinking, but, under normal circumstances, it will remain much the same as in Figure 2-3.

When the document is finalized, it serves a number of purposes within the athletic department:

- It represents mutually acceptable standards to use when supervising and evaluating coaches.
- It details the coaching philosophy of your school and can be distributed during informational meetings with student athletes and their parents as another element in the department's public relations program.
- It can be used to promote consensus among key persons and groups within the building, especially the school's administration. They are the ones most able to provide the time, money, and resources needed by coaches who engage in the activities listed in the Pledge, particularly numbers 8, 9, and 10.
- It provides the criteria to be used when hiring coaches, especially head coaches.

Figure 2-3
The Coach's Pledge

THE COACH'S PLEDGE

The Coach's Pledge extends beyond a knowledge of athletics and reaches into the life of each of his or her players. It is one of the most important responsibilities in the school and involves at least the same level commitment that coaches expect of their players. Mutual respect and team membership are to be expected equally of player and coach and, for the coach, involve the following promises:

As a coach in my school, I promise:

1. To be a model of appropriate language and behavior.
2. To respect and dignify each of my athletes as an individual.
3. To promote the safety of each athlete and to ask no more in practice or competition than each is capable of delivering, but. . .
4. To promote the conditions and circumstances that encourage each athlete to realize his or her full potential.
5. To impose time demands that acknowledge the primary importance of each athlete's academic and family responsibilities.
6. To promote among all athletes and coaches a solid sense of team membership.
7. To reflect in my coaching the best and most recent thinking / strategy in my sport.
8. To assist, whenever appropriate and mutually convenient, with the post-high planning of my players as it relates to athletics.
9. To be available to parents at times that are mutually convenient.
10. To work, whenever appropriate, with other school personnel to guarantee the best interests of each of my student athletes.

© M. D. Koehler

ASSESSING COACHING NEEDS

Before we get into the actual hiring of coaches, we should take the time to discuss the identification of coaching needs within the department. School systems are notorious for maintaining the status quo in the face of needed change. Those responsible for school curricula struggle for years to catch up to evident changes in social circumstances. Teaching methodology remains static in the face of startling new research suggesting strategies for improving student learning. New technologies shout for a reorientation of the teaching-learning process.

And, let's admit it, sports programs often maintain the same allocation of coaches, equipment, and facilities in spite of significant shifts in student participation and social expectations. Some sports, for example, experience a significant drop in student participation and maintain their original allocation of coaches. Others receive social mandates like Title IX and are unable or unwilling to make the necessary program adjustments to satisfy the emerging needs of female athletes.

Work closely with all coaches, therefore, to develop a set of criteria that can be used by athletic directors and others to make the kinds of adjustments in sports programs that are responsive to shifts in popularity and legal mandate. This is not to say that such criteria go into effect whenever student participation drops off in a particular sport. The first thing to do in such instances is determine the reasons for the shift in popularity and try to return it to its former level.

If such accommodations consistently fail, however, the athletic department must reduce the allocation of coaches and cut back on the program's budget. Such changes are essential if the athletic department is to have available personnel to accommodate inevitable participation increases in other sports programs, or if it is to adjust to decreases in revenues.

DEVELOPING HIRING CRITERIA

Once personnel needs have been assessed, coaches must be hired or found somewhere in the system to satisfy those needs. If hired, such coaches must be identified and selected based on established criteria. Figure 2-4 provides a form to distribute to persons involved in the process and used by them to consider the qualifications of candidates. Such a form should be developed in collaboration with the other coaches in the department. Unilateral decision making has surrendered in concept to collegiality and collaboration in much of the professional literature.

Interestingly enough, the athletic department, an expected bastion of authoritative leadership, was among the first in education to acknowledge and promote collaborative decision making. Head coaches are the recognized leaders in their respective fields and primary among those in the building who shape the school's culture. That they influence the ultimate selection of new coaches is very important to the morale as well as the effectiveness of the sports program.

The Coaches' Pledge (Figure 2-3) can be used as a starting point. It contains a list of desirable characteristics that already represent a consensus within the department. Figure 2-4, therefore, is a suggested composite. It may not be the exact one you use in your department, but it provides a good benchmark—a starting point for the one you and your coaches develop. If useful for nothing else, it identifies several areas that warrant your department's attention.

Distribute the Coaches' Pledge along with a survey, asking your department to suggest criteria to guide the interviewing and hiring process. Include their criteria, along with some of yours, in a form similar to the one in Figure 2-4. Be sure to list at least one or two criteria from each respondent, so that everyone in the department is represented on the form. You can include as many of your own criteria as needed as long as you acknowledge the input of your coaches.

WORKING WITH OTHER DEPARTMENTS TO FIND COACHES

The last criterion in Figure 2-4 acknowledges the need to find qualified teachers to fill coaching vacancies. Seemingly obvious, this is not as simple as it sounds. The *extra*curricular nature of coaching assignments in junior and senior high schools requires primary assignment in the classroom or elsewhere in the building. The task of hiring qualified teachers as well as coaches requires close cooperation with the academic departments in the building.

The athletic department, therefore, must never be regarded by other departments as a wing dangling unimportantly somewhere in the back of the building. The athletic director who works closely with the administration and other department chairs and is a visible and articulate spokesperson for academics is the ally of other departments and usually enjoys their cooperation.

Such cooperation is critical if administrators are to hire potentially successful coaches. Share the Coaches' Pledge and lists of hiring criteria with other department heads to enlist their understanding of the need to hire a "complete professional," a superior teacher *and* coach, and a person who will contribute to the culture of the school and community.

Effective cooperation normally involves periodic meetings with appropriate department heads to:

- Share information regarding special needs.
- Share hiring criteria established within each department.
- Develop informational materials for mailings to universities, placement offices, and other schools.
- Identify a promotional campaign to find the most qualified candidates.
- Discuss interviewing procedures and develop an interviewing schedule.
- Devise strategies for influencing the final decision-making process.
- Identify any shared responsibilities for future orientation activities for the person hired.

You will also want to meet with administrators, parents, and students who may be involved in the interviewing and hiring processes. You will want to share your department's criteria as well as the information you have developed in collaboration with other department chairs to promote an understanding of the kind of person the school should seek to fill the position.

Figure 2-4
Coaching Qualifications

Coaches will uphold the dignity, honor, and integrity of the coaching profession.

☆

Coaches will enlighten student athletes about the importance in order of family, academics, and extracurricular activities.

Coaches will encourage and promote sportsmanship among both the home and visiting teams, the coaching staff, and spectators.

☆

Coaches will encourage all aspects of safety before success.

☆

Coaches will work with and respect the officials in and out of the athletic arena.

☆

Coaches will take an active role in the prevention of use of drugs, alcohol, and tobacco.

☆

Coaches will be knowledgeable and adhere to the league and high school associations' rules and bylaws.

☆

Coaches will assist in discovering qualified teachers to fill coaching vacancies at the school.

RECRUITING AND HIRING QUALIFIED COACHES

The athletic department's involvement in the interviewing and selection processes should include several important steps. The hiring criteria already have identified the scope of the need within the department, and the cooperation with other departments has provided an all-school procedure to be followed. What is needed now is a procedure within the athletic department to interview and select the best candidate.

Before such interviewing begins, everyone involved must understand that the hiring process is a two-way street. You interview candidates to identify and select the most qualified person for the job; and the candidates, at least the *good* ones, evaluate you to determine if the job is right for them. Good interviews, therefore, involve both buying and selling. If the old saying, "Presentation is half the sell job," is correct, you have to do a little homework before interviewing candidates.

Figure 2-5 promotes consideration of the positive characteristics that must be shared with candidates, and it mentions the need for coaches and others to sell themselves as well as to question candidates during the interviewing process. The process itself involves several important considerations:

- **Be sure to structure the format.** Discuss the kinds of questions to be asked during the interview—questions that focus on the criteria established earlier. Also, identify a process for the interviewers to review all the candidates after meeting with them and to provide feedback to the athletic director. Figure 2-6 can be very helpful in this regard.

- **Be sure to engage a variety of people in the interview process.** Students and parents often can provide the most useful information regarding the qualifications of candidates. Have candidates meet with them after school or during lunch to assess their social skills. Such a process also gives the candidate a chance to evaluate the general characteristics of your school's students and parents.

- **Be sure to use the interview as only one part of your selection process.** Transcripts, biographical information, letters of reference, reference checks by phone, discussions with previous employers or opposing coaches, and pictures and newspaper articles complete the picture of candidates and provide important information.

- **Be sure to maintain written records.** First impressions fade; conversations with one candidate become confused with comments from another. Objective and nonevaluative records of interviews with candidates can promote good decision making when the interviewing process is concluded. Encourage everyone involved in the process to keep personal, anecdotal notes of interviews. Such documentation can be helpful later if legal action results from the rejection of a candidate.

Figure 2-5
Outline of Interview Procedures—
Positive Characteristics of High School

1. *Tour of Facilities—Indoor and Outdoor*

   View entire facilities and positive contributions of each area. Elaborate on practice facilities and times as well as competition areas.

2. *Tour of Faculty Facilities*

   Present faculty weight room, coaches' locker room, and office areas.

3. *Athletic Trophy Cases*

   Explore showcases to show history and athletic success of student athletes. Discussion of department philosophy—family first, academics second, and extracurricular activities third.

4. *Introductions of Support Staff*

   Introduce support staff and define and discuss their positive contributions to making the coaching job more effective.

5. *Discussion of Community and Positive Contributions*

   Socioeconomic background. Age group programs, park district programs, and feeder organizations. Community and spectator support. Parent Booster Club.

6. *Departmental Policy Discussion*

   Discussion of Policies, Handbooks, and departmental organization providing for a well-run unit.

7. *Additional Support Staff*

   Discussion of additional areas of support for the athletic department. Workers during season when the individual is not coaching—the sense of family and support for student athletes as well as the monetary support for support staff as announcers, ticket takers, supervisory personnel.

Figure 2-6
Interviewer Feedback on Candidate

Name of Candidate__________________ Date of Interview __________________

Position Interviewed for ______________ Name of Interviewer ______________

1. Coaching style ____

____

2. Philosophy of coaching ____

____

3. Overall goals ____

____

4. Basic values taught through coaching ______________________________

____

5. Philosophy of discipline______________________________________

____

6. Philosophy of tryouts ______________________________________

____

7. Organization of tryouts ______________________________________

____

8. Philosophy of drugs, alcohol and tobacco __________________________

____

9. Relationships with parents ______________________________________

____

10. Relationships with student athletes ______________________________

____

Any additional information: ______________________________________

____

Please list any additional information on back of page

A Word About the Evaluation of Candidates

Before we leave the interviewing and selection processes, mention must be made of a few considerations you should keep in mind when evaluating candidates:

- Although coaches are often noted for their personal charisma, such a quality can be very misleading. Spontaneous and witty people are often thought to be competent and intelligent. Some of the most charismatic people you will ever meet are among the least professionally competent. They often use personal charisma as a substitute for a well-developed conceptual framework, and can prove to be not only ineffective but actually harmful when working with young athletes.
- Always consider each candidate's position on the interviewing schedule when evaluating him or her for the position. A mediocre candidate following two bad candidates can look good by comparison.
- Guard against the blanket rejection of a candidate because of a single negative characteristic. The poor dresser or the relatively quiet candidate may prove to be the best person for the job. That's why it's important to identify hiring criteria and to secure the input of a variety of people throughout the process.

Finally, Figure 2-7 provides additional characteristics to keep in mind when evaluating the overall impression of candidates. It is useful for everyone involved in the interviewing process because it promotes the kind of objectivity that is required to make the right selection.

FINDING IN-HOUSE COACHES

Much of the identification and evaluation of candidates is made easier when they are found in house. This is true for at least three reasons:

- People identified in house are familiar with the culture of the school and community. Many of them already have contacts with feeder schools that can be useful during the process of rebuilding a sports program.
- People already in the school system tend to commit themselves to the athletic department when their past efforts are rewarded by assignment to key coaching positions.
- The athletic department and others involved in the interviewing process have more time and more resources to draw upon when determining the qualifications of candidates.

These are clear advantages when seeking to fill coaching vacancies, but avoid consideration of in-house candidates when:

- They are sponsored by one or more people in the administrative hierarchy, but fail to present the required qualifications for the job.
- They have the knowledge of strategy and fundamentals, but are unable to command the respect of their colleagues.

Figure 2-7
Additional Candidate Characteristics

Name of Candidate____________________ Date of Interview ____________________

Position Interviewed for ________________ Name of Interviewer __________________

Please list positive and negative characteristics of candidate

Pros	*Cons*
1.	1.
2.	2.
3.	3.
4.	4.
5.	5.
6.	6.
7.	7.
8.	8.
9.	9.
10.	10.
11.	11.
12.	12.
13.	13.

Please list any additional information on back of page

- They have everything the job requires, but lack the ability to promote the kind of change the program needs. Selecting people in house may do wonders for morale, but it does little to combat a sometimes formidable status quo that can stifle the growth of sports programs.

Finally, keep in mind that the general announcement of coaching vacancies is important to maintain morale in the school and among coaches. Unannounced vacancies that somehow keep being filled by outsiders send the wrong message to people already in the department. "Best practice" involves the posting of coaching vacancies and the acceptance of inquiries and applications, followed by a letter indicating your level of interest in the candidate.

ORIENTING NEW COACHES

New-teacher orientation is one of the first elements in any in-service training program. Coaches new to the department must be introduced to colleagues and oriented to the culture of the department. In essence, they have to learn "how we do business around here." Even minor misunderstandings of school or departmental protocol can result in major problems for new coaches. To avoid such problems, many athletic directors meet routinely with new coaches and introduce them to a mentor—someone who is available to answer questions and provide information as needed.

Such orientation meetings with the athletic director usually involve discussions of:

- Forms and procedures within the department and the school.
- Departmental expectations of coaches regarding the supervision of athletes in the locker room and during meetings.
- Attendance and behavior during departmental meetings.
- Methods for disciplining student athletes.
- The well-being of student athletes, from the sharing of insurance information to the filing of injury reports.
- The department's philosophy regarding multisport athletes and the possible interference of out-of-season conditioning programs.
- Expected behavior of the coach in the school and community.
- Departmental and school policies regarding absence, lesson plans, professional growth, and other considerations.
- Discussions of departmental and school standing committees and their functions.
- Budgetary procedures.
- Regulations governing travel.
- Use of secretarial time and telephone availability.
- Availability of such support programs as those provided by guidance and audiovisual departments.

Many other topics can be covered during new-coach orientation meetings. These are just a few. What is most important, however, is that the departmental processes and procedures that confront new coaches don't become hindrances to the performance of their primary responsibilities.

New coaches have a tough enough time energizing young athletes, other coaches, parents, booster clubs, the administration, and a host of others without struggling within a confusion of unexplained departmental expectations. Meet with your new coaches early in the school year to introduce them to the building, departmental philosophy and procedures, and expectations of coaches. This is a valuable meeting for new coaches and does wonders for their comfort levels! Use the New Coaches' Guidelines memo in Figure 2-8 as a model.

PROVIDING IN-SERVICE TRAINING PROGRAMS FOR ALL COACHES

Like other professionals in the building, coaches require involvement in comprehensive programs of professional growth. Such programs should consist of in-service training activities that introduce needed information, supervisory activities that give them the opportunity to practice what someone else has preached during the in-service component, and evaluation activities that assess their continued growth. In-service elements must, of course, have relevance for coaches if they are to be successful.

Relevant in-service activities usually engage coaches in an exploration of:

- **The fundamental purposes of coaching.** Sometimes it's important to revisit the goals of athletic participation and the relationships between coaches, players, parents, and others involved in the sports program. The coach, for example, who considers the teaching of strategy and fundamental skills her sole responsibility tends to disengage from athletes at the conclusion of the season. Sometimes it's important to involve such coaches in a restructuring of their "coaching platforms" to enhance their total contribution to the athletic department and the young athletes they serve.
- **An understanding of young athletes.** Motivation and discipline are key considerations for any coach. An understanding of how kids learn and what motivates them is critical if coaches are to be successful. This is one of those areas where a dependence on personal charisma can actually interfere with effective motivational strategies. Coaches require well-defined interpretive maps to lead them through the often complicated process of motivating kids. Good in-service training programs can provide them.
- **A knowledge of their sports.** Rules constantly change and new strategies are discovered almost every day. Coaches who expect to be successful must know how to incorporate or combat these new strategies. Again, in-service training is one of the answers.
- **A knowledge of technique.** Finally, like classroom teachers, coaches must understand methodology. A knowledge of fundamental skills and game strategy is relatively useless without the ability to teach both to young athletes. Good coaches are good teachers; they can benefit from periodic exposure to new ideas about instruction.

Figure 2-8
Memo Regarding New Coaches' Guidelines Meeting

Athletic Department

TO: New Coaching Staff

FROM: Athletic Director

RE: New Coaches' Guidelines Meeting

DATE:

As previously mentioned, I have scheduled a new coaches meeting for ____(date)____. Please mark your calendar to attend this important meeting.

Listed below is a tentative outline for the meeting. Please bring with you any questions that you might have regarding policy, procedures, etc. I look forward to meeting with you.

Tentative Agenda—New Coaches' Meeting

1. Introductions of support staff
   a. Support staff responsibilities
2. Facility tour
   a. Locations
   b. Keys
   c. Faculty wellness room
   d. Coaching offices/desks
3. Departmental expectations
   a. Department handbook
   b. School policies
   c. League guidelines
   d. State guidelines
4. Forms
   a. Physical forms
   b. Parent consent forms
   c. Accident reports
   d. Maintenance reports
   e. Space reservation request forms
   f. Score reporting forms
5. Student injury
   a. Special presentation from Certified Trainer
6. Departmental philosophy
   a. Multisport athletes
   b. Regulations on travel
   c. Regulations on professional leave
   d. Regulations for tryouts
7. New business

Before we continue, it's important to note that such in-service activities are not restricted to large-group presentations during or after school. Articles from professional journals, books, workshops, seminars, conventions, and consultants can provide in-service training at any time of the day and for any number of teachers. Anything that enriches a coach's understanding of aspects of his or her job can be described as in-service training. All that is necessary is that he or she has the opportunity to practice such new knowledge in a supervised situation with you or a colleague. More of that later.

Identifying In-Service Themes

Varying studies suggest that in-service programming is enhanced when:

- Coaches are actively engaged in the program and have opportunities to interact and to help one another. In-service programs tend to be least effective when they are passive "one-shot deals" conducted exclusively by outside personnel.
- Differential programming is offered for coaches. Because the coaches in any athletic department represent a variety of different sports, they require different programming to meet their needs. Often, therefore, one large-group presentation fails to accommodate the differential needs of coaches. Several programs, operating simultaneously and focused on individual sports, respond to the unique needs of coaches and provide the format for their increased involvement.
- Coaches can identify the goals for in-service programming. Such activities are additionally effective when coaches plan the programs or at least have input into a program's focus. Memos like the one in Figure 2-9 are helpful for engaging coaches in the identification of potential in-service topics.

Collaboration is an important element in the decisions affecting in-service topics. Certainly, the athletic director will have substantial input into the nature of the topics to be offered throughout the year, but his or her perceptions must be complemented by feedback from the coaching staff if the program is to engage coaches and meet their needs.

EVALUATING THE COACHING STAFF

Collaboration is also important during the evaluation process. The criteria in the Coach's Pledge (Figure 2-3) should be mutually acceptable if they are to serve as reasonable standards for coaching behavior. Having established agreement, athletic directors can use them as the substantive elements in the periodic evaluation that is so important to a good sports program.

Evaluation is quality control, an assurance of minimal expectations, a process that measures if coaches are achieving predetermined standards. Athletic directors must recognize that evaluation only *measures* growth. By itself, it doesn't *promote* growth. Only when evaluation is joined with supervision and in-service training do coaches grow professionally. They need the information that comes from in-service training, the practice that comes from supervision, and the sense of direction that comes from evaluation.

Figure 2-9
Memo Regarding In-Service Programs

Athletic Department

TO: Coaching Staff

FROM: Athletic Director

RE: In-Service Programs

DATE:

I am writing to ask for your assistance in identifying speakers and programs for continued coaching professional growth. Would you please assist the department by listing professionals, in-service programs, or activities that you would be interested in attending? Remember that these programs must be relevant to the purposes, strategies and skills involved with coaching young student athletes.

Please list your suggestions under the appropriate sections below and return to the athletic department no later than ________**(date)**________ so we may begin organizing and identifying in-service needs.

Thank you in advance.

Please list appropriate responses below and return to the athletic department.

In-Service Speaker Suggestions

In-Service Speaker Topics

In-Service Speakers

Evaluations of coaches, therefore, should involve the standards found in the Coach's Pledge and the job description. If such evaluations are to be useful for coaches, they must also include anecdotal and substantive observations of coaching performance—not just obscure marks on a checklist. The athletic director who increases his or her visibility by observing coaches during practice and contests and using such observations to evaluate performance makes a useful contribution to the professional growth needs of the coaching staff.

If the AD's observations include specific anecdotal accounts of coaching behaviors, coaches can review the observation notes and engage in needed self-evaluation before postobservation meetings with the athletic director. Such a process is particularly helpful to veteran coaches who are capable of assessing their own performance.

A good operational principle to keep in mind is that evaluation is most helpful *when it is requested by the coach.* When you're standing on the tee watching your fifth consecutive drive head into the woods, you want immediate evaluative help from a trusted someone who is willing to give it. The same is true of the coach who trusts you enough to request advice regarding team discipline, game preparation, game strategy, or the use of in-service information.

Such requested evaluations can be used to respond to a coach's immediate needs *and* to satisfy district requirements for annual assessments of teacher/coach performance, especially if you visit the coach's practice area to gather anecdotal information. Most important, when such observations involve self-evaluation, coaches tend to *own* the results—specifically any decisions to perform differently in the future.

Not all evaluations will be requested. Many will result from the routine need to document a coach's performance. Even these evaluations, however, will promote professional growth if you ask the kinds of questions during postobservation meetings that stimulate the coach's reflection about his or her behavior. Such self-reflection is one of the keys to professional growth.

Finally, you are primarily responsible for the evaluation of head coaches. Recognizing that head coaches provide the primary leadership within each sport, you should work carefully with them not only to evaluate their performance but to establish the framework for evaluations. Having done so, require your head coaches to evaluate their assistants using the same statement of philosophy as a frame of reference. More of this will be discussed in Section Eight.

SUPERVISING THE COACHING STAFF

Coaches engage in the most self-reflection during supervisory activities. Before we proceed, let's distinguish between supervision and evaluation. *Evaluation* is a process of quality control; it often involves value judgments about a coach's performance that are made by someone else, usually an administrator. *Supervision*, on the other hand, is a process of improvement that involves the making of value judgments by the individual coach.

In other words, supervision is the intermediary process that enables coaches to practice what they learned during in-service training activities before they are evaluated on how well they've learned them. Frankly, it is a process that, in many school systems, rarely receives the time and attention it deserves. Too often, athletic directors and other school administrators expect that occasional in-service programs, complemented by end-of-the-year evaluative write-ups, satisfy the professional growth needs of coaches.

Such a practice doesn't work for teachers, and it doesn't work for coaches. Schools across the country have recognized this and have begun trying to introduce collegial supervisory processes that engage teachers in self-evaluation and self-reflection. Such programs have become operational in many schools, and are still desirable in others.

Unfortunately, however, "professional growth" is a term associated more often with teachers than with coaches. The "subject matter" of a particular sport may be less significant educationally than English or math, but the higher order thought process that occurs during practice or contests (see Section Six) and the emotional and social development that young athletes experience through athletic competition are as important as anything in their lives. Coaches, therefore, must grow professionally every bit as much as classroom teachers.

Athletic directors must provide opportunities for such growth. The good news is that such opportunities don't always involve the athletic director. All you have to do is meet occasionally with coaches, particularly new ones, and provide a process for the rest that engages them in self-directed activities. Such activities can take advantage of everything from the video camera to the proximity of other coaches during practice and contests.

The athletic department that offers in-service training in coaching effectiveness, for example, is wasting its time if it fails to suggest follow-up activities for coaches to practice the principles offered during the in-service. A one-shot deal that emphasizes "disciplining with dignity" won't dent the behavior of hard-line veteran coaches who don't have follow-up opportunities to practice the concept.

They can be encouraged or required to:

- Ask you to observe a practice session in order to provide nonevaluative and anecdotal feedback for purposes of self-evaluation.
- Invite the audiovisual department to videotape one or more practice sessions, then use the videotapes for self-reflection at a later time.
- Ask coaching colleagues to provide periodic informal reactions to them during practice sessions.

These are only a few of the ways coaches can recreate their performance during practice or contests. There are other ways as well. The important element in the process of their total professional growth, however, is that they have opportunities to see "mirrors" of their performance that promote needed self-reflection. When combined with in-service training and evaluation, such a process of supervision completes the cycle of their learning experiences and results in improved coaching—a clear benefit to student athletes.

Any comprehensive attempt at supervision as defined in this section can meet with resistance, especially from coaches who already feel overworked and underpaid. In such instances, these concepts must be implemented thoughtfully. They can be used, however, for new coaches as an element in their orientation to the department, for "problem" coaches as a component in their remediation, or for other coaches who recognize the value of such activities in their total professional growth.

THE COACH'S ROLE IN THE COALITION

Opportunities for supervision and evaluation can happen at times other than during practices or contests. Many high schools across the country are engaging coaches, counselors, student athletes, their parents, and sometimes athletic directors in post-season meetings to help young athletes with the identification and ultimate selection of a college. This is especially true for highly recruited student athletes, and is becoming increasingly true for young athletes who seek to use their athletic talents to gain admission to one or more highly selective colleges and universities.

Commonly called "local coalitions," such meetings combine the expertise of coaches and counselors to guide student athletes through the sometimes confusing process of selecting the "right" college. Coaches bring to the coalition a knowledge of the requirements of the NCAA and other regulatory organizations, an understanding of the recruiting process, and possible acquaintance with college coaches. Counselors bring a knowledge of interest testing, vocational choice, and program planning.

Both bring a needed focus on academics and a future career as the primary reasons for selecting a particular college. Their knowledge of the college selection process and the influence they have on young athletes provide an invaluable complement to the planning activities of parents and coalesce the kind of power required to keep college recruiters focused on the academic as well as the athletic needs of student athletes.

The high school coach is particularly important in this coalition because he or she is generally responsible for the following tasks:

- Maintaining updated statistics for all of his or her college-bound student athletes.
- Providing early notification to colleges regarding up-and-coming student athletes who are likely to compete in college.
- Encouraging student athletes to conduct career and college searches during their junior year in order to be prepared for the selection process in the senior year.
- Motivating young athletes to excel in the classroom as well as on the field or court.
- Assuring appropriate press coverage and honors for deserving athletes.
- Meeting, as needed and as appropriate, with parents and young athletes to discuss the athletes' ability to play on the college level.
- Initiating college contacts for some athletes at the conclusion of senior year competition or coordinating college contacts for highly recruited athletes.
- Reviewing with athletes and their parents the NCAA bylaws regarding recruiting and financial aid.

Some coaches will do more. Many, for example, will act as intermediaries for highly recruited athletes in order to reduce or eliminate the number of phone calls and letters that can inundate parents or pester athletes during school hours. Others will make a succession of phone calls to prestigious schools to help athletically and academically qualified student athletes gain admission to schools that otherwise might not accept them.

Not all coaches can be required or even expected to go these "extra yards." Such behaviors are restricted to those few coaches who really do care about kids—who seek whatever is in their best interests. All coaches should, however, be encouraged to add their special brand of expertise to the planning activities of those few student athletes who do plan to continue their sports on the college level. The time commitment is not exhaustive, and the benefits they provide are invaluable.

The athletic director who takes the time to meet occasionally with one or more of these coalitions models the right kind of behavior for coaches and expands his or her opportunities to watch them "in action." Athletic directors can also provide expertise at those times when the meeting focuses on eligibility or recruiting requirements of the National Collegiate Athletic Association (NCAA), the National Association of Intercollegiate Athletics (NAIA), or the National Junior College Athletic Association (NJCAA).

Keeping Coaches Informed About Local, State, and National Policy

The mention of national regulatory organizations suggests a related concern. A primary responsibility of any athletic director is to keep coaches, counselors, and others in the building aware of changes in the requirements of regulatory organizations. That such requirements change with disturbing frequency is evident each year in the *NCAA Manual*. Debate at the NCAA national convention often results in significant changes in bylaws and procedures that affect high school and college student athletes.

The responsibilities of coaches and counselors are especially affected by such changes. The task of advising student athletes is difficult enough without yearly adjustments in NCAA policy. The athletic director who routinely shares information regarding such changes improves the delivery of services to student athletes and is perceived by others in the building as not only an expert in the field but a helpmate in providing excellent support services to students. Section Six provides a reproducible form for updates.

Because some school districts develop eligibility requirements that vary from state and national policies, you should routinely share them as well. Usually, a packet of information regarding local and state eligibility requirements shared in the beginning of each school year meets the needs of most coaches and counselors. Other information regarding insurance coverage, doctor's permission, or athletic codes can also be shared at that time.

Fortunately, the NCAA and other organizations mail relevant information to schools early each year, especially if they have recently implemented significant legislation. Forward such information to appropriate people within the building as soon as you receive it, and accompany it with further explanations as needed.

ENGAGING THE STAFF IN PROGRAM PLANNING

This aspect of working with coaches is relatively uncomplicated. Because head coaches have exclusive responsibility for maintaining their individual programs, the athletic director is generally perceived as a helpmate in finding the resources to make the program as successful as possible. Such resources can be tangible as with facilities, equipment, and budget dollars—or they can be intangible as with schedules, the coordination of travel, the selection of officials, and support systems like booster clubs and administrative backing.

This is not to say that the athletic department doesn't periodically reevaluate its philosophy and objectives, redesign its athletic code, update the school's eligibility requirements, or revise its training rules. The development or modification of such program requirements must always involve coaches if the changes are to be implemented successfully. More important, such involvement, if not intrusive and if organized thoughtfully, can be motivating to coaches to devote more of their time and energy to their programs and players.

The prominent psychologist Abraham Maslow indicated decades ago that the desire to satisfy social and ego needs is motivating to people. Coaches, therefore, seek involvement in their work and discover that the increased responsibility and recognition that accompany their contributions to the athletic department are rewards in themselves. Use sample memos like the one in Figure 2-10 to invite coaches to join in planning activities.

UNDERSTANDING MOTIVATION AND SHARING A TRINKET OR TWO

Because most athletic directors are former or current coaches, they understand the basics of motivation. You know, for example, that athletes play a sport primarily because it's fun, or at least it should be. They also play to satisfy their basic ego and social needs; sports can improve their self-esteem, and youngsters enjoy being members of a team. As a coach, you learned to capitalize on these needs, recognizing that real motivation is a whole lot more than pep talks and practice time.

You also probably learned not to confuse your need to win games with their needs for success, recognition, and self-esteem. You learned that motivating is like farming; you plant seeds, then work hard to cultivate them. You nourish them, provide the best possible environment, and remove any and all obstacles to their growth. And throughout the process, you remember that the predisposition to grow is in the *seeds*, not in the farmer.

So it is with motivation. A preoccupation with my needs often results in pushing other people in a certain direction—*extrinsically* motivating them. The problem with these occasional pushes is that invariably we have to push again—unless the person being pushed somehow enjoys the result of being pushed. When she or he does, the new-found *intrinsic* motivation provokes movement in the right direction—my direction—and I probably won't have to push that person again.

Coaches know this; so do good athletic directors. Coaches come to work each day with the same ego and social needs that youngsters bring to competitive sports. They need to feel responsible, to be recognized, and to feel a sense of professional and personal competence. They, too, want to be members of a team, to belong to a winning organization, to merge their identities with an athletic department that values them and reflects their basic beliefs.

When working with coaches, therefore, you must always acknowledge and accommodate the needs of the coaching staff, by supervising and evaluating them to improve their professional performance and by involving them in the decisions that most affect their jobs. So involved, coaches identify with the athletic department and are willing to contribute their time and energy to the realization of its goals and objectives.

Figure 2-10
Sample Memo Regarding Training and Discipline Rules

Athletic Department

TO: Coaching Staff

FROM: Athletic Director

RE: Update of Training and Discipline Rules

DATE:

The athletic department is looking for coaches who would like to volunteer their time in redesigning the school's training and discipline rules. The first meeting will be scheduled for Tuesday morning at 6:15 A.M. Juice, coffee, and rolls will be provided.

The following meeting times and dates will be scheduled by the group. I do not see the need to meet more than five times to complete this task. If you are interested in assisting the department in this task, please return the bottom of this page or call the athletic department to let us know. The group will be kept to the first seven individuals who express interest. I will notify you by phone of your involvement.

Thank you in advance for your assistance.

- -

________ Yes, I am interested in becoming involved on your committee.

Name ______________________________ Phone __________________

(Please return the bottom portion to the athletic department or call **number** if you are interested.)

Most important, they learn that you are a helpmate throughout each day; they learn to trust and respect you. At the end of the year, therefore, share an occasional trinket or two with your coaching staff, a key ring with your school's logo on it, a pen sporting the school's emblem, a nylon tote bag to carry materials to and from school. These tokens of your appreciation are inexpensive and are thoughtful ways to express your gratitude for another good year.

Never forget that genuine motivation recognizes the intrinsic needs of coaches and provides ways to satisfy them. Like the farmer, remember that your primary task is to cultivate and promote a healthy environment, to nourish, and to remove impediments to growth. Such a task recognizes that periodic evaluation, the *measurement* of performance, does little to promote this growth. The farmer doesn't measure each corn stalk to promote its growth, nor do we simply evaluate performance and expect it somehow to improve.

In essence, successful athletic directors realize that their work focuses on the needs of coaches. They decrease their own visibility by promoting processes that satisfy the needs of their coaching colleagues and lead to greater accomplishments by them. Consider this thought from the psychologist, Carl Rogers: "The degree to which I create relationships which facilitate the growth of others as separate persons is a measure of the growth I have achieved in myself."

LET'S WRAP IT UP

Coaches are the individual forces through which athletic directors influence the lives of young athletes. Uncommitted and incompetent coaches reflect poorly on your competence, and can actually compromise the efforts of others to guide teenagers through one of the most challenging times of their lives. Dedicated and skillful coaches generally are the products of trusting relationships, collaborative processes, and well-conceived professional growth programs.

Their influence on young athletes is increased whenever you help them grow personally and professionally, and when you use their collective talents to constantly improve the purposes and processes of the athletic department. Decades ago, Abraham Maslow emphasized the importance of "synergy" in organizations, the power that results when the combined efforts of persons is greater than the sum of their individual efforts, in essence when 2 + 2 = 5—or 6.

Collaborative processes create such organizational force. The athletic director who promotes the growth and participation of everyone on his or her staff maintains a top-notch athletic department. In addition, when he or she devises ways to engage the parent community, the athletic program promotes healthy communication and assures the support of a powerful community resource. This is the focus of Section Three.

SECTION THREE

Working with Parents

First, a quick story:

Friends and fans who find themselves "out of the sports loop" as you and I know it usually find their athletic thrills in front of a television set. As uneventful as this may sound to us, it does involve a level of creature comfort denied to coaches subjected to the elements in late fall or early spring. Several years ago, when still involved with football, Mike found himself coaching a playoff game in mid-November.

He discovered that "cold" is any outdoor sporting event in the Midwest in mid-November or early April, particularly for the coach confined to the sidelines or the infield. The experience must have been noticeably bone-chilling, because the school's athletic director called him in early the following week and gave him a nylon, fleece-lined jacket with "Coach Koehler" inscribed on the front. Every other coach in the school received one, too, accompanied by a small card, which read: "With sincere gratitude, from the Booster Club."

Mike still has that jacket. Whenever he wears it, he recalls the pleasant surprise of that mid-November morning in school when a group of parents was thoughtful enough to give the coaching staff a functional token of their appreciation. From that time on, whenever he and his colleagues mentioned the school's athletic "family," they invariably included the parents, who were perceived as helpmates in the development and operation of the school's sports program.

It's important to keep in mind that young athletes are not the only clients of the school's athletic program. Very often, parents—as well as teachers and administrators—receive a coach's help finding answers to the problems posed almost daily by teenagers. Most parents accept the task of raising junior high school and secondary students with very little preparation. Each day introduces a new set of unanticipated challenges, so parents often look to coaches for help.

They realize that the adolescent's love of sports can be a key to improved behavior at home and consistent achievement in the classroom. Although the character-building aspects of athletic participation are experiencing the same challenges confronting so many of our social institutions, they still work. Most coaches recognize that sport does, in fact, positively influence most young athletes.

The job is becoming increasingly difficult, however, in the face of so many social temptations and media influences. The bad news is that recent studies indicate increased drinking and drug use for young athletes; the good news is that sport still develops more "character" than "characters" and that the relationships among players, coaches, and parents positively influence the behavior of young athletes.

In light of the above, it's always surprising to us how many schools develop adversarial or, at best, laissez-faire relationships with the parent community, failing to use them as moral and financial advocates of the sports program. Effective athletic directors acknowledge parents as allies in the continuing struggle to maintain successful athletic programs. They seek their counsel and support when decisions must be made or equipment must be purchased to improve the quality of the total program.

This chapter suggests strategies for engaging selected parents in program planning activities and maintaining liaison with the entire community. It emphasizes the value of parent involvement and the power parents bring to program activities. It also suggests ways to harness such power for the good of coaches and players alike.

ORIENTATION: AN EARLY KEY TO SUCCESS

The Reasons Behind the Program

A good orientation program is the first important step in engaging parents in the operation of the athletic program. Any successful organization recognizes the need to establish shared values among its members, to achieve consensus among those who have an interest in determining its future. If parents are to work cooperatively with coaches and the athletic director to help the program realize its goals, it is critical that they share the values of the athletic department.

Before consensus building can be accomplished, parents must be introduced to the program and the people within it. The best time for such an introduction is at a meeting just before the start of the school year, when time is available and coaches and parents can talk informally without the stress of other meetings and activities that usually take place during the first several weeks of school. Figure 3-1 provides a sample letter to invite parents to the meeting and to give them a general idea of its purpose.

The Need for Preliminary Planning

The success of the meeting depends on the planning that precedes it, so we suggest a preliminary meeting among coaches to discuss the purposes of the meeting and to encourage an informal but detailed explanation of their schedules and their expectations for each athlete in their programs. Figure 3-2 provides an agenda for you to use as a guide. The athletic director's attitude at this point is critical if coaches are eventually to cooperate with parents and to encourage their involvement in program planning.

Figure 3-1
Letter to Parents of Prospective Athletes

Athletic Department

Date

Dear Parents of Glenbrook South Prospective Fall Student Athletes:

Welcome to interscholastic athletics at ________________ High School. Before the season gets underway, we ask that you attend a short athletic meeting in which we will discuss the athletic code of conduct, eligibility, scholastic endeavors, and the trainer's role. Immediately following the meeting, there will be a short break out session with the head coach from your son's or daughter's sport. Parents will need to sign an information card at the end of the meeting (only one parent need to attend with the athlete but we encourage both parents/guardians to attend the meeting).

Your encouragement and support of ____________ Athletics have always been the secret to our success. We ask you to continue that support by attending this important program with your son or daughter. The evening is scheduled to begin at 7:30 P.M. on Thursday, September 8, in the auditorium of the high school. The evening will conclude at 8:30 P.M. Athletes will not be able to participate in competition without attendance at this meeting by parent and athlete.

We look forward to seeing you and your son/daughter on Thursday, September 8, at 7:30 P.M. We believe you will find this program very beneficial.

Sincerely,

Athletic Director

Figure 3-2
Agenda for Head Coaches' Meeting

Athletic Department

Date: **August 14**
Time: **6:00 P.M.**
Place: **Athletic Office—Dinner will be provided**

AGENDA

I. **Welcome**

II. **Organizational Information**

a. Head Coaches' Meetings
b. Evaluations
c. Coaches Handbook
d. Eligibility/Parent Permission Slips/Physicals
e. NCAA Clearinghouse—Updated Standards
f. Score Reporting
g. Booster Club Dinner Dance
h. Support Staff
i. Custodial/Maintenance Staff
j. Supervision
k. Sportsmanship-IHSA Bylaw 6.0

III. **Old Business—Decision Items**

a. CSL Leadership Workshop
b. Construction Update

IV. **New Business—Dialogue Items**

a.

V. **Round Table Items—Informal Discussion**

a. Reminder to all Coaches that Cross Country is using home field for all competition—please advise all outdoor athletes to watch for safety consideration.
b. Coaching staff—please be courteous to others. If you are not using inside areas for practice on rainy days, please let the Asst. AD know so that others can practice in that area.
c. Any coach interested in participating on a committee to discuss disciplinary procedure should let the athletic director know of his or her interest.

VI. **Adjournment**—6:45 P.M. to Main Gymnasium for Fall Meeting with Parents and Athletes

Good athletic directors model the behaviors they expect of coaches. The AD who proposes collegial decision making with parents must also promote it with coaches, students, and others in the building. Advocating it is one thing; doing it is another. Expecting coaches to understand the NCAA's Clearinghouse, to help young athletes meet the eligibility requirements of Bylaw 14.3, and to assist families with the college selection process is unrealistic and unfair if the athletic director fails to understand and to assist with the same activities.

A Suggested Format

The other items on the agenda provided in Figure 3-2 promote an understanding not only of the upcoming meeting with parents and young athletes but of the Clearinghouse, eligibility requirements, and specific state rulings. Notice as well that the agenda is divided into "information," "decision," "dialogue," and "round table" items. Coaches understand, therefore, the nature of their involvement within each segment.

"Information" items are updates on previous decisions and specific details of activities that affect the department. Generally, no discussion or decision making is involved. "Decision" items involve discussion and eventual group consensus. "Dialogue" items involve the collaborative sharing of ideas without decision making, with eventual action to be taken after the athletic director has a chance to further clarify and establish the framework within which an eventual decision will be made. The "round table" segment provides the opportunity for any coach to put an item before the group for dialogue or information, generally to notify the group of upcoming events, alert them to important items, or seek their input regarding issues that affect that particular coach.

We mention the organization of the agenda at this point because the nature of the staff's involvement in departmental activities affects the success of the activities. Preliminary meetings to organize the student/parent orientation program, for example, probably will involve the staff in information sharing, dialogue, and several decisions about the goals and organization of the program. Coaches who are involved in decision making tend to "own" the programs they help develop and to work harder to assure their success.

More About the Program

Parents are often surprised at the fact that more than one-third of a school's student population is involved in the sports program (see Sample Letter to Parents, Figure 1-5). This statistic tends to be true of most schools. They also appreciate the fact that almost half the faculty finds the time after school to coach one or more sports, in effect, to work with students in something other than a purely academic setting.

This information can be imparted to parents during the meeting(s) and used to gain their support of the athletic program. Notice that the Athletic Profile (found in Figure 1-5, but have handouts available at the meeting as well) also has the names of relevant people to contact for answers to questions or for further information. Distribute this Profile at the meeting, even though parents received it initially, to emphasize its importance. It has good public relations value and does much to promote relationships between the school and the parent community.

It's also a good idea to print and distribute minifolders like the one in Figure 3-3. This particular schedule contains the dates, places, times, and opponents of all the fall sports. It is a handy reference for parents, teachers, and students who are interested in attending one or more functions during that time of the year. You will, of course, want to print similar schedules for the winter and spring sports.

You will also want to provide coaches with something similar to the schedule in Figure 3-4. It lists the names of all the head coaches and assistants in each sport and details relevant information about each contest. It encourages attendance and provides the names of persons to contact for information about specific teams.

REACHING OUT TO THE COMMUNITY

Welcoming parents and young athletes to the school's athletic program is essential in the beginning of the school year. Explaining and discussing the program to parents and other members of the community is equally important throughout the year. That's why it's a good idea to find the time to meet with service, fraternal, and other community organizations during the year to introduce new coaches, provide updates on the program, discuss the program in relation to current media emphases, or simply answer questions.

Make arrangements by contacting the presidents of local groups and volunteering to meet with them during luncheon meetings. Community organizations constantly search for speakers. The local athletic director and coaches within the program invariably provide informative and entertaining sessions. Such a practice also enables the AD to share information with influential members of the community in a way that avoids misinterpretation.

GETTING EVERYONE ON THE SAME PAGE

Athletic competition satisfies a diversity of vested interests. Parents seek values for their children; young athletes seek fulfillment; coaches seek associations with sports they love; fans seek excitement; boosters seek involvement; and athletic directors seek career opportunities! Much more is involved for all of us, but the point is that we each seek something a little different within the school's athletic program.

This is quite normal. Occasionally, however, the diversity of these expectations pushes us in different directions, even provokes conflict. Parents seek playing time and scholarships for their children; young athletes seek recognition; coaches seek victories by playing only the most talented; fans seek winning programs; boosters seek control; and athletic directors seek a few moments of peace and quiet! Again, each individual expectation is not bad. Problems occur when they conflict.

Conflicts are inevitable when our expectations are unreasonable. Coaches sometimes focus exclusively on winning and disregard positive associations with their athletes. Athletes sometimes look beyond the benefits of participation for increased status, awards, and scholarships. Parents sometimes seek their own athletic fulfillment through the accomplishments of their children. Each of these tendencies usurps the fundamental purposes of sport and can result in a devaluing of the athletic experience for students—even in athletic abuses.

Figure 3-3
Sample Sports Schedule

BOYS' SOCCER

DATE		LEVELS	OPPONENT	TIME	SITE
Aug.	26	V/S	Lake Forest (V @ 7:00 pm)	5:00 pm	H
Aug.	29	V	Titan Invitational	4:00 pm	H
Aug.	30	V	Titan Invitational	4:00 pm	H
Aug.	31	V	Titan Invitational	4:00 pm	H
Sep.	1	S/F	GBN Invitational	3:30 pm	A
Sep.	1	JV	Loyola	4:00 pm	A
Sep.	2	V	Titan Invitational	10:00 am	H
Sep.	2	S/F	GBN Invitational	10:00 am	A
Sep.	5	V/S	Leyden	4:30 pm	H
Sep.	5	JV/F	Leyden	4:30 pm	A
Sep.	6	FB	Loyola	4:00 pm	A
Sep.	9	V/S	Hinsdale Central	12:00 pm	A
Sep.	11	JV/FA	Niles North	4:30 pm	A
Sep.	12	V/S	Niles North	4:30 pm	H
Sep.	13	JV/FA/FB	Glenbrook North	4:30 pm	H
Sep.	15	V/S	Glenbrook North (V @ 7:00)	5:00 pm	A
Sep.	15	JV/FB	Lake Forest	4:30 pm	A
Sep.	18	JV/FA/FB	Highland Park	4:30 pm	A
Sep.	19	V/S	Highland Park	4:30 pm	H
Sep.	20	JV/FA	Niles West	4:30 pm	A
Sep.	21	V/S	Niles West	4:30 pm	H
Sep.	26	V/S	Deerfield	4:30 pm	A
Sep.	26	JV/FA	Deerfield	4:30 pm	H
Sep.	27	FB	Notre Dame	4:30 pm	H
Sep.	28	V	Glenbard Invitational	4:30 pm	A
Sep.	29	JV/FA/FB	Evanston	4:30 pm	A
Sep.	29	V	Glenbard Invitational	4:30 pm	A
Sep.	30	V	Glenbard Invitational	9:30 am	A
Oct.	2	V/S	Maine South	4:30 pm	H
Oct.	2	JV/F	Maine South	4:30 pm	A
Oct.	5	JV/FA	Maine East	4:30 pm	H
Oct.	5	V/S	Maine East (V @ 7:00)	5:00 pm	A
Oct.	7	V/S	Evanston (V @ 12:00)	10:00 am	A
Oct.	10	V/S	Maine West (V @ 7:00)	5:00 pm	A
Oct.	10	JV/FA	Maine West	4:30 pm	H
Oct.	11	JV/FA/FB	New Trier	4:30 pm	H
Oct.	12	V/S	New Trier	5:00 pm	A
Oct.	13	V/S	Warren (V @ 7:00 Homecoming)	5:00 pm	H
Oct.	16	JV/FA	Waukegan	4:30 pm	H
Oct.	17	V/S	Waukegan	4:15 pm	A
Oct.	19	V	IHSA Regional Begins	TBA	
Oct.	26	V	IHSA Sectional Begins	TBA	
Oct.	31	V	IHSA Supersectional Begins	TBA	
Nov.	3	V	IHSA State Finals Begins	TBA	

GIRLS' CROSS COUNTRY

DATE		LEVELS	OPPONENT	TIME	SITE
Sep.	2	V/S/F/Open	Fenton Invite	9:30 am	A
Sep.	9	V	Resurrection Invite	9:30 am	A
Sep.	12	V/JV/FR	Waukegan	4:30 pm	H
Sep.	19	V/JV/FR	GBS & EV @ New Trier	4:30 pm	A
Sep.	23	V/JV/F/Open	Niles North Invite	9:00 am	A
Sep.	27	V/JV/FR	Niles West	4:30 pm	A
Sep.	30	V	Peoria Invitational	11:15 am	A
Oct.	5	V/JV/FR	Maine East	4:30 pm	H
Oct.	7	V/JV/FR/So	Niles West Invite	9:25 am	A
Oct.	14	V/JV/FR	CSL @ Waukegan	TBA	
Oct.	21	V	IHSA Regional Begins	TBA	
Oct.	28	V	IHSA Sectional Begins	TBA	
Nov.	4	V	IHSA State Final		

GIRLS' SWIMMING

DATE		LEVELS	OPPONENT	TIME	SITE
Aug.	31	V/JV/F	Deerfield	5:00 pm	H
Sep.	15	V/JV/F	Glenbrook North	5:00 pm	H
Sep.	16	V	GBN College Events Diving	10:00 am	A
Sep.	16	V	GBN College Events Swimming	1:00 pm	A
Sep.	18	F/S	Stevenson Invite	5:00 pm	A
Sep.	22	V/JV/F	Evanston	5:00 pm	H
Sep.	26	V/JV	Lake Forest	5:00 pm	A
Sep.	29	V/JV/F	New Trier	5:00 pm	A
Oct..	6	V/JV	Waukegan	5:00 pm	A
Oct..	7	V/JV	Titan Relays - Diving	10:00 am	H
Oct..	10	V/JV/F	Loyola Academy	4:30 pm	H
Oct..	13	V/JV	Maine East	5:00 pm	A
Oct.	14	V	Trevian Relays	2:00 pm	A
Oct..	20	V/JV	Niles West	5:00 pm	H
Oct..	21	F	NT Freshman Invite	1:00 pm	A
Oct..	27	V	CSL Diving @ Evanston	3:30 pm	A
Oct.	27	V	CSL Swim @ Evanston	6:00 pm	A
Oct..	28	JV	CSL Diving @ Evanston	10:00 am	A
Oct	28	JV	CSL Swim @ Evanston	1:00 pm	A
Nov.	11	V	IHSA Sectionals	1:00 pm	A
Nov.	17	V	State Swim Prelims	4:00 pm	A
Nov.	17	V	State Diving Prelims	9:00 am	A
Nov.	18	V	State Finals	1:00 pm	A

High School
TITANS

Fall Sports Schedule

Donated by
The ________ Booster Club

COACHES

Girls' Swimming
Head Coach — Don Allen
Junior Varsity — Robin Doyle
Freshmen — TBA
Diving — TBA

Boys' Cross Country
Head Coach — Kurt Hosenstein
Assistant — Ken Kerr

Girls' Cross Country
Head Coach — Tom Neville
Junior Varsity — Valerie Ruth

Football
Head Coach — Ron Harris
Assistants — John Davis, Terry Simons, Jim Torsiello, Jeff Aaron
Sophomore — Jack Sims, Jeff Yardy, Ron Fearn
Freshmen — Matt Johlie, Al Bulow, Steve Weissenstein, TBA

Boys' Golf
Head Coach — Rich Gregory
Sophomore — Ed Young

Girls' Golf
Head Coach — Jon Fuller
Assistant — John Lewis

Boys' Soccer
Head Coach — Jim Walter
Assistant — Mark Daniels
Junior Varsity — Hector Carabez
Sophmore — John Arko
Freshmen — Sharon Sheehan
Freshmen — TBA

Girls' Tennis
Head Coach — Tom Henderson
Junior Varsity — Kreg Yngst

Volleyball
Head Coach — Patty Iverson
Junior Varsity — Karen Hill
Freshmen — Cathy Cabot
Freshmen — TBA

Figure 3-3, continued
Sample Sports Schedule

FOOTBALL

DATE		LEVELS	OPPONENT	TIME	SITE
Aug.	5	V/S	Barrington	11:30 am	A
Aug.	26	FA/FB	Barrington	9:00 am	A
Sep.	1	V/S	Niles North	5:00 pm	H
Sep.	2	FA/FB	Niles North	9:30 am	H
Sep.	8	V/S	Maine West	5:00 pm	H
Sep.	9	F	Maine West	9:30 am	H
Sep.	9	JV	Maine West	9:30 am	A
Sep.	16	V/S	Glenbrook North	11:30 am	A
Sep.	16	F	Glenbrook North	9:30 am	A
Sep.	22	V/S	Niles West	5:00 pm	H
Sep.	23	F	Niles West	9:30 am	H
Sep.	23	JV	Niles West	9:30 am	A
Sep.	29	F	Maine East	4:30 pm	A
Sep.	29	V/S	Maine East	5:00 pm	A
Oct.	7	V/S	Evanston	11:30 am	A
Oct.	7	FA/FB	Evanston	9:30 am	A
Oct.	9	JV	Evanston	10:00 am	A
Oct.	14	V/S	New Trier (Homecoming)	11:30 am	H
Oct.	14	FA/FB	New Trier	9:30 am	H
Oct.	21	V/S	Waukegan	11:30 am	A
Oct.	21	FA/FB	Waukegan	9:30 am	A
Oct.	28	V	IHSA 1st Round Playoff	TBA	
Nov.	4	V	IHSA 2nd Round Playoff	TBA	
Nov.	11	V	IHSA Quarter Final Game	TBA	
Nov.	18	V	IHSA Semi Final Game	TBA	
Nov.	25	V	IHSA State Final Game	TBA	

BOYS' CROSS COUNTRY

DATE		LEVELS	OPPONENT	TIME	SITE
Sep.	2	V/S/F	Fenton Invitational	9:30 am	A
Sep.	12	V/S/F	Waukegan	4:30 pm	H
Sep.	19	V/S/F	Evanston & New Trier	4:30 pm	A
Sep.	23	V/S/F	Niles North Invitational	9:00 am	A
Sep.	27	V/S/F	Niles West	4:30 pm	A
Sep.	30	V	Peoria Invitational	10:30 am	A
Oct.	5	V/S/F	Maine EastNiles	4:30 pm	H
Oct.	7	V/JV	West Invitational	9:15 am	A
Oct.	14	V/S/F	CSI Conference @ Waukegan		
Oct.	21	V	IHSA Regional Begins		
Oct.	28	V	IHSA Sectional Begins		
Nov.	4	V	IHSA State Finals Begin		

BOYS' GOLF

DATE		LEVELS	OPPONENT	TIME	SITE
Aug.	21	V	Rolling Green High School Invite	3:00 pm	A
Aug.	22	V/S	GBN @ St. Charles	10:00 am	A
Aug.	24	V/JV	Highland Park	4:00 pm	A
Aug.	29	V/JV	New Trier	4:00 pm	A
Aug.	30	V	Hersey	3:15 pm	H
Sep.	1	V/S	Prospect	3:30 pm	A
Sep.	2	V	Hersey-Rolling Meadows	10:30 am	A
Sep.	6	V/S	Waukegan	4:00 pm	A
Sep.	8	F/S	Hersey Invite	3:30 pm	A
Sep.	9	V	Batavia	8:00 am	A
Sep.	9	F/S	Hersey Invitational	9:30 pm	A
Sep.	12	V/S	Evanston	4:00 pm	H
Sep.	16	V	GBS Invitational		
Sep.	19	V/S	Maine East	4:00 pm	H
Sep.	23	V	Canant Invitational	7:30 am	A
Sep.	27	V/S	Niles West	4:00 pm	A
Sep.	28	V/S	CSI Conference @ Maine East		
Sep.	30	S	Lockport Invitational	10:00 am	A
Oct.	3	V	IHSA Regional Begins	TBA	
Oct.	10	V	IHSA Sectional Begins	TBA	
Oct.	13	V	IHSA State Finals Begin		
Oct.	14	V	IHSA State Finals Begin		

GIRLS' GOLF

DATE		LEVELS	OPPONENT	TIME	SITE
Aug.	29	JV	St. Charles	4:00 pm	H
Sep.	1	V/JV	Libertyville	4:00 pm	H
Sep.	5	V/JV	Evanston	4:00 pm	A
Sep.	7	V/JV	Hindsdale Central	4:00 pm	H
Sep.	9	V	Waukegan Invite	11:00 am	A
Sep.	13	V/JV	Waukegan	4:00 pm	H
Sep.	14	V/JV	Lake Forest	4:00 pm	H
Sep.	16	V	Rockford Guilford Invite	10:00 am	A
Sep.	19	V/JV	Glenbrook/North Antioch	4:00 pm	A
Sep.	21	V/JV	New Trier	4:00 pm	H
Sep.	23	V	Fremd/New Trier/Region/ GBS @ Old Orchard		
Sep.	26	JV	Regina	4:00 pm	A
Sep.	27	V/JV	Deerfield/Prospect	4:00 pm	H
Sep.	30	V	Champaign Invitational	8:30 pm	A
Sep.	30	JV	St. Charles JV Invite		
Oct.	5	V	IHSA Regional	TBA	
Oct.	10	V	IHSA Sectional	TBA	
Oct.	13	V	State Finals	TBA	
Oct.	14	V	State Finals	TBA	

GIRLS' TENNIS

DATE		LEVELS	OPPONENT	TIME	SITE
Aug.	29	V	Stevenson	4:30 pm	H
Aug.	29	JV	Stevenson	4:30 pm	A
Aug.	31	V	Deerfield	4:30 pm	H
Aug.	31	JV	Deerfield	4:30 pm	A
Sep.	2	V	New Trier Invite	8:30 am	A
Sep.	2	JV	GBS JV Quad		
Sep.	6	V	Glenbrook North	4:30 pm	A
Sep.	6	JV	Glenbrook North	4:30 pm	H
Sep.	8	V	Maine South	4:30 pm	H
Sep.	8	JV	Maine South	4:30 pm	A
Sep.	9	V	Fremd Invite	8:30 am	A
Sep.	9	JV	Wheeling		
Sep.	11	V	Highland Park (Fr @ Fink Park)	4:30 pm	A
Sep.	12	V	Highland Park	4:30 pm	A
Sep.	12	JV	Highland Park	4:30 pm	H
Sep.	14	V	Waukegan	4:30 pm	A
Sep.	13	JV	Waukegan	4:30 pm	H
Sep.	16	V	New Trier Invite	8:30 am	A
Sep.	19	V	Evanston	4:30 pm	H
Sep.	19	JV	Evanston	4:30 pm	A
Sep.	21	V	Niles West	4:30 pm	A
Sep.	21	JV	Niles West	4:30 pm	H
Sep.	26	V	New Trier	4:30 pm	H
Sep.	26	JV	New Trier	4:30 pm	A
Sep.	28	V	Maine East	4:30 pm	H
Sep.	28	JV	Maine East	4:30 pm	A
Sep.	30	JV	Downers Gr. South JV Invite	8:30 am	A
Oct.	2	V	Hersey	4:30 pm	A
Oct.	2	JV	Hersey	4:30 pm	H
Oct.	6	V	CSI Conference	TBA	
Oct.	6	JV	CSI Conference	TBA	
Oct.	7	V	CSI Conference	TBA	
Oct.	7	JV	CSI Conference	TBA	
Oct.	13	V	IHSA Regional Begins	TBA	
Oct.	14	V	IHSA Sectional Begins	TBA	
Oct.	19	V	IHSA State Finals Begin	TBA	
Oct.	20	V	IHSA State Finals Begin	TBA	
Oct.	21	V	IHSA State Finals Begin	TBA	

GIRLS' VOLLEYBALL

DATE		LEVELS	OPPONENT	TIME	SITE
Aug.	29	V/JV	Good Counsel	4:30 pm	A
Aug.	29	FA/FB	Good Counsel	4:30 pm	H
Sep.	1	V	New Trier Summers End Invite	5:00 pm	A
Sep.	1	FA/FB	Loyola	4:30 pm	H
Sep.	2	V	New Trier Summers End Invite	9:00 am	A
Sep.	6	V/S/FA/FB	Maine West	5:00 pm	A
Sep.	8	V/S/FA/FB	Maine South	5:00 pm	H
Sep.	12	V/S/FA/FB	Evanston	5:00 pm	H
Sep.	14	V/S/FA/FB	Waukegan	5:00 pm	A
Sep.	15	JV	Glenbrook North JV Invite	5:30 pm	A
Sep.	16	JV	Glenbrook North JV Invite	9:30 am	A
Sep.	19	V/S/FA/FB	Maine East	5:00 pm	H
Sep.	21	V/S/FA/FB	Niles West	5:00 pm	A
Sep.	23	V	Schaumburg Invite	8:30 am	A
Sep.	26	V/S/FA/FB	Glenbrook North	5:00 pm	A
Sep.	28	V/S/FA/FB	New Trier	5:00 pm	H
Oct.	2	V/S/FA/FB	Maine East	5:00 pm	A
Oct.	5	V/S/FA/FB	Evanston	5:00 pm	A
Oct.	6	V	GBN Discovery Tourn	5:00 pm	A
Oct.	7	V	GBN Discovery Tourn	9:00 am	A
Oct.	9	V/JV	Immaculate Conception	6:00 pm	H
Oct.	11	V/S/FA/FB	Waukegan	5:00 pm	H
Oct.	16	V/S/FA/FB	Niles West	5:00 pm	H
Oct.	18	V/S/FA/FB	New Trier	5:00 pm	A
Oct.	20	JV	Evanston JV Invite	5:00 pm	A
Oct.	20	JV	Evanston Invite	5:00 pm	A
Oct.	21	FA	New Trier Invite	8:00 am	A
Oct.	21	JV	Evanston JV Invite	9:00 am	A

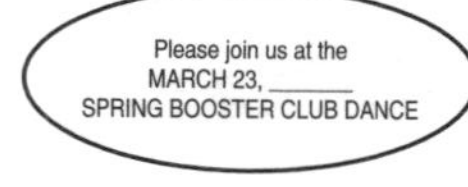

Please join us at the
MARCH 23, _______
SPRING BOOSTER CLUB DANCE

Figure 3-4
Sample Coaching Assignments and Schedule

HIGH SCHOOL
Coaching Assignments
Winter Sports

Superintendent:
Principal:
Athletic Director:
Asst. Athletic Director:
Athletic Trainer:
Asst. Athletic Trainer:
Athletic Secretary:
Conference: **Central Suburban League**
Colors: **Navy and Gold**
Nickname: **Titans**

BOYS BASKETBALL

Head Coach:	Steve Weissenstein
Jr. Varsity:	Geoff Falk
Sophomore:	Ed Young
Freshmen A:	Neil Schmidgall
Freshmen B:	Todd Hansen

WRESTLING

Head Coach:	Tim Cichowski
Assistants:	Craig Swenson
	Max Farley
	Ron Harris

BOYS SWIMMING

Head Coach:	Robin Doyle
Assistants:	Bill Wolff
	Jack Simms
Diving:	Arnie Cajet

GIRLS BASKETBALL

Head Coach:	Howard Romanek
Asst. Coach:	Terry Benjamin
Freshmen A:	Bob Schoenwetter
Freshmen B:	Bernie O'Donnell

GIRLS GYMNASTICS

Head Coach:	Jan Osowski
Assistants:	Phil Carello
	Tom Neville

Figure 3-4, continued
Boys' Basketball Schedule

Date	*Levels*	*Opponent*	*Time*	*Site*
Mon, Nov 20	V	Fenton Tournament		Away
Tue, Nov 21	V	Fenton Tournament		Away
Wed, Nov 22	S	Notre Dame Tournament		Away
Fri, Nov 24	V	Fenton Tournament		Away
Fri, Nov 24	S	Notre Dame Tournament		Away
Sat, Nov 25	V	Fenton Tournament		Away
Sat, Nov 25	S	Notre Dame Tournament		Away
Tue, Nov 28	V/S	Deerfield (Varsity @ 7:30)	6:00 PM	Home
Tue, Nov 28	FA/FB	Deerfield	4:30 PM	Home
Fri, Dec 1	V/S	Niles North	6:00 PM	Away
Fri, Dec 1	FA/FB	Niles North	4:30 PM	Away
Sat, Dec 2	JV	Niles North	9:30 AM	Away
Sat, Dec 2	V/S	Prospect	6:00 PM	Home
Mon, Dec 4	JV/FA/FB	Prospect (JV @ 7:30)	6:00 PM	Home
Fri, Dec 8	V/S	Maine East	6:00 PM	Away
Sat, Dec 9	JV/FA/FB	Maine East (JV @ 11:00)	9:30 AM	Away
Sat, Dec 9	V/S	Glenbrook North	6:00 PM	Home
Mon, Dec 11	FA	Loyola Tournament		Away
Tue, Dec 12	FA	Loyola Tournament		Away
Wed, Dec 13	FA	Loyola Tournament		Away
Fri, Dec 15	V/S	Evanston	4:30 PM	Away
Sat, Dec 16	JV/FA/FB	Evanston	9:30 PM	Away
Mon, Dec 18	S	Zion Benton Tournament		Away
Tue, Dec 19	S	Zion Benton Tournament		Away
Wed, Dec 20	S	Zion Benton Tournament		Away
Wed, Dec 27	V	Elgin Tournament		Away
Thu, Dec 28	V	Elgin Tournament		Away
Fri, Dec 29	V	Elgin Tournament		Away
Sat, Dec 30	V	Elgin Tournament		Away
Fri, Jan 5	V/S	Waukegan	6:00 PM	Away
Sat, Jan 6	JV/FA/FB	Waukegan	9:30 AM	Away
Mon, Jan 8	JV/FA/FB/SB	Lake Forest	5:30 PM	Away
Tue, Jan 9	JV/SB	Glenbrook North	6:00 PM	Home
Tue, Jan 9	FA/FB	Glenbrook North	4:30 PM	Home
Fri, Jan 12	V/S	Niles West	6:00 PM	Home
Sat, Jan 13	JV/FA/FB	Niles West	9:30 AM	Home
Fri, Jan 19	V/S	New Trier	6:00 PM	Away
Sat, Jan 20	JV/FA/FB	New Trier	9:30 AM	Away
Sat, Jan 20	V/S	Barrington	6:00 PM	Away
Mon, Jan 22	JV/SB/FA/FB	Barrington	6:00 PM	Away
Fri, Jan 26	V/S	Maine East	6:00 PM	Home
Sat, Jan 27	JV/FA/FB	Maine East	9:30 AM	Home
Sat, Jan 27	V/S	Elk Grove	6:00 PM	Home
Mon, Jan 29	JV/SB/FA/FB	Elk Grove	5:30 PM	Home
Fri, Feb 2	V/S	Evanston (Pac the Place)	4:30 PM	Home
Sat, Feb 3	JV/FA/FB	Evanston (Pac the Place)	9:30 AM	Home
Fri, Feb 9	V/S	Waukegan	6:00 PM	Home
Sat, Feb 10	JV/FA/FB	Waukegan	9:30 AM	Home
Sat, Feb 10	V/S	Fremd	6:00 PM	Away
Tue, Feb 13	FB	Niles North Tournament	4:30 PM	Away
Wed, Feb 14	FB	Niles North Tournament	4:30 PM	Away
Fri, Feb 16	V/S	Niles West	6:00 PM	Away
Sat, Feb 17	JV/FA/FB	Niles West	9:30 AM	Away
Sat, Feb 17	V/S	Lake Forest	6:00 PM	Home
Fri, Feb 23	V/S	New Trier	6:00 PM	Home
Sat, Feb 24	JV/FA/FB	New Trier	9:30 AM	Home
Mon, Feb 26	V	IHSA Regional Begins		TBA
Tue, Mar 5	V	IHSA Sectional Begins		TBA
Fri, Mar 8	V	IHSA Supersectional Begins		TBA
Fri, Mar 15	V	IHSA State Finals Begin		Away

Figure 3-4, continued
Girls' Basketball Schedule

Date	*Levels*	*Opponent*	*Time*	*Site*
Mon, Nov 13	V/JV/F	Schaumburg Tournament		Away
Thu, Nov 16	V/JV/F	Schaumburg Tournament		Away
Sat, Nov 18	V/JV/F	Schaumburg Tournament		Away
Mon, Nov 20	V/JV/F	Schaumburg Tournament		Away
Fri, Nov 24	V/JV/F	Schaumburg Tournament		Away
Tue, Nov 28	S/V	Maine West	6:00 PM	Away
Tue, Nov 28	FA/FB	Maine West	5:00 PM	Away
Fri, Dec 1,	V/S/FA/FB	Niles West	6:00 PM	Home
Tue, Dec 5	V/S/FA/FB	Glenbrook North	5:30 PM	Away
Fri, Dec 8	V/S/F	Maine East	6:00 PM	Home
Sat, Dec 9	V/FB	Maine South	2:30 PM	Away
Sat, Dec 9	S/FA	Maine South	1:00 PM	Away
Tue, Dec 12	FA/FB	New Trier	4:30 PM	Away
Tue, Dec 12	V/JV	New Trier	6:00 PM	Away
Fri, Dec 15	V	Evanston (Pac the Place)	6:00 PM	Away
Fri, Dec 15	S	Evanston (Pac the Place)	4:30 PM	Away
Sat, Dec 16	JV	Maine East	9:30 AM	Away
Sat, Dec 16	FA/FB	Evanston (Pac the Place)	1:00 PM	Away
Tue, Dec 19	V/S/FA/FB	Waukegan	6:00 PM	Home
Wed, Dec 27	V	Wheaton North Invite.		Away
Thu, Dec 28	V	Wheaton North Invite.		Away
Frid, Dec 29	V	Wheaton North Invite.		Away
Tue, Jan 9	Fr	Regina	4:00 PM	Away
Tue, Jan 9	JV	Regina	5:30 PM	Away
Tue, Jan 9	V	Regina	7:00 PM	Away
Fri, Jan 12	V/S/FA/FB	Niles West	6:00 PM	Away
Sat, Jan 13	V	Chicagoland Prep Classic	2:30 PM	Away
Fri, Jan 19	V/S/FA/FB	New Trier	6:00 PM	Home
Sat, Jan 20	F	Good Counsel	11:30 AM	Away
Sat, Jan 20	JV	Good Counsel	1:00 PM	Away
Sat, Jan 20	V	Good Counsel	2:30 PM	Away
Fri, Jan 26	V/S/F	Maine East	6:00 PM	Away
Sat, Jan 27	JV/F	Hoffman Estates	1:00 PM	Away
Sat, Jan 27	V	Hoffman Estates	2:30 PM	Away
Tue, Jan 30	S/FA	Deerfield	5:00 PM	Away
Tue, Jan 30	V/FB	Deerfield	6:30 PM	Away
Fri, Feb 2	V	Evanston (Pac the Place)	6:00 PM	Home
Fri, Feb 2	S	Evanston (Pac the Place)	4:30 PM	Home
Sat, Feb 3	FA/FB	Evanston (Pac the Place)	1:00 PM	Home
Tue, Feb 6	V/S/FA/FB	Waukegan	5:00 PM	Away
Tue, Feb 13	V	Regionals start		Away
Mon, Feb 19	V	Sectionals start		Away
Mon, Feb 26	V	Supersectionals		Away
Thu, Feb 29	V	State Finals start		Away

Figure 3-4, continued
Wrestling Schedule

Date	*Levels*	*Opponent*	*Time*	*Site*
Fri, Nov 24	V	Conant Invitational	12:00 PM	Away
Sat, Nov 25	V	Conant Invitational	12:00 PM	Away
Thu, Nov 30	V/JV/F	Loyola	5:00 PM	Away
Fri, Dec 1	V/JV/F	Glenbrook North	6:00 PM	Away
Sat, Dec 2	S	Deerfield, Elmwood Park @ Niles North	9:00 AM	Away
Sat, Dec 2	V	Prospect, Weber @ Stevenson	1:00 PM	Away
Tue, Dec 5	FB	Glenbrook North Invitational	5:00 PM	Away
Tue, Dec 5	V/JV/F	Notre Dame	5:00 PM	Home
Fri, Dec 8	V/JV/F	Highland Park	6:00 PM	Home
Sat, Dec 9	JV	Niles North Invitational	9:00 AM	Away
Sat, Dec 9	V	Buffalo Grove Invitational	9:30 AM	Away
Sat, Dec 9	F	Deerfield Invitational	9:00 AM	Away
Thu, Dec 14	V/JV/F	Waukegan	6:00 PM	Home
Fri, Dec 15	V	Russ Erb Tournament	3:30 PM	Home
Sat, Dec 16	V	Russ Erb Tournament	12:00 PM	Home
Sat, Dec 16	FA	Frosh Invitational @ MS	10:00 PM	Away
Thu, Dec 21	V/JV/F	Evanston	6:00 PM	Home
Sat, Jan 6	V	Jacobs Invitational	8:30 AM	Away
Sat, Jan 6	S	Reavis Tournament	9:00 AM	Away
Fri, Jan 12	V/JV/F	Niles West	6:00 PM	Away
Sat, Jan 13	V	Lake Foret, Mundelein @ GBN	10:00 AM	Away
Sat, Jan 13	F	Wheeling @ Lake Forest	10:00 AM	Away
Fri, Jan 19	V/JV/F	Maine East	6:00 PM	Away
Sat, Jan 20	V/JV/F	Holy Cross @ Niles North	9:00 AM	Away
Fri, Jan 26	V/JV/F	New Trier	6:00 PM	Away
Sat, Jan 27	V	Deerfield	10:00 AM	Away
Fri, Feb 2	V	IHSA Regional Begins		Away
Fri, Feb 2	V	IHSA Regional Begins		Away
Fri, Feb 9	V	IHSA Sectional Begins		Away
Fri, Feb 9	V	IHSA Sectional Begins		Away
Fri, Feb 16	V	IHSA State Finals Begin		Away

Girls' Gymnastics Schedule

Date	*Levels*	*Opponent*	*Time*	*Site*
Mon, Nov 27	V/JV/F	Glenbrook North	6:00 PM	Home
Thu, Nov 30	V/JV/F	Deerfield	5:30 PM	Away
Tue, Dec 5	V/JV/F	Evanston	5:30 PM	Away
Thu, Dec 7	V/JV/F	Niles West	5:30 PM	Away
Sat, Dec 9	V	Hersey Invite	1:00 PM	Away
Thu, Dec 14	V	Niles West Invite	6:00 PM	Away
Sat, Dec 16	V	Palatine Invite	11:00 AM	Away
Tue, Dec 19	V/JV/F	New Trier	5:30 PM	Away
Sat, Jan 6	V	Lake Forest Invite	6:00 PM	Away
Mon, Jan 8	F	Niles West Invite	6:00 PM	Away
Thu, Jan 11	V/JV/F	Waukegan	6:00 PM	Home
Mon, Jan 15	V/JV/F	Maine East	10:00 AM	Home
Fri, Jan 26	V	CSL @ NT		Away
Sat, Jan 27	JV	CSL @ MS	11:00 AM	Away

Figure 3-4, continued
Boys' Swimming Schedule

Date	*Levels*	*Opponent*	*Time*	*Site*
Fri, Dec 1	V	Deerfield Invitational (Diving @ 4:30 pm)	5:30 PM	Away
Mon, Dec 4	V/S/F	Conant	4:30 PM	Away
Fri, Dec 8	V/JV/F	Glenbrook North	5:00 PM	Home
Sat, Dec 9	V	GBN Invitational (Diving @ 10:00 am)	1:00 PM	Away
Fri, Dec 15	V/JV/F	Niles North	5:30 PM	Home
Thu, Dec 21	V/JV/F	Maine East	5:30 PM	Home
Tue, Jan 9	F	Frosh Invite @ Lyons Township	5:00 PM	Away
Fri, Jan 12	V/JV/F	Niles West	5:00 PM	Home
Sat, Jan 13	V	Titan Invitational (Diving @ 9:00 am)	1:00 PM	Home
Fri, Jan 19	V/JV/F	New Trier	5:30 PM	Away
Tue, Jan 23	V/JV/F	Lake Forest	5:00 PM	Away
Fri, Jan 26	V/JV/F	Evanston	5:00 PM	Home
Sat, Jan 27	V/JV/F	Conant Invitational (Diving @ 9:00 am)	1:00 PM	Away
Tue, Jan 30	V/JV/F	Waukegan	5:00 PM	Away
Sat, Feb 3	F	South Division Invite (Diving @ 9:30 am)	1:00 PM	Away
Fri, Feb 9	V	CSL Conference (Diving @ 3:30 pm)	6:00 PM	Away
Sat, Feb 10	JV	CSL Conference (Diving @ 9:30 am)	1:00 PM	Away
Sat, Feb 17	V	IHSA Sectional	1:00 PM	Home
Sat, Feb 17	V	IHSA Sectional Diving		Away
Fri, Feb 23	V	IHSA State Finals Begin		Away

We avoid such a tendency by seeking optimal consensus among all the parties involved in the athletic program. We shared the "Coach's Pledge" in Section Two, and indicated that one of its purposes is to achieve consensus among coaches and the athletic director regarding coaches' responsibilities to student athletes. The Pledge is also appropriate for distribution to parents and young athletes during orientation or other meetings throughout the school year.

In addition to the consistency it promotes within the school's sports program, the Pledge has significant public relations value within the parent community. Parents appreciate the Pledge's commitment to academics and family responsibilities. It also promises availability to parents throughout the season and afterward, when college planning may require the coach's experience.

Students and parents should be asked to make similar pledges. The Athlete's Pledge in Figure 1-2 should also be distributed and discussed during the orientation meeting. Each student should be given two copies—one to take home, the other to sign and return to the athletic director. The Pledge not only informs student athletes of the expectations of the program but enables reasonable consequences if the training rules are broken, or if misbehavior or unexcused absence becomes a problem.

The Pledge also has important public relations value. It lists the expectations of young athletes in the school and suggests the reasons for such behaviors. Training rules, for example, are tied to health and fitness levels, and appropriate language is linked with good breeding. The commitments also emphasize the primacy of academics and the importance of family relationships and responsibilities.

Parents like the Athlete's Pledge. It is generally consistent with their values and identifies the school and the child's coach as valuable resources in the school. They also appreciate the Parents' Pledge (Figure 3-5). It anticipates several sensitive issues that sometimes cause conflict between coaches and parents, and it promotes discussion of them with coaches and the school's athletic director.

Consider, for example, the coach's authority to determine strategy and player selection. This is a sore spot for many coaches and some parents. Someone in the stands invariably knows more than anyone else on the field—and usually shares his or her observations by shouting to the coach and players and expecting fellow fans to enjoy his or her antics. Most often, the adults in the stands ignore such a person; some few laugh. Unfortunately, others may believe and support him or her.

When a group of such people approaches the athletic director to criticize the coach or the team, some athletic directors find themselves in difficult positions. They sense the need to acknowledge and, perhaps, respond to parent concerns, but they also feel loyalty to their coaches. Their ability to resolve such a problem is especially difficult when they have failed to achieve consensus with the parent community before such problems occur. The Parents' Pledge helps to avoid such problems.

It also deters a parent from talking to the athletic director about a coach's failure to play his or her child. Certainly, not all parents will be dissuaded from complaining when the coach's selection of players seems unfair, but most, having read and perhaps discussed the Pledge, will be less inclined to expect the athletic director to intervene, especially if the athletic director has publicly supported the Pledge early in each school year.

Figure 3-5
The Parents' Pledge

Cooperation among coaches, athletes, parents, and school personnel is essential if students are to realize the values of athletic participation. Like coaches and athletes, parents must make commitments to the athletic program to assure such cooperation. We ask that you read the following Pledge and, as needed, discuss your reactions with your child's coach or the school's Athletic Director. Thanks for your help.

As the parent of an athlete in this school, I promise:

- To accompany my child to as many orientation and informational meetings offered by the athletic department as my schedule will permit.
- To work closely with all school personnel to assure an appropriate academic as well as athletic experience for my child while he or she is in high school.
- To assure that my child will attend all scheduled practices and athletic contests.
- To require my child to abide by the athletic department's training rules.
- To acknowledge the ultimate authority of the coach to determine strategy and player selection.
- To promote mature behavior from students and parents during athletic contests.
- To work cooperatively with other parents and school personnel to assure a wholesome and successful athletic program for our school.
- To work closely with coaches and other school personnel to identify a reasonable and realistic future for my child as a student athlete, both in school and in college.

This Pledge was endorsed by the Booster Club on (date).

Notice that the Pledge also carries an endorsement from the booster club. The endorsement verifies the acceptance of the Pledge among the parents in the community who are most involved in the activities of the athletic department, and thus appears more acceptable to all parents of student athletes. It also commits the members of the booster club to the principles outlined in the Pledge. We will offer more information on booster clubs later in this section.

The principle of consensus building, then, is essential within many of the responsibilities of athletic directors. Parents who agree with school personnel that young athletes should commit to regular attendance at practice and contests are less inclined to take them on vacations during the season. They also are more willing to accept the coach's opinion of the young athlete's ability to play in high school or in college.

Those of us who are involved in sport realize only too well that only 1 in 100 to 150 young athletes ever receives a scholarship to play in college, and many of those are partial scholarships. We also recognize that only *four one-thousandths of one percent* of today's high school seniors will ever play for the National Basketball Association (NBA). The same percentages are true for other sports as well.

Given this awareness, we seek the best for young athletes, and acknowledge and promote the value of academics in high school and in college. The Parents' Pledge asks them to do the same thing; it de-emphasizes with young athletes and their parents the urgency of athletics and promotes a realistic and reasonable approach to athletics now and in the future. Without consensus-building meetings early in the school year, such a balance is difficult to achieve.

THE FOUR STEPS TO EFFECTIVE PUBLIC RELATIONS

The need for good public relations is evident in everything we do. The promotion of positive relationships with young athletes, school personnel, and the parent community is the biggest and most important step in developing effective public relations. Successful athletic directors, however, complement those efforts with other activities that magnify the strengths of the athletic program and attract young athletes and parents.

Effective public relations consist fundamentally of four steps. One: Do something good. Two: Tell everybody. Three: Tell everybody. Four: Tell everybody. "Horn tooting," if sufficiently loud and pleasing, invariably attracts attention and usually draws people to your program. Coaches must recognize this fact as well. Discuss it early in each school year and remind coaches to notify you of newsworthy items, such as honors and awards, inspirational stories, humorous and revealing anecdotes, accomplishments, statistics, and other topics that will draw attention to the program.

A frequent sharing of information with the papers also cuts down on the possibility of misinformation's being spread throughout the community. A friend once told us that he never appreciated newspapers until he learned "to read between the lies." He acknowledged that mistakes are inevitable but suggested that doctors bury them, lawyers hang them, and newspapers print them all over the front page. The more we clarify news items, therefore, the better the coverage. The list of potential topics is endless.

Possible PR Topics

Anything that is remotely newsworthy should be forwarded to the local media. Topics that seem only marginally interesting within the school sometimes have great potential within the community. Emphasize that with coaches and parents by sharing the form in Figure 3-6 early in the school year.

Consider the following as examples of possible topics:

- Record-breaking performances by athletes or coaches.
- Notable statistics for a single season or career for athletes.
- Hall of Fame recognition for coaches.
- Team MVP honors and awards for athletes.
- Workshops and conventions attended by coaches.
- Articles or books written by coaches.
- Presentations made by coaches at workshops or conventions.
- Outstanding single-season or career win-loss records of coaches.
- Local, state, or national awards for coaches.
- Departmental activities, such as field trips and workshops involving student athletes or coaches.
- Donations received by the athletic department and the names of the donors.
- Honors or awards recently conferred on athletes or coaches, including academic awards for athletes and nonsport recognition for coaches.
- Recent election of coaches to local, state, or national office.
- Scholarship offers or acceptances by student athletes.
- Schools to be attended by student athletes, whether or not scholarships are involved.
- Post-junior high school or -high school honors and accomplishments by former student athletes, including academic honors.
- Babies born to coaches' families.

The PR Process

Coaches and others having newsworthy items to share can use the form in Figure 3-7 to inform you of such topics. Distribute it to them weekly or biweekly, perhaps at department or individual meetings. Emphasize the value of frequent news releases, not just to attract people to the program but to garner the kind of community support successful athletic programs require.

Also distribute the form to parents at the first orientation meeting of the year. Inform them that you're interested in receiving information about their children's athletic or academic accomplishments. Impress upon them the importance of information about academics. A thoughtful mixture of athletics and academics piques the interests of newspaper editors—especially now, when so much attention is devoted to the negative aspects of athletic competition.

Figure 3-6
A Reminder from the Athletic Department

Just a quick note to remind you to forward to the athletic department as much information as possible about coaches and athletes. We receive phone calls periodically from the local newspapers requesting information. They remind us that the community is very interested in the "Good News according to __________________ Junior High School/High School."

More important, we feel that the hard work our coaches and athletes perform on a daily basis should be recognized.

So if you hear of anything that you think is even remotely newsworthy, share it with us!

Thanks for your help!

Figure 3-7
Athletics Public Relations Form

(Fill out sections A & C if you are honoring a coach; please fill out sections A & B if you are honoring a student athlete)

A. Coach

Coach's Name ______________________________ **Phone Ext.** _________

Address ____________________________________

No. of Years Coaching at GBS _________________

B. Student Athlete

Student Athlete's Name _______________________ **Year in School** _______

Address ____________________________________

Sport _________________________ **Coach's Name** ___________________

C. Honors

(Please fill out the appropriate section below noting the following: Record-breaking performances; Notable statistics; Hall of Fame recognition; MVP honors or awards; Articles or books published; Presentations at workshops or conventions; Outstanding career win-loss records; local, state, or national awards, Scholarship offers; Schools attended by athletes; etc. Please use back if necessary.)

____

____

____

____

____

____

____

____

(Please fill out the appropriate information and forward this sheet to the Athletic Secretary. This sheet will be forwarded to the media)

- -

Athletic Use Only

___Pioneer Press
___Daily Herald
___Oracle

___Chicago Tribune
___Chicago Sun-Times
___Yearbook

Let both the coaches and the parents know that newspaper, television, or radio coverage is uncertain once you forward the press release to the media. Media people have differing ideas about what is newsworthy, so parents and coaches should be aware that you can only forward the information to the papers; coverage is not guaranteed. Without a preliminary indication that coverage is uncertain, parents and coaches will be disappointed when they fail to see their information in the papers, and they are unlikely to notify you of future activities or accomplishments. Avoid this by tempering their expectations about media coverage and by forwarding them a copy of the press release before you send it to the papers.

A copy of the completed release is provided in Figure 3-8. Before you mail the release to the papers, share a copy with the person who provided the information. Use the cover note in Figure 3-9 to thank the person for the information, to notify him or her of the mailing date to the newspapers, to invite any changes in the copy, and to encourage a continued sharing of information. Such a practice will help promote the PR program and underscore your assistance with the local media.

BOOSTERS CAN MAKE THE DIFFERENCE

Boosters are local people, generally nonschool personnel, who donate their time and energies on behalf of the athletic program, sometimes the entire extracurricular program. Like the coaches and players they assist, they have vested interests in the success of the athletic program. Their evident goals are to provide personal and financial support for athletics; their less obvious goals sometimes are to identify personally with program successes and to influence program decision making.

Boosters, therefore, can make a difference. Usually, the difference is good; sometimes it is bad. Boosters who seek only to complement the program by remedying or responding to needs are invaluable resources within the community. Because they have only the best interests of athletes and coaches in mind, they are welcomed adjuncts of the athletic program and should have routine involvement in some of the decisions made by the athletic director.

When boosters are self-serving, however, and support athletics only to indulge a need to influence the program or the people within it, they interfere with its success. Such self-indulgent people often violate the spirit and the rules governing interscholastic athletics. Athletic directors and coaches must do all they can to control the involvement of all boosters, especially those manipulative few who can do more harm than good.

Securing the booster club's endorsement of the Parents' Pledge influences not only the parents of student athletes, particularly those new to the program, but also those few boosters who are involved in athletics more to advance themselves than the program. Athletic directors stand on solid ground, therefore, when parents criticize coaching strategy or player selection or when they seek the AD's help for an athlete to miss practice because of a family vacation. Reference to the Pledge is the AD's best response.

Figure 3-8
Sample Completed Athletics Public Relations Form

(Fill out sections A & C if you are honoring a coach; please fill out sections A & B if you are honoring a student athlete.)

A. Coach

Coach's Name Coach Ron Harris **Phone Ext.** 1234

Address H.S.

No. of Years Coaching at GBS 20

B. Student Athlete

Student Athlete's Name ____________ **Year in School** ______

Address ____________

Sport ____________ **Coach's Name** ____________

C. Honors

(Please fill out the appropriate section below noting the following: Record-breaking performances; Notable statistics; Hall of Fame recognition; MVP honors or awards; Articles or books published; Presentations at workshops or conventions; Outstanding career win-loss records; local, state, or national awards, Scholarship offers; Schools attended by athletes; etc. Please use back if necessary.)

Ron Harris has been asked to speak at the Illinois Football Coaches Association Annual Conference regarding the excellent showing of the Glenbrook South Football Team in the 1995–96 Illinois State Football Playoffs. In addition to this excellent honor, Ron has also been asked to coach the Illinois East-West Shrine All Star Football Game this summer. Ron will accompany one of his linemen, Andy Lee, who has also been named to the team.

(Please fill out the appropriate information and forward this sheet to the Athletic Secretary. This sheet will be forwarded to the media)

Athletic Use Only

X Pioneer Press
X Daily Herald
X Oracle
X Chicago Tribune
X Chicago Sun-Times
X Yearbook

Figure 3-9
Thanks for the Information!

- First of all, thanks for sharing information with the Athletic Department. A positive relationship with the community has always been very important to us, and we think they'll be interested in the information.

- The attached press release is scheduled to be mailed to the papers on ______________. If you have any corrections or additions you want to share with us, please forward them to us before that time.

- Please recognize that the attached press release may not become a feature article in the papers. What they do with our press releases is up to them. The important thing is that we keep sharing the information and the "Good News" that's happening almost every day in our school.

- So please keep sharing information. The Athletic Department will continue sending reminders, and we hope to keep receiving information from you. Thanks again.

Fortunately, the vast majority of boosters are involved with the athletic program to further the interests of young athletes and coaches. Even then, however, lack of organization can result in occasional problems. To avoid such problems, we recommend the development of a set of bylaws, such as those contained in Figure 3-10. These are the bylaws of the Glenbrook South Booster Club and can be duplicated, with appropriate name changes, for your school—or you can use them as a model for the development of your own.

What is important is that you establish organizational guidelines that define and limit areas of booster responsibility. Such bylaws and policy statements avoid future problems and establish your booster club as a viable but complementary part of the athletic program. The group can be of help to the athletic director and coaches with other areas of the school's extracurricular program as well

Other programs in the school sometimes become resentful of the support received by the athletic program, particularly if athletics receives a great deal of media and school attention. You can avoid such resentment by encouraging the booster club to provide handouts or booklets to parents, teachers, and students that detail other activities in the school on a monthly basis. The sample calendar in Figure 3-11 provides one page from such a booklet and can serve as a model for something similar in your school.

Notice that the month contains nothing about athletics. As indicated earlier in this section, that kind of information has been provided elsewhere. Such a booklet or handout emphasizes the involvement and support of the booster club in all school activities—not just in athletics. Notice that it highlights debate, band, drama, and parent group meetings; it expresses booster club interest in a range of student and parent programs and identifies itself as an organization for the entire school.

Finally, use the sample letter in Figure 3-12 early in the year to welcome members to the club. It identifies the scope of the athletic program, thanks the member for his or her involvement, provides and explains the athletic pass that you will include in the mailing, and lists a few of the items that past booster donations provided for the athletic program. The letter does much to establish a positive relationship and to promote active involvement in future booster club activities and donations.

THE PARENT ROLE IN THE COALITION

Such positive relationships are important with every member of the parent community. They help promote athletics in the school and community and, eventually, they help develop coalitions of parents, coaches, and other school personnel to help student athletes find athletic experiences that complement their educational interests beyond junior high or high school. Finding the right college is particularly difficult because of the many factors that affect an eventual decision.

The parents are the prime players in coalition activities. They are the critical link between the school and home and, in spite of the possibility that coaches are God-figures, parents generally influence final decisions. This is just another reason why coaches and athletic directors must establish positive relationships with parents. Some parents wear out faster than their children's gym shoes, but they all have a reserve of power that energizes decisions about their kids.

Figure 3-10
Sample Booster Club Bylaws

General Statement

The Glenbrook South Titan Booster Club is a nonprofit organization of interested parents who voluntarily assist in the furtherance of interscholastic athletics as an integral part of the educational process at Glenbrook South High School.

Article I—Name, Purpose, Powers, Offices

Section 1 *Name*—The name of the Club is the Glenbrook South Titan Booster Club.

Section 2 *Purpose*—The purpose of the Club is as follows:

(a) To engender, foster, and promote the athletic program and school spirit at Glenbrook South High School

(b) To assist and support the faculty members involved in the administration and conduct of the interscholastic athletic program.

(c) To raise funds for special equipment and programs deemed desirable by the Athletic Director not specifically provided for by the District School Board. No part of the funds raised shall inure to the benefit of the Club members.

Section 3 *Powers*—In support of the stated purpose, but not in limitation thereof, the Club shall have the power:

(a) To solicit contributions including in-kind donations on behalf of the Glenbrook South Athletic Program.

(b) To engage in activities which will assist or contribute to the furtherance of the Glenbrook South Athletic Program.

(c) To cooperate with the principal, Athletic Director or other designated official of Glenbrook South High School in programs that further the welfare of the student body. Such programs not to be limited to interscholastic sports.

Section 4 *Offices*—The Club shall have and maintain offices on the school premises. Such offices may be within the Athletic Department with the Athletic Director as the Club representative on campus. Other arrangements as deemed appropriate by the Principal are also acceptable.

Article II—Membership

Section 1 *Eligibility*

(a) Regular membership in the Club shall be open to all parents of students at Glenbrook South High School.

(b) Associate membership in the Club shall be open to adults subscribing to the objectives of the Club. Associate members cannot hold office in the Club, although they may become members of a committee and special work groups authorized by the Club's Board of Directors.

Printed with permission from the Glenbrook South Titan Booster Club.

Section 2 *Members in Good Standing*—A member shall be deemed in good standing when annual dues are paid.

Section 3 *Termination of Membership*—Membership in the Club may be terminated:

(a) For nonpayment of dues.
(b) Through resignation—any member may voluntarily resign from the Club.
(c) For cause—any member that engages in activities detrimental to the Club may be terminated as a member after an appropriate hearing, if requested, before the Board of Directors and an affirmative vote of not less than three fourths of the members of the Board of Directors.

Article III—Meetings

Section 1 *Annual Meeting*—An annual meeting of members shall be held during the month of June in each year, on such a day and at such place and hour as determined by the Board of Directors for the purpose of electing officers. It is recommended that the June meeting of the Executive Board be held as the Annual Meeting.

Section 2 *Regular meetings*—Regular Directors meetings shall be held each month on the second Tuesday at such place and hour as determined by the Board of Directors.

Section 3 *Special meetings*—Special meetings may be called by the Chairman, the President, or by a vote of not less than 40 percent of the members.

Section 4 *Place of meetings*—The Board of Directors may designate any place, either within the school building, or without, as the place of meeting of the members.

Section 5 *Notice of meetings*—A written notice stating date, day, time, and place of the meeting will be sent to each Board Member not less than 7, nor more than 15 days prior to the meeting. Meetings of the general membership require a written notice to be published not less than 15, nor more than 30 days prior to the meetings.

Article IV—Board of Directors

Section 1 *Election*—The affairs of the Club shall be managed by the Board of Directors, which shall consist of no less than nine (9) elected members in good standing, plus the immediate past President who shall serve ex-officio. The exact number of elected Directors each year is to be determined by the Board of Directors at least thirty (30) days before the Annual Meeting. A new Board of Directors shall be elected each year for a term of office for one year. The new Board of Directors will begin its term of office on July 1st and preside over the July meeting.

Section 2 *Composition of the Board*—As much as possible, the Board of Directors shall be made up of parents representing the sports comprising the Glenbrook South Athletic Program. It is not necessary that each sport be represented by a separate parent. The assistant Athletic Director shall serve as a member of the Board.

Section 3 *Officers*—The officers of the Club shall be a Chairman of the Board, a President, Vice President, Secretary, and Treasurer. No two offices may be held at the same time by the same person.

Section 4 *Nominations*—The Nominating Committee shall consist of the Chairman of the Board, the President and Three Directors. The Nominating Committee shall nominate the Directors and officers of the Board. The names of the prospective nominees shall be presented to the Board of Directors and the general membership at least 30 days prior to the Annual Meeting. Additional nominations may be made from the floor at the Annual Meeting. In the event there are more nominees than vacancies on the Board of Directors, election shall be by written ballot. A simple majority is required to win the election.

Section 5 *Qualifications*—To be eligible as an Officer or Director, an individual must be a member in good standing.

Section 6 *Vacancies*—In the event a vacancy in the Board of Directors occurs as a result of death, resignation, disability, or termination for cause of a Director, such vacancy shall be filled by the Board of Directors, who shall elect a Director to serve until the next Annual Meeting. In the event a vacancy occurs as a result of an increase in the number of elected Directors, such vacancy shall be filled by vote of the Board of Directors at any meeting.

Section 7 *Quorum*—One-half of the Board of Directors shall constitute a quorum for the transaction of business at any meeting of the Board. If a quorum is not present, any lesser number may adjourn the meeting without further notice.

Section 8 *Action by Directors*—The act of a majority of the Directors present at a meeting at which a quorum is present, shall be the act of the Board of Directors, except where otherwise provided by law of these Bylaws.

Section 9 *Compensation*—Directors and Officers shall not receive any compensation for their services.

Section 10 Two Board Members whose children have graduated from Glenbrook South may remain on the Board of Directors for a period of no longer than two years. As Alumni Board Members, they can not be officers but may be placed on committees as other Board Members are. The two Alumni positions do not have to be filled. If more than two members request Alumni status, the Board shall determine who will fill these positions. The President shall notify all who requested alumni status on the Board.

Article V—Officers—Duties and Responsibilities

Section 1 *Chairman of the Board*—The Chairman of the Board of Directors shall be the Glenbrook South High School Athletic Director or such other representative as designated by the School Principal. The Chairman shall be entitled to vote only in the event of a tie vote of the other Directors. The office of Chairman is an appointive office.

Section 2 *President*—The President shall be the principal executive officer of the organization and shall in general supervise and control all the business and affairs of the Club. He shall preside at all meetings. At the expiration of the President's term of office, he will serve as an ex-officio member of the Board of Directors. The President may sign, with the Secretary or any other proper officer of the Club, any contracts, leases or other instruments which the Board of Directors have authorized to be executed, except in cases where the signing and execution thereof shall be expressly delegated by the Board or by these Bylaws. The President shall perform all duties incident to the office and such other duties, as may be prescribed by the Board of Directors from time to time.

Section 3 *Vice President*—In the absence of the President, or in the event of his inability or refusal to act, the Vice President shall perform the duties of the President, and when so acting, shall have all the powers of the President and be subject to the same restrictions. The Vice President shall perform such other duties as shall from time to time be assigned to him by the President of the Board of Directors.

Section 4 *Secretary*—The Secretary of the Club shall be responsible for the proper mailing of notices of meetings to the Board of Directors and members as appropriate; shall take and publish, in good form, the minutes of all meetings; shall be custodian of the Club seal; and in general, perform all duties incident to the office of Secretary.

Section 5 *Treasurer*—The Treasurer shall be in charge of the Club funds and financial records. As Treasurer, he shall collect all member dues and assessments, shall have established proper accounting procedures for the handling of the Club funds, and shall be responsible for the keeping of the funds in such banks, trust companies and/or investments as are approved by the Board of Directors. He shall report the financial condition of the Club at all meetings of the Board of Directors, and at other times when called upon by the President. At the end of the fiscal year, he shall deliver over to his successor all books, monies, and other property in his charge, or, in the absence of a successor, he shall deliver such properties to the President.

Article VI—Fiscal and Elective Year

Section 1 The Fiscal Year shall be from July 1st through June 30th, inclusive. The Elective Year shall be from July 1st through June 30th, inclusive.

Article VII—Committees

Section 1 *Executive Committee*—There shall be an Executive Committee consisting of the Chairman and elected officers. The Executive Committee shall conduct the affairs of the Club under the chairmanship of the President in accordance with the policies of the Board of Directors and may exercise the authority of the Board in all matters delegated to the Committee by it. The Executive Committee shall meet no less frequently than quarterly, to chart the course of the Club's activities.

Section 2 *Nominating Committee*—The Nominating Committee shall consist of the Chairman of the Board (presiding officer), the President and three Directors. The Directors shall be elected to the Nominating Committee by the Board of Directors at its first official meeting in July.

Section 3 *Other Committees*—The President shall appoint from the Board of Directors, such other committees as deemed necessary to conduct the affairs of the Club. He shall prescribe the Committee functions and designate the Chairman. No Committee shall act on behalf of the Board of Directors unless specifically authorized to do so. Any member of any Committee may be removed by the President whenever, in the judgment of the President, the best interests of the Club shall be served by such removal.

Section 4 *Rules*—Each Committee may adopt rules for its own government, not inconsistent with these Bylaws, or with rules adopted by the Board of Directors.

Article VIII—Dues

Section 1 *Annual Dues*—The rate of dues shall be established by vote of a majority of the Board of Directors.

Article IX—Accounting

Section 1 *Books, Records, Chart of Accounts*—The Club shall keep correct books and records of account and shall also keep minutes of the proceedings of its Board of Directors and Committees having any of the authority of the Board of Directors. A record book shall be kept by the Secretary.

A Chart of accounts that accurately reflects the income, revenue, expenses, assets, and liabilities of the Club, shall be prepared and maintained by the Treasurer. Such chart of accounts may be prescribed by the Executive Committee.

An archives of books, records, financial statements, and relative documents will be maintained in the Club office on the school premises.

All books and records of the Club may be inspected by any member in good standing for any proper purpose at any reasonable time.

Article X—Contracts, Checks, Deposits, and Funds

Section 1 *Contracts*—The Board of Directors may authorize any officer or Director, in addition to those so authorized by these Bylaws, to enter into any contract or execute and deliver any instrument in the name and on behalf of the Club. Such authority may be general or confined to specific instances.

Section 2 *Checks, Drafts, etc.*—All checks, drafts, or other orders for the payment of money, notes, or other evidence of indebtedness, issued in the name of the Club, shall be signed by such officer or officers of the Club, as determined by resolution of the Board of Directors.

Section 3 *Deposits*—All funds of the Club shall be deposited from time to time to the credit of the Club in such banks, trust companies, or other depositories as the Board of Directors may select.

Section 4 *Gifts*—The Board of Directors may accept on behalf of the Club, any contribution, gift, bequest, or device for the general purpose or for any special purpose of the Club.

Article XI—Amendments to Bylaws

Section 1 *Procedure*—These Bylaws may be altered, amended, repealed, and new Bylaws may be adopted by a majority of the entire Board of Directors at any meeting of the Board, provided that at least seven (7) days written notice is given of intention to alter, amend, repeal, or to adopt new Bylaws at such meeting.

Section 2 *Notice*—When any amendments of the Bylaws have been made, copies of such amendments, or a complete revised copy of the Bylaws as amended, shall be mailed within thirty (30) days to each member of the Board of Directors.

- -

THESE BYLAWS WERE ACCEPTED IN A MEETING OF THE BOARD OF DIRECTORS ON May 12, 1992

____________________ ____________________

President Athletic Director

MEMBERS OF THE BOARD

Figure 3-11
Sample Calendar of School Activities

SEPTEMBER

_______________ High School

Experientia docet (experience teaches)
-Tacitus

SUN.	MONDAY	TUESDAY	WEDNESDAY	THURSDAY	FRIDAY	SAT.
			AUGUST S M T W T F S 1 2 3 4 5 6 7 8 9 10 11 12 13 14 15 16 17 18 19 20 21 22 23 24 25 26 27 28 29 30 31	OCTOBER S M T W T F S 1 2 3 4 5 6 7 8 9 10 11 12 13 14 15 16 17 18 19 20 21 22 23 24 25 26 27 28 29 30 31	1	2
3	4 LABOR DAY No School	5 SENIOR PHOTO RETAKES → Band Rehearsal 6:30 - 8:30 pm	6 → Senior Assembly	7 → Academy Assembly	8 →	9
10	11 Fall Sports Assembly Band Rehearsal 6:30 - 8:30 pm	12 Marching Band Festival	13	14	15 Back to School Dance	16 Debate Presentation
17	18 HEARING/VISION SCREENING → Department Meetings	19 → Band Rehearsal 6:30 - 8:30 pm	20 →	21 →	22 →	23 Fall Begins
24	25 ROSH HASHANAH No School	26 Band Rehearsal 6:30 - 8:30 pm	27 Junior High Band Day Parent Association General Meeting	28 ESL Parent Orientation Night Mini-Musical "The Fantastics"	29 Mini-Musical "The Fantastics"	30 Mini-Musical "The Fantastics"

Figure 3-12
Sample Welcome Letter to Booster Club Member

Athletic Department

Dear Booster Club Member: Date

On behalf of the more than 60 coaches and over 1,100 athletes, I would like to personally thank you for becoming a member of the High School Booster Club.

Your membership entitles you and your family to enter any district #225 event for athletic competition. A reminder that this pass may not be used at Illinois High School Association sanctioned tournaments such as Regionals, Sectionals, and State Competition due to the fact that we send the revenue from these events to the IHSA.

Also included in this packet is the Booster decal that fits in your automobile window and the AD Book which has the directions to many of the schools that we compete against.

Your money that you have generously contributed will go toward assisting our student athletes with many additional opportunities that we normally would not be able to supply. Here are just a few of the items that have been provided in the past years because of your donations:

Athletic/academic award plaques each year (46)
$500 scholarships for college bound athletes each year
Championship patch for each member of all league championship teams
Pocket sport calendar sent to members each season
Pictures of senior athletes and their parents
Orthatron knee machine for the Training Room
Whirlpool for the Training Room
Mettler Sonicator (Ultrasound Equipment) for the Training Room
Baseball dugouts
Track record boards for the gymnasium
Scoreboards for the lower and main gymnasiums
VHS Systems (Camera, Recorder, TV)
Guide Booklet for College Bound Student Athletes
Membership in the Collegiate Athletic Network

Again, thank you for your patience in the distribution of the AD book, and I look forward to working with you.

Sincerely,

H.S. Athletic Coordinator

If high school parents, coaches, and others use their collective power on behalf of student athletes, much of the unprincipled recruiting that sometimes clouds intercollegiate athletics will never get started. Knowledge of the college selection and recruiting processes is the first thing parents, coaches, and counselors need to deal effectively with college coaches. Parents and high school personnel already have the power, but most of them just don't realize it. The same is true of elementary and junior high school parents. The decay occurring in much of American sports is eating its way from the professional to the elementary and junior high levels. High school coaches are now beating the feeder-school bushes for promising young athletes, disregarding their educational needs in order to focus on athletics.

Street agents are identifying younger and younger athletes, specifically 6' 5" eighth graders, in order to be able to "represent" them in high school and beyond, when these children grow into scholarships and multimillion dollar contracts. Needless to say, money is influencing the direction of sports in this country. The enlightened intervention of parents, coaches, and other school personnel can be a powerful force to reverse the trend.

Consider Figure 3-13, the "Working Together" Checklist for Parents. Similar lists can be found for coaches and counselors in Mike's *Advising Student Athletes Through the College Recruitment Process*, published by Prentice Hall in 1996. It lists the responsibilities of parents before and during the recruitment process, including assurances that their child has taken career inventories, has met the NCAA eligibility requirements, has selected a college irrespective of sports, and has made arrangements with coaches and counselors to deal with the college selection and recruitment processes.

Coaches and counselors have related responsibilities. In essence, if everyone does his or her job, young athletes will attend college for the right reasons, not simply to satisfy an adolescent need for athletic recognition. In addition, if parents invest themselves in the process and work closely with coaches and counselors, they will coalesce the power each brings to the process.

Put it this way: If parents and school personnel influence young athletes to focus on college as primarily an academic experience, the insidious distractions and the often empty promises of intercollegiate and professional sports will have less influence on their decisions to attend a particular college. We have learned over the years that if coaches and parents—for whatever reasons—tell young athletes *not* to attend certain colleges, the athletes will not attend those colleges.

That's power. Many college coaches may have more than their share of charisma; they may command the media spotlight, even expect or realize legendary status in their sports. They are still, however, dependent on high schools for their supply of talent, so they *recruit* "blue chippers," young athletes who benefit from, and often are bewildered by, their own athletic gifts. High school coaches *mold* blue chippers, and enlightened parents control their destinies.

Parents and coaches must use this power in order to assure the right college experiences for young athletes. Athletic directors must realize that parents and coaches do so when they work together to select the right schools for students. Be sure, therefore, to share the information in Figure 3-13 with any parent who anticipates athletics for his or her child in college.

Figure 3-13
"Working Together" Checklist for Parents

Use the following checklist to remind yourself through the year if you have met your child's college needs.

DURING MY CHILD'S JUNIOR YEAR,
DID I:

________ Meet with the counselor in the spring of the junior year to discuss the college search process?

________ Develop a calendar with my child to assure completion of career inventories?

________ Discuss senior year registration with the counselor to assure compliance with NCAA requirements?

________ Discuss with my child the list of colleges developed with his or her counselor?

________ Visit selected college campuses?

EARLY IN MY CHILD'S SENIOR YEAR,
DID I:

________ See that my child gains admission to at least one college in the event college sports fail to materialize?

________ Check with the counselor to assure compliance with the NCAA?

________ Check with teachers to assure good academic progress?

________ Meet with the coach, as necessary, to deal with persistent recruiters?

WHEN MY CHILD'S COMPETITION WAS COMPLETED,
DID I:

________ Revise our list of schools to reflect possible scholarship offers?

________ Meet with the coach to assess my child's athletic potential and to determine the kinds of questions we should be asking of recruiters?

________ Meet with the coach to deal with persistent recruiters?

________ Accompany my child on all college visits?

________ Maintain contact with the counselor and coach as needed?

The parents of gifted elementary or junior high student athletes require the same kind of assistance. The checklist in Figure 3-14 lists the kinds of questions they must ask in order to assure an appropriate experience for their children in high school. Parents in inner cities must be particularly aware of "street agents," who lure young athletes to the brink of abuse by promising them money and recognition if they attend the "right" high school.

Parents who oversee high school course selection and the academic progress of their children and are alert to the possibility of unprincipled agents or coaches do much to refocus athletic competition on the needs of young athletes, not the colleges that eventually recruit them. You, therefore, are well advised to work closely with parents to secure their support of athletic programs and to help them use their power to reaffirm the basic values of athletic competition.

LET'S WRAP IT UP

As we've already told you, too many coaches and athletic directors regard parents as occasional interferences. Many of them see parents as "outsiders" who ask tough questions, have unrealistic ideas of their children's ability, expect scholarships for them to the strongest sports programs in the country, and seem always to be "lurking around" during practice sessions and games.

Well, much of this probably is true—and, generally, we should be pleased that it is. The unrealistic assessments of their children's ability and potential for college are occasionally tough to handle, but the presence of parents during practice and their occasional questions signal an interest and a concern that can benefit both the program and the student. Most parents are genuinely concerned about the welfare of their children and will do anything possible to help them.

If their young athletes need a new seven-man sled on the football field, new field hockey uniforms, or a whirlpool for the training room, many parents will do what they can to satisfy the need. If the athletes and coaches require moral support to struggle through a difficult season, many parents will provide it. And if athletic directors require input from knowledgeable people in the community to maintain top-notch athletic programs, many parents are available to offer it.

Parents, therefore, are not faceless figures in the crowd during contests. They are allies in the school's efforts to develop and maintain the best possible athletic experiences for young athletes. Successful athletic directors promote parent involvement on booster clubs and parent advisory councils. They maintain friendly relationships with them in school and throughout the community.

They also work with them at the conclusion of the young athlete's participation to assure an appropriate academic and athletic experience in high school or in college. The closer athletic directors, coaches, and parents work together, the better our sports programs will be, benefiting from the collective knowledge and involvement of all the concerned adults in the community.

Figure 3-14

"Working Together" Checklist for Junior High Parents

Use the following checklist to remind yourself through the year if you have met your child's high school needs.

DURING MY CHILD'S LAST YEAR IN JUNIOR HIGH,
DID I:

________ Review my child's achievement and aptitude test scores to assess his or her readiness for certain programs of study?

________ Discuss the actual course selection with the junior high school and the high school counselor?

________ Discuss with the counselor or college consultant the appropriateness of my child's selection with changing college admissions requirements?

________ Meet with the high school counselor to discuss orientation activities and identify important information?

________ Discuss with the high school counselor a process for monitoring NCAA requirements?

______ Meet with the high school coach(es) to discuss time demands before and during athletic competition?

________ Other

SECTION FOUR

Scheduling and Related Organizational Duties

First, a quick story:

During Nancy's first few years as a high school athletic director, she found herself pressured by several opposing forces. Each was pushing for the best times and facilities for practice sessions. She knew, of course, that all head coaches seek only the best for their athletes and that their normal biases can provoke a conflict or two in the department, so she accepted such conflict as inevitable. She also realized, however, that she didn't want to be the exclusive decision maker every time a conflict arose involving the allocation of facilities. She knew that people who make such decisions eventually alienate everyone who has a vested interest in them, so she decided to head off conflicts by having the coaches help make the decisions.

Before the start of each sports season, therefore, she asked the head coaches of each sport to meet with her one afternoon after school. After announcing the reason for the meeting, she distributed information on the relevant legal expectations of Title IX, provided a few ideas to guide their thinking, and listed all the available facilities both inside and outside the building. Some of the problems confronting the group were resolved by the need for specialized facilities; for example, the football team had its practice field, and the field hockey team had its practice and game field. On occasion, the football team would have to make some concessions to the soccer team—especially on soccer game days—but the demands of the game-day schedules always took precedence over the other team's practice needs.

As you can no doubt see, from the practice considerations outlined in Figure 4-1, the problems normally occurred when the boys' and girls' basketball teams or the boys' and girls' swim teams wanted the gyms or the pool right after school. With more than a little negotiating, however, and a whole lot of consensus building, the coaches developed mutually acceptable practice schedules.

Once comprehensive schedules were developed, they often served from year to year, with only slight modification (see Figure 4-2, Sample Practice Schedule). When such was the case, Nancy would convene the coaches, ask if any changes had to made in practice schedules, revise them as needed, then thank everyone for their time. The process proved to be very successful for her because it introduced the coaches to the problems involved in the allocation of facilities, it reaffirmed the importance of Title IX, and it promoted cooperation within the coaching staff.

The storm generated by Title IX, although a couple of decades old, probably is as turbulent as ever. Like most storms, it finds a way to hit just about everyone in its path. Although women have benefited from expanded opportunities for athletic participation, they still struggle against powerful forces that cite inadequate revenue production as a reason to return to pre-Title IX days, when the sun shone more brightly—unfortunately, almost exclusively on men's programs.

Men, too, battle the winds of change. Many try to accept the inevitability of women's athletics and to acknowledge the benefits that women realize from athletic participation. But a significant number struggle with the concept of "separate but equal" and cling desperately to the traditional notion that "revenue producers" deserve preferential treatment, including the best facilities when they need them.

That conflict is one of the focuses of this section. Adding to the problem, however, is the fact that most schools are experiencing significant increases in the numbers of students participating in interscholastic athletics. Girls are realizing the benefits of athletic participation, and so are the boys who find themselves influenced by society's increasing awareness of the importance of improved physical fitness through exercise and a well-rounded diet. Interscholastic athletics is the logical choice for such students because of its emphasis on training rules and physical conditioning.

The result is significant numbers of students joining a variety of sports programs every year. They may not all be totally committed to the concepts of physical sacrifice, the will to win, or team membership, but they're on our doorsteps, and they deserve everything we have to offer them, including fair treatment and the best equipment and facilities available in our schools. We have discovered that the least committed freshman athlete often becomes the most dedicated upperclass student, and even the "conscientiously uncommitted" realize significant physical, emotional, and social benefits from their involvement in interscholastic athletes.

MORE ABOUT THE PRACTICE SCHEDULE

Fortunately, our experience has been that most coaches are wonderfully capable of some give and take during the allocation of facilities. They may maneuver a little bit when the planning session starts, but they generally make willing concessions when the actual decisions have to be made. This is especially true in athletic departments that have fostered a family concept and that have engaged coaches in a variety of decisional activities. The more coaches are involved in making decisions and in having access to the information required for such decisions, the more willing they are to cooperate with athletic directors and other coaches to handle problems.

Figure 4-1
Sample Practice Considerations

Multiple Number of Levels

Boys Basketball (BBB)	5 levels	VAR, JV, SO, FA, FB
Girls Basketball (GBB)	5 levels	VAR, JV, SO, FA, FB
Wrestling (WR)	3 levels	VAR, JV, F
Gymnastics (GYM)	3 levels	VAR, JV, F
Swimming (SW)	3 levels	VAR, JV, F
Track and Field (TR) (begins in January)	3 levels	VAR, JV, F

Previous Year's Competitor Numbers

Boys Basketball	60	Girls Basketball	60
Wrestling	45	Swimming	40
Gymnastics	40	Track and Field	200

Additional Considerations

Freshmen need to practice early—transportation problems.

Competition days take precedence over practice days.

Even practice schedules as much as possible for all sports.

Coaches share in decision-making process.

Late contests should result in early practice on the following days if possible.

Keep weekly practices as similar as possible by weeks—e.g., freshmen practice late every Tuesday.

Swimming will be in pool and will not need facility space.

Figure 4-2
Sample Practice Schedule

Monday 2/5	*N Main*	*S Main*	*East Gym*	*W FH*	*E FH*	*WR*	*Weight*
3:00	BBB	BBB	GYM mt	TR	TR	WR	Open
5:30	GBB	GBB	GYM mt	TR	TR	WR	INT
8:00	INT	INT	GYM mt	A Ed	A Ed	x	x
Tuesday 2/6							
3:00	BBB	BBB	GYM	TR mt	TR mt	WR	Open
5:30	GBB gm	GBB gm	GBB gm	INT	INT	WR	INT
8:00	GBB gm	GBB gm	Night	School	Night	x	x
Wednesday 2/7							
3:00	GBB	GBB	GYM	TR	TR	WR mt	Open
5:30	BBB	BBB	BBB	TR	TR	WR mt	INT
8:00	INT	INT	x	A Ed	A Ed	x	x
Thursday 2/8							
3:00	GBB	BBB	GYM mt	TR	TR	WR	Open
5:30	GBB	BBB	GYM mt	INT	INT	x	INT
8:00	GBB	BBB	Night	School	Night	x	x
Friday 2/9							
3:00	GBB gm	GBB gm	GBB gm	TR mt	TR mt	WR mt	Open
5:30	GBB gm	GBB gm	GBB gm	TR mt	TR mt	WR mt	INT
8:00	BBB gm	BBB gm	BBB gm	Dance	Dance	Dance	x
Saturday 2/10							
8:00	BBB gm	BBB gm	BBB gm	TR	TR	x	Open
11:00	GBB gm	GBB gm	GBB gm	Rental	Rental	WR	Open
2:00	GBB gm	GBB gm	GBB gm	Rental	Rental	WR	x
5:00	BBB gm	BBB gm	BBB gm	x	x	x	x

N Main—North end of main gym
S Main—South end of main gym
East Gym—East gymnasium
W FH—West end of field house
E FH—East end of fieldhouse
WR—Wrestling room
Weight—Weight room
x—Closed for cleaning
Night School—Evening high school

INT—Intramural program
Open—for sports program
A Ed—Adult education
gm—game/contest
mt—meet/contest

The actual allocation of facilities, therefore, is generally not a big issue. Most coaches recognize the needs of their colleagues and make reasonable concessions in their own practice schedules to accommodate them. All they need is the opportunity to understand how limited facilities can affect everyone in the department, then to plan cooperatively to meet everyone's needs. Given the opportunity, most people are considerate of one another. They can, however, be forgetful, which suggests additional considerations about practice.

Before Practice Starts

Athletes and coaches have certain responsibilities before the season actually begins. Athletes must not be permitted to practice until:

- They show evidence of a physical examination (Figure 4-3).
- They return the form in Figure 4-4, which provides information in case of a medical emergency.
- They return a signed Athletic Code (see Figure 1-4).
- They have met the school's and the state's eligibility requirements.
- They show evidence of having attended a "liability" or "risk" meeting, which explains the potential for injury in all athletic participation. Athletic directors should organize and hold such meetings before the start of each sports season, and involve as many coaches as possible in each meeting.

In addition, coaches must submit to the athletic director a final team roster before the first practice can begin. A sample form for such a roster is provided in Figure 4-5. This is also the time to distribute to coaches a form such as the one in Figure 4-6, which explains locker room responsibilities—the supervision of athletes before and after practice, and the maintenance of the facility—and transportation regulations.

Remind coaches, too, to distribute to each player a form concerning the athletic department's expectations of athletes' behavior in the locker room (see Figure 4-7). Coaches soon learn that the locker room rivals the practice field for injuries to athletes. It also is the place for intimidation of younger athletes and an occasional fight. The behavior of athletes in the locker room *must* be outlined and coaches must supervise the facility carefully.

When Practice Begins

Once each athlete has received permission to practice and the team roster has been submitted, the next important issue involves the practice sessions themselves. Coaches, more than anyone else in the school building, must recognize the potential legal and procedural problems that exist during practices and contests. Practice is a time when coaches must be especially alert to problems involving player safety, eligibility, departmental expectations of locker room behavior, and family needs regarding vacations and religious holidays.

Distribute a form similar to the one in Figure 4-8, which outlines the policies that coaches should follow to assure reasonable compliance with the expectations of the school and the needs of each athlete's family. Such a form should be discussed in a departmental meeting prior to distribution in order to achieve the consensus needed to guarantee its use by coaches.

Among the very important topics addressed are:

- The need to ensure that coaches are the first to arrive at practice and the last to leave. Practice areas are invitations for horseplay, and horseplay is an invitation for injury. Coaches must be available at all times to prevent such problems.
- The need to begin and end practice at a reasonable time. Student athletes have family and academic responsibilities that (excuse the apparent heresy) are often far more important than soccer or field hockey practice. Coaches certainly can expect total commitment and hard work from each athlete during practice, provided the practice is reasonably scheduled and appropriate in length.
- The need to store all equipment in an appropriate place. Sports equipment is generally very expensive and should be protected between practices from the elements and theft. Lying around unprotected, it also is a temptation to neighborhood children, who risk serious injury by playing with it.
- The need to follow departmental and school policy regarding athletes who may have been absent from school on the day of practice. Figure 4-8 details the procedure to be followed.
- The need to accommodate the religious requirements of athletes, who, for example, may not be permitted to practice until after sundown on certain religious holidays or who have other religious proscriptions that preclude practice.

Practices Involving Scrimmages

Many sports promote preseason scrimmages involving other schools. Such scrimmages enable coaches to assess personnel under game conditions, making it easier to identify starters or to evaluate the success of certain strategies. Scrimmages, particularly intrasquad scrimmages prior to the start of the season, promote community interest and serve as a gathering point for athletes, coaches, teachers, administrators, and parents to meet informally and to share their excitement about a new season.

Coaches must realize, however, that the number of scrimmages per season is normally limited by either state or school policy, so it's important to provide coaches with a set of guidelines, similar to those in Figure 4-9, to avoid potential problems.

Figure 4-3
Medical and Parent Consent Form

NOTE: THIS FORM IS TO BE USED FOR THE INTERSCHOLASTIC ATHLETIC PHYSICAL ONLY

INTERSCHOLASTIC ATHLETIC MEDICAL AND PARENT CONSENT FORM

To the Parents: Both sides of this form must be completed before your son/daughter can participate in Interscholastic Athletic practices or contests. Your cooperation is appreciated.

Coordinator of Athletics

TO BE COMPLETED BY THE STUDENT Name of Sport ____________________

Name ____________________ I.D. No. __________ Year in School 1 2 3 4

Last, First—Please Print

Birth Date __________ Place of Birth—County __________ State __________

School Attended Last Year ____________________ Sex: Circle One M F

Name of Doctor ____________________ Phone Number __________

Doctor's Address ____________________ Town __________

I hereby apply to participate in Interscholastic Athletics at Glenbrook South High School. I agree to abide by the Constitution, Rules, and Bylaws of the Illinois High School Association and the Glenbrook South Code of Conduct.

____

Student's Signature

TO BE COMPLETED BY THE DOCTOR

Name of Student ____________________ Height __________ Weight __________

Disease History: Allergies ____________________

Seizures ____________________

Comments: ____________________

____

Athletics Allowed:

All Sports ______	Football ______	Soccer ______
Badminton ______	Golf ______	Tennis ______
Baseball ______	Gymnastics ______	Track ______
Basketball ______	Softball ______	Volleyball ______
Cross Country ______	Swimming ______	Wrestling ______

I hereby certify that I have examined the above-named student and there appears to be no medical reason why he/she is not physically able to compete in supervised athletic activities checked above at Glenbrook South.

Doctor's Signature ____________________

Please use hand stamp with signature

Date of actual physical __________

If the physical is more than 1 year old, it is not acceptable.

PARENT CONSENT FOR PARTICIPATION IN INTERSCHOLASTIC ATHLETICS

Student's Name: ______________________________

Address: ______________________________

I, as parent, understand that the school district has made available an accident insurance program in which my child may enroll and that the program is optional and limited to the coverage specified in the brochure. I (We) realize there is a possibility that a child may suffer injury, including permanent paralysis or death, as a result of participation in athletic activities.

I further understand that the school district disclaims any financial responsibility for the costs of medical treatment, hospitals, ambulances, or paramedics, etc., arising out of or by virtue of an injury to my (our) child while participating in such interscholastic competition or preparation thereof.

My (Our) above named child has my (our) approval to participate in the following interscholastic sports. (Please use an X).

______All Sports	______Football	______Swimming
______Badminton	______Golf	______Tennis
______Baseball	______Gymnastics	______Track
______Basketball	______Softball	______Volleyball
______Cross Country	______Soccer	______Wrestling

I (We) are aware of the opportunity to view the film "Informed Consent" which is available at the school offices should I (we) wish to view it, upon request. I further acknowledge that before my child can participate in such school-sponsored sport(s) this consent must be executed by me (us) and filed at the school, together with the result of a physical examination indicating that my child is physically fit to participate in such school-sponsored activity.

______________________	______________________
Date	Name—Parent or Guardian
______________________	______________________
Telephone Number	Signature—Parent or Guardian

Printed with permission from Glenbrook South High School.

Figure 4-4
Emergency Information and Parent Consent Form

ATHLETIC DEPARTMENT
EMERGENCY INFORMATION AND PARENT CONSENT

Name ______________________ Birthdate ____________ Age _________

Parent's Name ______________________ Home Phone ______________

Address ______________________ City ______________ Grade _______

Day Phone of Parents: Father ______________ Mother ______________

In an emergency, if the parents cannot be reached, notify:

______________________ Phone ______________

Family Doctor ______________________ Phone ______________

Known Allergies ____

Permission is hereby granted to the attending physician to proceed with any medical or minor surgical treatment, x-ray examination and immunizations for the above-named student. In the event of an emergency arising out of serious illness, the need for major surgery, or significant accidental injury, I understand that an attempt will be made by the attending physician to contact me in the most expeditious way possible. If said physician is not able to communicate with me, the treatment necessary for the best interest of the above-named student may be given.

Permission is also granted to the Certified Athletic Trainer to provide the needed emergency treatment prior to the student's admission to the medical facilities.

Parent Signature ______________________ Date ______________

Printed with permission from Glenbrook South High School.

Figure 4-5
Sample Team Roster

Girls' Varsity Soccer Roster

#	PLAYER	YEAR	POSITION
18	Jane Smith	Junior	Defender
16	Player 2	Sophomore	Midfielder
10	Player 3	Senior	Defender
21	Player 4**	Senior	Defender
13	Player 5	Junior	Forward
5	Player 6	Senior	Forward
2	Player 7	Junior	Midfielder
15	Player 8	Senior	Defender
19	Player 9**	Senior	Defender
12	Player 10	Sophomore	Midfielder
G	Player 11	Sophomore	Goalie
7	Player 12	Junior	Midfielder
23	Player 13	Junior	Forward
8	Player 14	Senior	Midfielder
9	Player 15	Junior	Forward

**Denotes Team Captain

Coaches: Head Coach, Asst. Coach

Figure 4-6
Coaches' Supervision and Transportation Responsibilities

SUPERVISION

All school athletic activities must be supervised by a coach employed by the School Board.

1. A coach must be present at all games and practice sessions.

2. Coaches must make every effort to prevent accidents. Negligence is invariably judged more harshly by a court of law than by the average coach. It can lead to liability suits that award large sums to the injured person.

3. Individuals are not to be given permission to use school facilities for activities such as shooting baskets, running on the track, weight lifting, etc. Such activities can be carried on only when they are under the supervision of a coach or instructor.

4. A coach is responsible for the conduct of squad members in the locker room. Whenever possible, he/she should be in the locker room with them. When this is not possible, an assistant should be present.

5. Coaches who use the facilities on a Saturday, or a holiday, are responsible for the team leaving the building.

6. When your practice has concluded, you must stay until the last athlete is out, and make sure that all doors are locked. Turn out all lights when you leave.

STUDENTS SHOULD NOT BE IN THE BUILDING AT ANY TIME UNLESS THEY ARE SUPERVISED.

TRANSPORTATION

All contestants must travel to and from athletic contests with the coach. School buses will be used for most trips. No athlete should be allowed to drive or ride with others unless written permission is given by parents and athletic director. Under certain circumstances and with prior approval from the coach or athletic director, an athlete may return home with his/her parents.

Reprinted with permission from District #225 Coaches' Handbook.

Figure 4-7
Locker Room Expectations of Student Athletes

1. A coach will be present at all times when student athletes are in locker room area.

2. Students athletes are responsible for their behavior in the locker room area as well as on the field or court. We strongly disapprove of rough play and expect the athletes to demonstrate responsible actions in the locker room area.

3. Use of towels and other equipment supplied by the locker room attendant will be taken care of as if the equipment were the student's own property. All equipment will be returned to the attendant before students leave the area.

4. The above rules are also effective at away contests where student athletes have the privilege to use the opposing team's locker room facilities.

5. Any infractions of the above expectations will result in a hearing before the athletic board, and the violation could result in severe consequences.

Figure 4-8
Duties and Responsibilities of Coaches

HEAD COACHES

You are responsible for all coaches and levels within your sport. The duties listed below are important. Many of them should be completed by your assistants. Your assistants should help you in every way possible. Be certain that they are aware of their duties.

ASSISTANT COACHES

Many of these duties will be your responsibility. Loyalty, cooperation, and support are essential to any successful program. Assist your head coach at all times. Your concerns or complaints should be discussed privately with him/her and with us.

Before the Season Begins You Must:

1. Check your practice area and equipment to be certain it is ready for use.
   A. Work orders must be signed by the Athletic Director before they are submitted.
   B. Purchases must *not* be made by individuals. All purchase requests must be initiated from the Athletic Director's office.
2. Registration of athletes:
   A. Athletes *must* turn in the completed gold physical/medical history forms before they are allowed to practice. No equipment should be issued before these forms are in.
   B. An accurate list of all participants must be on file in the athletic office at all times. This list must be turned in by the end of the first week of practice so that an accurate eligibility list can be prepared. ***You must inform the athletic secretary of additions or deletions.***
3. Assist in arranging for the systematic issuance of equipment. Communicate with our equipment personnel. This system varies by sport. Ask questions if you are not sure what to do.
4. Discuss the athletic program with your athletes and your assistants. Make certain that they are aware of any rules or policies which pertain to your sport and your department. If you have any special rules for your team, be sure that the athletic director is aware of them before distribution and has a written copy on file. Winter and spring family vacations often present problems for the athlete. An athlete should not be dismissed from a team or adversely treated because of family obligations. However, absent athletes may have to work hard to regain their previous playing status. The athletes who remain here during vacations must be given consideration for their commitment. Athletes should inform their coach well beforehand if they plan to miss practice or contests because of family vacations.
5. Submit a copy of your schedule with bus times listed. Be realistic about these times. Buses should not have to wait more than 5 minutes for your team.
6. Meet with your staff to standardize techniques, drills, system of play, etc. to ensure consistent teaching within your sport.

Reprinted with permission from District #225 Coaches' Handbook.

During the Season You Must:

1. Make certain that the athletes in your program are supervised at all times. Locker room supervision before and after practice and on away trips is your responsibility. Assign assistants as needed.
2. Use sound judgment and coaching practices at all times. If you see lightning, practice or contests should immediately be suspended or terminated. Seek safe shelter for everyone.
3. Assist in the care and security of your equipment, practice area, and locker room.
4. Schedule and organize daily practices. Gym space is assigned by sport; you are to assign it by level.
5. Turn in the result sheet after each contest and provide any publicity information which might be helpful. This report must be in by noon on the first day of school following the contest.
6. Attend Booster Club and other meetings as requested.
7. Keep accurate team and individual records. Turn in a summary at the conclusion of your season.
8. Keep your eligibility list accurate and up to date. If an athlete drops from your squad, make certain that the equipment is collected and the name is removed from the list. Be sure to review the eligibility prior to the banquet letters being mailed home.
9. An accident report must be filled out for each injury. This report should be turned in to the athletic trainer within 24 hours of the accident.

At the Conclusion of the Season You Must:

1. Assist in the collection of all equipment. This is your responsibility. Do not leave it for others to do. Have your athletes turn in all equipment/uniforms immediately following the final contest. In delinquent cases, please follow these procedures:

   Step 1—Coach contacts athlete in school.
   Step 2—Coach phones parents before banquet.
   Step 3—Coach withholds awards at banquet.
   Step 4—Athletic office mails letter home.
   Step 5—Semester grades will be withheld.

   If an athlete quits your team, be sure to collect his/her uniform/equipment immediately. Communicate with the equipment personnel and athletic secretary.
2. Prepare for and conduct the awards presentation. Submit a list of award winners to the athletic secretary for preparation at least one week before the banquet.
3. Turn in a summary of the season and the information needed to complete the differential responsibility report.
4. Assist in the evaluation of each coach on your staff.
5. Schedule end-of-year evaluation with the athletic director or assistant athletic director. Bring completed evaluations of assistant coaches to this meeting.
6. Check major equipment and facilities. Make recommendations for repairs and improvements.
7. Prepare a tentative budget for the next year. This must include exact specifications, sizes, and prices.
8. Assist in the preparation of the schedule for the next season.

Figure 4-9
Sample Summary of League Contest Limits

Badminton	All levels—16 dates
Baseball	Varsity—35 games in 25 dates Freshmen and Sophomore—28 games Junior Varsity—10 games
Basketball	Varsity—21, 19/1, 18/2 Sophomores—18/2 Junior Varsity 17/1 Freshmen—17/1
Cross Country	All levels—15 dates
Football	All levels—9 dates
Golf	All levels—16 dates
Gymnastics	Varsity—15 dates Junior Varsity—15 dates Freshmen—12 dates
Soccer	Varsity—17-0, 16-2, 15-2 Sophomores—same as above Freshmen—14, 12-1
Softball	All levels—35 games
Swimming	Varsity—14 dates Junior Varsity—14 dates Freshmen—12
Tennis	All levels—18 dates
Track and Field	All levels—18 dates
Volleyball	Varsity—21, 19-2, 18-2, 16-3, 15-4 Junior Varsity—18, 17-1 Freshmen 16, 15-1
Wrestling	Varsity—18, 17-1, 16-2, 15-3, 14-4 All other levels—16 dates

SCHEDULING CONTESTS

The primary consideration regarding the scheduling of contests is the state's maximums permitted for each sport. Normally, these maximums involve the number of contests per season as well as the number permitted during any given week in the season. Schools belonging to a conference must plan in conjunction with other athletic directors and school principals to determine athletic contests during any given year. Such contests take priority over nonconference contests, for example, when a league contest has been postponed for whatever reason and must be made up before the conclusion of the season.

The scheduling of nonconference contests—even the decision of what conference to join—involves several important considerations, including:

- **The distance between the schools.** Schools in rural areas sometimes must travel considerable distances to the nearest schools. Their decisions to form a conference are dictated almost exclusively by geographical location, and, because they are in predominantly rural areas, they tend to be similar in size.
- **The sizes of the schools.** On occasion, one or more of these schools is considerably larger than any of the others. This invariably poses problems. Conferences must be constantly alert to opportunities to add or delete schools as new schools are built or as some grow or diminish in size. Size is a critical factor because it often provokes inequities in the numbers and talent levels of the athletes in the respective schools.
- **Expected income.** On occasion, smaller schools, especially those with outstanding athletic programs, like to play larger schools because of the challenge and the additional money to be realized from gate receipts. Although money is always an important consideration, equitable levels of competition are much more important for the reputations of the respective programs as well as for the safety of the athletes in the smaller school. Teams with considerably more players can wear down and eventually injure players from smaller schools, even if the starting teams are comparable in size and talent.
- **Traditional rivalries.** The excitement and increased income generated by traditional rivalries make them scheduling "musts." If promoted appropriately and if maintained for their friendly and wholesome competition, they stimulate community involvement and can be among the highlights of each school year. On the other hand, if they provoke conflict and hard feelings, the financial benefits they guarantee are not worth the need for increased security or the potential harm they involve.

You must realize, however, that all traditional rivalries are potentially destructive. Students can be highly creative when it comes to devising pranks for rival schools. One of the keys to maintaining a wholesome rivalry is to promote "zero tolerance" for pranks by distributing and explaining disciplinary procedures. Another way is to emphasize school spirit by supporting the home team, not by antagonizing the opposition. Well-coordinated and supervised pep rallies can be very helpful in this regard.

We knew a principal, for example, who allowed his students to leave the campus and conduct a midday Homecoming parade through the community. Most of the cars ended up in the parking lot of the neighboring rival, and no fewer than twenty fights broke out before the teachers from both schools finally were able to get everyone back into their cars and returned to their own campuses. That we maintain traditional rivalries, therefore, is desirable; that we promote them intelligently is even more important.

Finally, the best way to identify schools for nonconference contests is to meet with the head coaches of each sport and discuss the needs of their programs. Many coaches like to schedule easier opponents before beginning conference play; others have to schedule smaller schools because of state regulations governing play-off competition. Some states, for example, determine what class or division a school will be in during play-off competition based upon the average size of the schools against which it competed that year. These kinds of factors require some serious thinking before actual decisions are made.

Whatever the rationale for your decisions, use the Scheduling Form in Figure 4-10 as a guide for determining which school or schools you would like to schedule.

ORGANIZING INVITATIONALS

Organize one or more invitational tournaments or meets during the school year. Such tournaments may involve considerable preliminary planning and a great deal of work during the actual invitational, but they provide several benefits:

- Foremost for coaches, invitationals provide a great deal of exposure for sports programs. If the teams invited are among the best in the area, state, or nation, the invitational can attract a significant number of people, many of whom will help promote the program in the community and encourage larger numbers of students to participate.
- The more people who attend the invitational, the more money for the athletic department. Often, the receipts for the gate and concessions are significantly larger than the money budgeted for expenses such as security, crowd control, and guarantees for participating schools. The profits from a successful invitational can be used for "carrot money" in the department (see Section Five), specifically to purchase equipment that breaks unexpectedly or to defray expenditures for coaching clinics or other travel.
- Invitationals can involve excellent competition for your school's athletes. Even if your athletes don't fare well against the other schools, they will experience the excitement of high-level competition and gain a vision of what it takes to achieve athletic excellence. If they are embarrassingly outclassed every year, you may want to rethink the merits of sponsoring the invitational or of participating in it.

Use the letter in Figure 4-11 to invite schools and to provide the information they need to make their trip and visit more comfortable.

Figure 4-10
Scheduling Form

(This form is to be completed by head coach and brought to fall scheduling meeting to assist athletic director)

Sport ______________________ Date of Meeting ______________

League Contest
Limitations ______________________

Mandated Cross
Over Contests ______________________

Date(s) of
Cross overs ______________________

______________________ ______________________

Scheduled
Schools ______________________

Possible
Date(s) & Levels ______________

______________________ ______________________
______________________ ______________________
______________________ ______________________
______________________ ______________________
______________________ ______________________
______________________ ______________________
______________________ ______________________
______________________ ______________________
______________________ ______________________
______________________ ______________________
______________________ ______________________
______________________ ______________________
______________________ ______________________

(Please add any additional scheduling information on back of form—this will assist athletic director in scheduling process.)

Figure 4-11
Invitational Letter

Athletic Department

DATE:

TO: Girls Athletic Director
Head Girls Swim Coach
Head Girls Diving Coach

FROM: Athletic Director

RE: Swimming and Diving Relays

Scheduled of Events:	7:30—9:00	Diving Warm-ups
	9:00	Diving Preliminaries & Finals
	12:00	Swimming Warm-ups
	1:00	Swimming Finals
Competing Schools:	1	2
	3	4
	5	6

Entry Fee: $65.00. If you have not already sent in the fee, please do so at this time.

Trophies & Medals: Medals will be awarded for first, second, and third places.

Admission: Adults $2.00, Students with ID $1.00.

Locker Room: All teams will be assigned to lockers in either the boys' or girls' locker room. Each girl should bring her own lock and towel.

Coaches' Information: Diving—Each school may enter three divers in the diving event. The sum total of the three divers will determine their place. All divers will perform all 11 dives in the morning session.

Diving Entry Sheets: These must be turned in with swimming entries on (date) so that we may enter the dives into the computer system.

Entries: Entry sheet must be faxed or received by host school by 12:00 noon on (date). Written changes accepted up until 8:00 A.M. on (date). After 8:00 A.M., only substitutions for illness or injury will be accepted as per National Federation Rules. Diving sheets must be sent/faxed with swim entries on (date).

Rules of the Meet:

1. A school may enter only one relay team per event.
2. A contestant may participate in no more than 4 events. Diving counts as an event.
3. A school may enter no more than 3 contestants in the diving.
4. Scoring for the swimming and diving will be 14, 10, 8, 6, 4, and 2.
5. Swimmers may swim on more than one level, as long as they do not drop below their school class level.
6. Diving judges will include one from each team plus the referee. Judges will not judge their own divers.
7. Order of events is as listed on the enclosed entry sheet.

Questions: Call the Girls Athletic Coordinator at xxx-xxxx or the Head Swim Coach at xxx-xxxx.

ACCOMMODATING TEAMS FOR CONTESTS

Hospitality is the warmth that forges lasting relationships. It is one of the surest signs of class, and it makes for wholesome and exciting rivalries. Hospitable coaches and athletic directors are unaffected by a win-at-all-costs philosophy; they realize that personal dignity and self-respect are more important than a field hockey or football game, so they treat visiting teams with as much hospitality and respect as possible. This includes:

- Having a team manager meet the visiting team's bus to escort them to their locker room and to determine if the coach has any equipment needs.
- Having the athletic director or the school's head coach meet with the opposing coach to see if he or she has any requests for materials or equipment.
- After the opposing team is settled, having the team's manager ask the opposing coaches if they would like a cup of coffee or a soft drink.
- Mailing each team a form that contains all the information they'll need to find their way around your campus and to plan for pregame and half-time activities. Use the reproducible in Figure 4-12 for individual sports or, appropriately modified, for all sports.

POSTPONING AND RESCHEDULING CONTESTS

Contests must occasionally be postponed because of factors that are beyond the control of the athletic director, coaching staff, or school administration. Decisions to postpone must always be made in conjunction with the athletic director and usually the school principal, unless otherwise specified in the policies of the athletic department. If a contest is be postponed, the athletic director is responsible for rescheduling it, always in conjunction with the AD from the opposing school. If two or more contests are postponed, any rescheduling decisions must give priority to conference teams. Following are some factors that may cause postponements:

- Inclement weather for outside contests.
- The conditions of the field resulting from earlier weather conditions.
- The safety of your athletes, opposing athletes, officials, or support personnel at the contest.
- The safety of spectators.
- Inadequate or damaged facilities or equipment.

The decision to postpone a contest is rarely an easy one; a variety of circumstances can lead to any of the factors listed above, ranging from gang activity in the community to impending lightning storms. The many factors that influence the decision require close collaboration among coaches, the athletic director, and usually the school principal. See Figure 4-13 for a sample form to use when a change of schedule is necessary.

Figure 4-12
Contest Information

HIGH SCHOOL ATHLETIC DEPARTMENT

TO: ______________________________

Athletic Director, ____________________ High School

FR: (Your Name)

RE: Our upcoming contest

Sport: ____________________

Date: ____________________

INFORMATION REGARDING:

JERSEYS: Please wear dark-colored jerseys.

LOCKER ROOM: Please use the girls' locker room located on the east side of the Exhibition Gym.

NAMES OF OFFICIALS: __________, __________, __________, __________.

PARKING: Please park buses or other forms of transportation in the southwest corner of the parking lot behind the gym.

PRESS BOX AND/OR VIDEOTAPING: I will escort you to the appropriate area.

PREGAME SCHEDULE:

Time	Activity

HALF-TIME SCHEDULE:

Time	Activity

Good luck, and we're looking forward to an enjoyable experience. Please call me if you have any questions or specific needs.

Figure 4-13
Notice of Athletic Schedule Change

ADDITION ______________________ POSTPONED ______________________

CANCELLATION ______________________ RESCHEDULED ______________________

SPORT ______________________

OPPONENT ______________________

LEVEL ______________________

SITE ______________________ CHANGE TO ______________________

DATE ______________________ CHANGE TO ______________________

TIME ______________________ CHANGE TO ______________________

RE: (explanation of athletic schedule change)

SEND NOTIFICATION TO:

_____Opposing School(s)

_____Assignment Chairperson

_____Coaching Staff

_____Plant Manager

_____Athletic Director

_____Asst. Athletic Director

_____Ticket Manager(s)

_____Other______________________

_____Main Office

_____Principal

_____Assoc. Principal

_____Student Activities Director

_____Athletic Trainer(s)

_____Athletic Secretary

_____Dean of Students

ADDING OR DELETING SPORTS IN THE ATHLETIC PROGRAM

Sometimes sports must be added to, or deleted from, the school's sports program. Some sports experience a resurgent popularity or, like soccer several years ago, suddenly "come into their own." Other changes are made necessary by changing social conditions, which are provoked by new philosophies, federal and state legislation, and landmark court cases. The most obvious example is the women's movement, which resulted in Title IX and improved basketball, softball, soccer, and other sports programs for women and, less obviously, sports like volleyball for men.

New and better-equipped sports programs and athletic opportunities emerged for both men and women, and athletic participation in this country increased dramatically. A consequence of this growth was a shortage of facilities, equipment, transportation, and coaching personnel for women's and, in some instances, men's sports. Some sports, particularly for women, are still seeking qualified coaches. All this continues to pose sizable challenges for athletic directors.

Adding Sports

One of these challenges was to create or reevaluate criteria for adding new sports to the athletic program. Most have used something like the following criteria:

- The sport should be approved by the state athletic association. Most states provide materials that detail acceptable programs. This is one more reason why continuing liaison with the state organization is a good idea.
- The sport should be a competitive and physically challenging athletic activity, and one that is being organized in enough neighboring schools to permit scheduled competition.
- There should be sufficient student interest to guarantee continuing participation as well as spectator appeal and revenue generation. The potential or actual growth of the sport can be determined by contacting organizations like the NCAA or the sport's state or national federations.
- The school must have facilities and funding to accommodate the sport. New sports must not drain funding or facilities from existing sports. Compromises may be necessary, as when new soccer programs use the school's football stadium for contests, but anticipated scheduling conflicts must be minimized if new sports are to be incorporated into the athletic program.
- Finally, sports that assure gender equity should receive highest consideration.

Eliminating Sports

Sometimes sports must be dropped from athletic programs. Such decisions normally result from consideration of the following criteria:

- Student interest is insufficient to continue the sport.
- The sport has become too dangerous to permit continued student participation. Many high schools, for example, discontinued gymnastics competition for boys because of the increased incidence of injury—particularly during trampoline practice and competition.
- The school's program is consistently unable to compete successfully with neighboring schools, and a periodic change of coaches has not improved the program. It may also be difficult to find qualified coaches.
- Schools in the area are dropping the program and scheduling is no longer possible.
- The sport fails to generate revenue and funding becomes inadequate.

Establish procedures for discussion about adding or eliminating certain sports. Such decisions should be made in collaboration with coaches and the school's administration and, sometimes, with students and parents. The addition of a new sport or the deletion of an old one can be a sensitive issue within the community and warrants the time and the involvement of all relevant parties.

CONCLUDING THE SEASON

Evaluation of coaches and the athletic program was discussed in Section Two. An end-of-the-year meeting with head coaches is necessary to discuss significant events during the year and to anticipate the needs of next year's program. This is also the time to receive from coaches a final roster and a summary of the season record, both conference and nonconference, the names of the head and assistant coaches, the names of captains and the team manager, any championships won, and all significant accomplishments, such as honors for players or coaches or record-breaking performances.

Such information is useful for press releases and upcoming speeches with community organizations. It is particularly helpful, however, if you receive requests for information ten years from now. Certainly, the school yearbook provides similar information, but it may not include the record-breaking performances of athletes or coaches, and it generally is not as immediately accessible as information from the athletic director's office.

Distribute the Athletic Season Report in Figure 4-14 to head coaches before all end-of-the-year meetings and ask that they return it to you before the meeting if they want to discuss it. Otherwise, ask that it be returned to the athletic department sometime before the end of the school year.

Figure 4-14
Athletic Season Report

SPORT ____________________ **YEAR** ____________________

PERSONNEL

Head Coach ____________________

Assistants ____________________

____

____

RECORDS

Season Record ____________________ League Record ____________

Team Honors ____________________ League Standing____________

____

Lower Level Records: JV_____ Soph_____ FA_____ FB_____

AWARDS

Captain(s)/Yr in School ____________________

Most Valuable ____________________ Most Improved ____________________

Other Individual Awards ____________________

____

All-Conference Awards ____________________

____

Booster Club Academic Awards ____________________

____

CSL Scholar Athletes ____________________

____

Figure 4-14, continued
Athletic Season Report

STATE TOURNAMENT

(Circle the final series of competition)

Regional Sectional Super-Sectional State

List Scores, Opponents, and Highlights ______________________________

____

____

____

SUGGESTIONS/CONCERNS

Scheduling:

Facilities:

Safety:

Equipment:

Administrative:

Other:

PLEASE ATTACH ANY SUMMARY INFORMATION YOU WISH TO INCLUDE IN REPORT

PUBLICIZING CONTEST SCHEDULES IN THE COMMUNITY

Section Three discussed the importance of distributing game schedules within the school and community in order to promote spectator interest in the athletic program. Additional mention is warranted. Aside from maintaining exciting and winning sports programs, this is perhaps the best way to generate interest within the school and community. Following are a few ways to assure that schedules will be distributed:

- Have coaches distribute them to players with instructions to bring them home to share with family and relatives.
- Distribute schedules to influential members of the community during speeches to fraternal and other community organizations. Following such presentations, ask the organization to help publicize schedules, perhaps even to consider a project to improve attendance at the school's athletic contests.
- Place stacks of schedules in drug stores, local restaurants, and other popular establishments in the community. Determine if store owners or managers will allow them to be placed near check-out stations or cash registers.
- Mail schedules to presidents of fraternal and community organizations, such as the Chamber of Commerce, League of Women Voters, Jaycees, Optimists' Club, Lions, Rotary, Knights of Columbus, and others. You or your coaches are unlikely to speak to all of these organizations during any given year, and you'll need their help publicizing all athletic contests throughout the year.
- Create large posters of schedules, appropriately designed, and place them in such prominent locations in the community as store windows and bulletin boards in local establishments, particularly those frequented by students and parents.
- Share schedules with local-access television stations and ask that they publicize them throughout the week. Some local-access TV stations simply re-run games; ask that they also publicize them during the week of a game.
- Meet with the booster club to discuss ways to promote athletic contests and provide schedules to them for distribution throughout the community.
- Meet with your school's student council and class executive boards to create publicity activities for the distribution of schedules.
- Meet with the school's chapter of the National Honor Society and suggest the publicizing of athletic events as a way to meet their Leadership and Service responsibilities.
- Share schedules with local newspapers for their columns on upcoming events.
- Ask local radio stations to mention upcoming games and contests each week. Perhaps send them PR notices that contain copy for radio personnel to read on the air.

This last activity highlights the value of an effective process for distributing press releases—the focus of Section Seven. A successful and exciting athletic program sells itself within the community, if it receives the kind of press it deserves.

LET'S WRAP IT UP

Scheduling is the meat and potatoes of the athletic director's daily menu. Appetizers are great and dessert is always fun, but the meal itself is what sustains us, and scheduling and publicity sustain the good health of the athletic department. Schedules for practice sessions must be developed during the year, and facilities must be allocated. Contest schedules must be organized and distributed each year, and they must recognize the competitive skills of the school's athletes as well as the financial needs of the program. These are the primary reasons why practice and contest scheduling are collaborative activities within the athletic department.

Good athletic directors meet with head coaches to discuss scheduling priorities and to share decisions regarding the allocation of facilities for practices, nonconference opponents, schools to invite to invitationals, and offers to accept from other schools. Collaboration has been a continuing emphasis throughout this book. It is the process that broadens the base of the department's leadership and promotes trust and commitment among coaches. Use the information in this section to establish processes that promote collaboration. Such processes will result in both acceptable schedules and positive relationships within the department.

SECTION FIVE

Developing the Budget

First, a quick story:

Bob was well intentioned if ineffective. He had been a high school principal for twelve years and had developed all the survival techniques of a veteran administrator. He had learned to substitute charisma for artistry, management for leadership, and a good-old-boy slap on the back for genuine concern about his colleagues. He was moderately well liked for his personality but generally disregarded as a leader and educator.

One of the reasons for this absence of respect was his inability to develop a well-conceived school budget. The money Bob allocated to each department in the school was dictated by tradition. Every year, each of the departments received an allocation similar to that of the previous year, and, as the end of each year approached, most of them frantically spent the remainder of their allocations to assure similar allocations the next year.

A few departments, headed by well-meaning but surprisingly naive administrators, spent only what they needed for their programs. Because proper performance is often punished in organizations, each of these department heads was given a reduced allocation the following year. Bob simply assumed they didn't need it and gave it to other department heads who were always short of funds and who were quick to manipulate him with a good-old-boy joke at lunch. Organizations also reward improper performance.

Because allocations are so vital to the sports program, the athletic department budget brings out the competitive spirit in even the most docile coaches—particularly those who perform well. Everyone in Bob's school knew how he determined the budget. If departments wanted more money, they cajoled him during lunch or in the halls and squeaked a lot of wheels, particularly when Bob could hear them.

The situation certainly wasn't good. The budget in Bob's school was not a planning document. It failed to relate expenditures to goals; it neglected the early anticipation of long-term needs; it disregarded accountability; it isolated departments, rather than promote their cooperation. And it provoked school-wide satisfaction with the status quo. Few of his departments assessed their needs, developed short and long-range goals, and considered the budget as the one way to realize them.

MONEY AS THE UNIVERSAL CURE

Like everyone else in our society, many educators seem too predisposed to resolving their problems with money. Politicians are convinced that more money for welfare will help overcome poverty. Big city school boards are convinced that more money will improve the achievement of inner-city students. And some coaches are convinced that new high-tech equipment will result in improved team performance and in winning records.

To some extent, they are all correct. That's the problem. The element of truth in their arguments obscures the real dimensions of the problem. The poor do need money for shelter and food, but money alone fails to break their cycle of poverty. Inner-city students do need the best teachers, textbooks, and materials available, but money alone fails to address the personal and social influences that affect their learning. And young athletes may benefit from high-tech equipment, but the improvement of team performance and the development of winning records result as much from coaching competence, team commitment, and well-planned programs as from generous budgets. Additional money is important, if it is used to promote the identification and resolution of problems. All too often, it is used to treat symptoms, not the problems themselves. Medical doctors know only too well that when they treat only symptoms, the patient dies.

Politicians pour extra dollars into outdated welfare programs; school boards funnel additional monies into poorly organized schools; and athletic departments sometimes allocate funds to failing sports programs. The assumption that such funds will improve these programs often proves frustrating to politicians, school boards, and athletic directors! The budget is only one means of treating the organizational ills of different programs. If it is used to treat only symptoms, the program continues to suffer and sometimes dies.

WHERE MOST OF THE MONEY GOES

In most schools, only 2 percent to 3 percent of the total district budget is allocated to athletics. Those of us who have been in the business for a while understand that the payback to the community is enormous—far in excess of their initial investment. Many sports programs excite the entire community and do as much as any other organization to unite citizens in a common interest and cause. And while this is happening, the students themselves are enjoying their associations and integrating the values that only athletic competition can provide.

What most coaches have to understand is that the significant majority of the total budget is eaten up by coaches' salaries and transportation costs. Equipment needs, uniform replacements, travel expenses, and other miscellaneous items come from the remainder of the budget and must be carefully scrutinized. The budget, especially for the athletic department, is not a cornucopia that dispenses its plenty whenever a need arises. That's just one reason why careful planning is an essential when making budget decisions.

The Athletic Budget: An Overview

What are the components of the athletic budget? Important components of the budget—in addition to the major elements of coaches' salaries and transportation costs—that must be provided for in the athletic department's budget include:

- The planning and operation of school-sponsored tournaments and workshops.
- Awards and other forms of recognition to be given to athletes and coaches.
- Officials for all athletic contests.
- Medical supplies and related equipment.
- Anticipated gate receipts from tournaments and contests to defray and complement budget projections.
- The construction, maintenance, and repair of physical facilities.
- The payment of school personnel to assist with ticket help, concessions, and security at contests.
- Secretarial help, postage, office supplies, banquets, equipment needs related to individual sports, and other such specific, but important items.

Budget Criteria

Decisions regarding each of these components are based upon reasonable and realistic criteria. Following are a few criteria that must be kept in mind during budget planning activities:

- The current inventory of equipment and uniforms.
- Any changes in rules that may influence equipment purchases.
- Condition of equipment and availability of improved equipment.
- Rotation plans in force for uniforms and equipment.
- The total number of athletes involved in the program.
- Anticipated new sports.
- Rotational plan for major equipment items.
- Long-range needs of the program.
- Anticipated gate receipts.
- Expected assistance from the school board and booster club.

Some of these criteria are dependent upon the assistance of others, but effective planning can reduce the uncertainty of program needs. Such planning should be done on both a short-term and a long-term basis and should involve head coaches throughout much of the process.

THE BUDGET AS A PLANNING DOCUMENT

A friend of ours refers to his family budget as a mathematical confirmation of his greatest fears. You and I know what he means. When financial cuts come filtering down the school's hierarchy and when coaches are lined up outside the door clutching their budget requests, athletic directors earn their salaries. They also earn their stripes when they handle budget battles intelligently.

To handle the budget well, the first thing ADs must recognize is the tendency of many coaches to regard the athletic budget as a secret account with hidden pockets of cash that can always yield more money for coaches who *really need it*. This perception prevails in many schools, particularly in those that fail to introduce coaches to the realities of "fiscal fitness." When coaches regard the athletic budget as a mysterious source of warm fuzzies instead of cold cash, everyone has problems. The coaches are disappointed, then angry about their inability to get what others seem to be getting; the athletic director is viewed as an irresolute bean counter who caves in to the strongest coaches; and the school's administration is regarded as the enemy in the "we-they" dichotomy, the organizational force that allows the athletic department to cling desperately to the lowest rung of the school's hierarchical ladder.

So what do we do? At the risk of sounding professorial, let's turn for the moment to theory, specifically to Abraham Maslow, who told us years ago that the continued deprivation of truth is pathogenic. The absence of truth makes us sick, even paranoid. It would seem, then, that an obvious way to avoid many of the above problems is to explain the budget to coaches and to engage them in the department's financial planning.

First Things First

The first step is to share with the coaching staff your statement of goals for the school year. If your school requires an annual report at the end of each year, share some of it with the coaches to let them know that you, too, are accountable and that you routinely share your vision of student athletics with the school's administration and the school board. If your school does not require an annual report, develop a report of your own that lists goals for the year. Use the form provided in Figure 5-1.

Such a report might also include some of the other budget forms provided in this section. Most important, the report shares your vision with coaches and the administration, and affirms your knowledge of program planning. Any effective plan must begin with goal statements and must relate subsequent activities and expenditures to the realization of the goals. Sharing this document with your coaches, therefore, gives them a sense of departmental priorities and leads them through the first step of achieving consensus with others in the school and within the department.

Examples of effective goal statements include:

- To promote positive student behavior at all athletic contests.
- To engage interested coaches in coaching effectiveness training programs.
- To promote a better understanding of the goals of the athletic program among all professionals within the school.
- To address the needs of student athletes and their parents in the college recruitment process.

Figure 5-1
Memo Regarding Yearly Goals

Athletic Department

TO: Building Principal

FROM: Athletic Director

RE: Yearly Goals

DATE:

Listed below are the goals for the school year in the athletic department:

1. To increase student athlete participation within the scope of the athletic program.
2. To promote sportsmanship within the spectator crowd as well as the athletic teams.
3. To promote drug awareness activities for both parents and athletes.
4. To provide a better understanding of the academic admission requirements of NCAA Division I, II, and III schools.
5. To provide ongoing coaching effectiveness training for coaches of all levels and sports.
6. To provide ongoing liability information for coaches of all levels and sports.
7. To address the needs of gender equity and assure that each sport is in compliance.

- To promote drug awareness activities within the entire athletic program.
- To increase student participation within the entire program (or a specific team).

None of these goals explains *how* it will be accomplished; each simply represents a generalized expression of intent. The specifics of how each will be achieved depends on the input of coaches and the degree of commitment each is willing to make to the realization of the goal(s). The degree of their commitment is usually directly proportional to the knowledge they have and the ownership they feel in the purposes of the athletic program.

Getting Key People Involved

Head coaches *must* have a hand in the development of the athletic program's annual goals if consensus is to be achieved within the program each year. Distribute the memo in Figure 5-2 to coaches at the end of each school year to get their assessment of program needs. Once their needs have been tallied, include statements of the needs you identify, then return the composite form in Figure 5-3 to them and ask that they rank the needs in priority order.

You can then translate each need into a goal for the following school year and list them in the Yearly Goals statement provided in Figure 5-1. Include that form with your annual report to the administration and board of education to inform them of the results of departmental planning activities. Such documentation informs decision makers of program needs, promotes their willingness to help meet them, and impresses everyone with your administrative skills!

Share these finalized goal statements with the entire coaching staff at a meeting in the beginning of the year. This is also the time to pave the way for the year's budget discussions by informing them of any changes in the district's financial picture, such as budget cuts. It's also a good idea to share the anticipated budget figures and ask their cooperation when budget discussions commence in December or January.

Working with Individual Coaches

The next step is to share relevant information with individual coaches. Head coaches must have an idea of how much money is available and how important it is that expenditures relate to the department's goals as well as to their team's needs. We all realize that equipment and uniforms require replacement, that facilities must be maintained or improved, and that such specifics as scouting stipends must be increased.

These are "givens" and generally constitute the primary focus of most budget discussions. Other elements in the budget, however, are equally important—perhaps more important to the success of the program. Coaches require periodic in-service training. Travel budgets to conventions, contests, and other events require coordination. Incoming students have to be invited to participate in the school's athletic program. Schedules have to be distributed within the community. And many of the new goals that emerge each year from planning activities require financing.

Figure 5-2
Annual Goals for Athletic Department Memo

Athletic Department

TO: Head Coaching Staff

FROM: Athletic Director

RE: Annual Goals for Athletic Department

DATE:

It is time once again to begin working on the goals for the athletic department for the new school year. Please use the following list to help the athletic administration identify the needs not only for your specific sport but for the overall athletic department.

Goal Statements

Examples:
Improved field maintenance

1. ______________________________

2. ______________________________

3. ______________________________

4. ______________________________

5. ______________________________

(Please return form to the athletic department no later than May 1.)

Figure 5-3
Goal Statements Memo

Athletic Department

TO: Head Coaching Staff

FROM: Athletic Director

RE: Annual Goals for Athletic Department

DATE:

Thank you for your assistance in identifying the annual goals for the athletic department. Please rank in order the following list, so that we can clarify the most important goals. Remember to rank the goals in order of the overall athletic department, and not only your specific sport.

Please rank in order of importance

1 = most important to 10 = least important

Goal Statements

Improved field maintenance	________
Increased student athlete participation	________
Promotion of drug awareness programs	________
Promotion of NCAA entrance standards	________
Address gender equity concerns	________
Increased coaching education programs	________
Improved uniforms for indoor sports	________
Liability information for coaches	________
Improved press and media coverage	________
Development of student athlete handbook	________

(Please return form to the athletic department no later than May 15.)

COORDINATING THE BUDGET WITH HEAD COACHES

Head coaches must understand that these issues are equally important to their equipment needs if the athletic program is to be a success. After they receive the final copy of the program goals for the year, therefore, you should meet with each of them individually, usually near the end of the first semester, to discuss their requests and to determine how those requests relate to the goals of the total program.

This is also the time for the coaches to explain and, on occasion, defend, their budget requests. To prepare for the meeting, distribute the memo in Figure 5-4, which asks coaches to make budget requests. Include with it the supply and uniform requests in Figures 5-5 and 5-6. Notice that the forms ask coaches to prioritize their requests in the event the budget can't accommodate all of them. Figures 5-7 and 5-8 provide examples of what these forms might look like when they have been submitted. Then, use Figure 5-9 to record the bids you receive from suppliers for each corresponding item on Figures 5-5 and 5-6.

Finally, the Jersey Inventory, Figure 5-10, should also be included with the memo in Figure 5-4—or you can use the form in Figure 5-11. Both are especially useful because they can be updated as the team supplements its supply of jerseys. After these materials have been distributed and received, meet with each coach and inform him or her of decisions within one or two days after the meeting. Coaches appreciate immediate notification of decisions.

Establish some kind of rotating system for large-ticket items. Coaches should be aware of the system and should incorporate it into their budget planning each year. The coach who realizes, for example, that next year is his or her year for major purchases will focus on other items during the current year. Such a process avoids needless disagreement and guarantees each coach an opportunity to purchase major items.

Each coach should be encouraged to work with his or her staff to identify the items that are most important to the success of their team. New football helmets may seem at first to be their number-one priority, but with some mutual planning, they may decide to recondition the helmets and use the money from the rotating system to purchase a new seven-man sled. The safety of the athletes is, of course, the major consideration. That's always our most important criterion regarding budgeted items; once it is accommodated, however, new items may emerge from staff planning activities.

A Word About the Fall, Winter, and Spring Seasons

Budgets that are returned by the fall and winter coaches and that are finalized in midyear meetings with them usually are etched in stone. Expecting a spring coach to finalize a budget document prior to the start of the current season is unreasonable. Ask spring coaches to provide a tentative list of items they probably will need; Figure 5-12 provides a sample letter. Before the coach leaves at the end of the school year, meet with him or her to complete final purchase orders.

Figure 5-4
Budget Requests Memo

Athletic Department

TO: Head Coaching Staff

FROM: Athletic Director

RE: Athletic Budget Requests

DATE:

Attached are the necessary forms for you to complete your portion of the budget process. Please make your requests based upon your present inventory and your needs to operate your program. Good planning always pays off for everyone. I have various athletic catalogs in my office that will assist you. Please feel free to borrow these at any time.

Use only the forms provided for your requests. For those individuals who feel comfortable with the computer, please feel free to place your requests on the disk provided. There is a separate form for supplies and a separate form for uniforms/warm-ups. You must provide clear, concise descriptions, prices, manufacturers, sizes, and quantities for each item. Use whole dollar amount whenever possible.

Please indicate a priority ranking for each item in case any deletions have to be made. Any questions, please feel free to call the athletic office. I will be happy to assist you.

Sample:

QUANTITY	DESCRIPTION AND SPECIFICATIONS	UNIT COST	TOTAL COST
24	#8709 Name brand Hooded Sweatshirts. Navy with gold lettering on front—4 inch full block "School" arched. Underneath numbered 96-1 to 96-24. Sizes 12/L 12/XL.	$12.00	$288.00
48	Name brand Winger Hose-Heavy Weight Nylon; Navy with 2 Gold Stripes at Top	$3.00	$144.00

Figure 5-5
Athletic Budget Requests

SUPPLIES

Sport ______________________ Year ______________

PRIORITY	QUANTITY	DESCRIPTION & SPECIFICATIONS (Manufacturer, #, color, sizes, etc.)	UNIT COST	TOTAL COST

Figure 5-6
Athletic Budget Requests

UNIFORMS

Sport ____________________ Year ____________________

PRIORITY	QUANTITY	DESCRIPTION & SPECIFICATIONS (Manufacturer, #, color, sizes, etc.)	UNIT COST	TOTAL COST

Figure 5-7
Sample Submitted Athletic Budget Requests

SUPPLIES

Sport Boys' Cross Country Year ____________

PRIORITY	QUANTITY	DESCRIPTION & SPECIFICATIONS (Manufacturer, #, color, sizes, etc.)	UNIT COST	TOTAL COST
1	1	Megaphone from name brand catalog #4540A	$89.95	$89.95
2	8	5 × 3/8 Spikes—100 Count #4632A 3 × 1/2 Spikes—100 Count #4633A	$6.95	$55.60
3	1	Book "Cross Country"	$34.96	$34.95
4	1	Book "Cooking Method Excellence"	$18.95	$18.95
			Total	$199.45

Figure 5-8
Sample Submitted Athletic Budget Requests

UNIFORMS

Sport Girls' Swimming and Diving Year ________

PRIORITY	QUANTITY	DESCRIPTION & SPECIFICATIONS (Manufacturer, #, color, sizes, etc.)	UNIT COST	TOTAL COST
1	12	Name-brand warm-ups to match current warm-ups. Warm-ups to be numbered 25–36. #2602 Jacket Bomber Supplex 2 tone waistband. Sizes 2 S, 2 M, 8 L. Navy/Gold with Gold Lettering. All trim navy—shoulder gusset/Gold. Slash welt pocket wind collar option shell outer knit. Gold outside/Navy Zipper. Sewn on Tackle Twill lettering—Navy.	$71.60	$859.20
2	12	160 E Supplex 8 panel Elastic Pants with braid. Navy. Navy Zipper. Sewn on Tackle Twill lettering.	$46.00	$552.00
3	24	Large name-brand zipper bags. Gold sewn-on Letters—"GBS Swimming" Gold sewn-on numbers—Numbered 1 thru 36.	$18.00 $5.00	$432.00 $120.00
			Total	$1963.20

Figure 5-9
Record of Bids

Item #													
1													
2													
3													
4													
5													
6													
7													
8													
9													
10													
11													
12													
13													
14													
15													
16													
17													
18													
19													
20													
21													
22													
23													
24													
25													
26													
27													
28													
29													
30													
31													
32													
33													
34													
35													
36													
37													
38													
39													
40													
41													
42													
43													
44													
45													
46													
47													

Figure 5-9, continued
Record of Bids

48													
49													
50													
51													
52													
53													
54													
55													
56													
57													
58													
59													
60													
61													
62													
63													
64													
65													
66													
67													
68													
69													
70													
71													
72													
73													
74													
75													
76													
77													
78													
79													
80													
81													
82													
83													
84													
85													
86													
87													
88													
89													
90													
91													
92													
93													
94													

Figure 5-10
Jersey Inventory

JERSEY NUMBER & SIZE		
SPORT:	COLOR:	LEVEL:
DATE:		
1	34	67
2	35	68
3	36	69
4	37	70
5	38	71
6	39	72
7	40	73
8	41	74
9	42	75
10	43	76
11	44	77
12	45	78
13	46	79
14	47	80
15	48	81
16	49	82
17	50	83
18	51	84
19	52	85
20	53	86
21	54	87
22	55	88
23	56	89
24	57	90
25	58	91
26	59	92
27	60	93
28	61	94
29	62	95
30	63	96
31	64	97
32	65	98
33	66	99

Figure 5-11
Uniform/Jersey Inventory

Sport ______________________________ Year______________________

Level: Var JV F

Away Uniform
Jerseys/Tops

Size	*Quantity* Good	Replace	*Comments*
XS			
S			
M			
L			
XL			
XXL			

Numbers: Place an "x" through the number on the jerseys found in your inventory.

01	02	03	04	05	06	07	08	09	10	11	12	13	14	15	16	17	18	19	20
21	22	23	24	25	26	27	28	29	30	31	32	33	34	35	36	37	38	39	40
41	42	43	44	45	46	47	48	49	50	51	52	53	54	55	56	57	58	59	60

Additional Numbers:

Away Uniform
Pants

Size	*Quantity* Good	Replace	*Comments*
XS			
S			
M			
L			
XL			
XXL			

Numbers: Place an "x" through the number on the jerseys found in your inventory.

01	02	03	04	05	06	07	08	09	10	11	12	13	14	15	16	17	18	19	20
21	22	23	24	25	26	27	28	29	30	31	32	33	34	35	36	37	38	39	40
41	42	43	44	45	46	47	48	49	50	51	52	53	54	55	56	57	58	59	60

Additional Numbers:

Figure 5-12
Budget Requests Letter

Athletic Department

TO: Head Spring Coaching Staff

FROM: Athletic Director

RE: Budget Requests

DATE:

Attached you will find a tentative list of items that you requested for next year's budget. Please check this list over carefully to make sure that these are indeed the items you need for next year. As we previously discussed, it is hard for you as a coach to plan two year's in advance for your budget needs.

Please bring in writing any changes that you want made for your budget. I will be available all week to meet with you regarding any changes.

Thank you in advance.

ATHLETIC BUDGET REQUESTS FOR

Sport ______________________ Year ______________

PRIORITY	QUANTITY	DESCRIPTION & SPECIFICATIONS	UNIT COST	TOTAL COST

DISCUSSING THE BUDGET WITH THE PRINCIPAL

The next step is to secure bids from manufacturers and suppliers. Two or three competing bids are normally appropriate for expensive items. Figure 5-13 provides a letter for contacting suppliers. Any practicing athletic director knows that finding manufacturers and suppliers is never a problem; they invariably find you. You usually will establish a relationship with two or three who find a way to meet your equipment needs.

Having finalized the athletic department's budget and secured bids for equipment, the athletic director, in most schools, then meets with the building principal or his or her designate. At that time, the AD is expected to explain and defend the athletic department's budget. Because this meeting often deals with specific requests, it's always a good idea to bring copies of coaches' requests and the bids received from suppliers.

Rarely does this meeting involve any serious disagreement regarding budgeted items, especially if you understand the reasons for each request and can defend them to the principal. It's also important to bring a finalized budget to the meeting that is consistent with the amount of money normally allocated to the department each year. Use the final budget format provided in Figure 5-14.

Figure 5-15 shows you what the final proposed budget might look like. Deviations from your final amounts require a clearly documented need and are generally accepted if the reasoning behind them is sound. Finally, any adjustments in the budget resulting from this meeting must be communicated immediately to the coach(es) involved.

FINAL STEPS

Usually, the budget goes to the board of education for final approval sometime near the start of the second semester. After that time, the final bids are secured and decisions must be made regarding which ones to accept. The lowest bids are almost always the most desirable, but, occasionally, safety or quality issues may require a supplier other than the lowest bidder. Again, it's a good idea to document the reasons behind such decisions in the event an administrator or board member questions the decision at some time in the future.

For example, Nancy was questioned one year by a new board member who wondered why she was purchasing new football jerseys when she had just purchased new ones for the current year. She shared a memo with him, explaining that football players were allowed to keep their jerseys if they paid the replacement costs. Her answer satisfied the board member's curiosity. He even congratulated her for promoting what appeared to be an excellent public relations decision.

When the bids have been accepted and any deviations from the lowest bids are documented, you are ready to mail purchase orders to the suppliers. Use the purchase order in Figure 5-16, or one like it. Keep copies of the purchase orders in each team file in the event coaches request information about budget items. A good filing system is the basis for an athletic director's memory.

It's also a good idea to distribute copies of the Guidelines for Purchasing in Figure 5-17. Anything that clarifies the roles of persons in the athletic department avoids future confusion and misunderstanding. A copy of this statement should be included in the coaches' policy book, if your school has one. If not, you are well advised to develop one.

Figure 5-13
Sample Contact Letter to Suppliers

Athletic Department

Sales Representative
Company Name
Address
City, State, ZIP

Date

Dear Sales Representative,

Attached is a copy of the athletic bids for the sports program at *(name)* school. All proposals are due on March 2 at 2:00 P.M. Prices shall be firm for a period of 90 days.

Any questions concerning specifications of items listed should be directed to the Athletic Director.

Thank you for your assistance.

Respectfully,

Athletic Director

Figure 5-14
Final Budget Format

Proposed 1997–98 Athletic Budget 7/9/96

Activity-Acct. #	Officials	Repair	Travel	Entry Fee	Supplies	Equipment	Total	Coach	Tickets	Security
General							0			
Training Room							0			
Badminton							0			
Baseball							0			
Boys Basketball							0			
Girls Basketball							0			
Boys C.Country							0			
Girls C.Country							0			
Football							0			
Boys Golf							0			
Girls Golf							0			
Boys Gymnastics							0			
Girls Gymnastics							0			
Boys Soccer							0			
Girls Soccer							0			
Softball							0			
Boys Swim							0			
Girls Swim							0			
Boys Tennis							0			
Girls Tennis							0			
Track							0			
Boys Volleyball							0			
Girls Volleyball							0			
Wrestling							0			
Totals	**0**	**0**	**0**	**0**	**0**	**0**	**0**	**0**	**0**	**0**
Long-Range Plan										
	Equipment	**Facilities**	**Personnel**	**Total**				**Grand Total**		

Figure 5-15
Sample Completed Final Budget Format

Proposed 1997–98 Athletic Budget 7/9/96

Activity-Acct. #	Officials	Repair	Travel	Entry Fee	Supplies	Equipment	Total	Coach	Tickets	Security
General		2,500	3,500	1,150	8,000	1,500	16,650			
Training Room			400		7,200		7,600			
Badminton		100	100	80	2,200		2,480			
Baseball	2,500	150	150	0	3,200		6,000			
Boys Basketball	3,000		150	650	2,600		6,400			2,800
Girls Basketball	2,800		150	600	450		4,000			
Boys C.Country			750	280	300		1,330			
Girls C.Country			200	50	0		250			
Football	2,500	7,000	275	0	7,300		17,075			
Boys Golf			1,000	815	800		2,615			
Girls Golf			1,200	275	1,800		3,275			
Boys Gymnastics	600	100	100	375	600		1,775			
Girls Gymnastics	500	100	100	300	1,450		2,450			
Boys Soccer	3,500		200	150	3,400		7,250			
Girls Soccer	2,400		140	0	2,400		4,940			
Softball	1,800		125	110	1,800		3,835			
Boys Swim	700	50	125	375	1,500		2,750			
Girls Swim	700	50	125	210	1,500		2,585			
Boys Tennis			125	75	1,200		1,400			
Girls Tennis			100	155	1,200		1,455			
Track	1,300	100	1,000	800	2,500		5,700			
Boys Volleyball	1,500		100	300	1,200		3,100			
Girls Volleyball	1,600		100	560	1,600		3,860			
Wrestling	800		800	675	1,400		3,675			
Totals	**26,200**	**10,150**	**11,015**	**7,985**	**55,600**	**1,500**	**112,450**	**0**	**0**	**2,800**
								Grand Total		**115,250**
Long-Range Plan										

Figure 5-16
Purchase Order

#####

Supplier: ______________________ Date: ______________________

Address: ______________________ Ship To: ______________________

______________________ ______________________

______________________ ______________________

Quantity	*Description*	*Unit Cost*	*Total Cost*

Athletic Director's Signature ______________________

Account No. ______________

Figure 5-17
Policy Guidelines for Purchasing

The purchase of all athletic equipment will be done through the office of the Athletic Director and must be within budgeted amounts for each team.

Please follow these guidelines when involved in the purchase of equipment or supplies:

1. Coaches will be asked to complete budget requests for each year and to meet with the Athletic Director to determine final amounts. The forms that result from these meetings will be used to secure bids and submit purchase orders.

2. The Athletic Director, in consultation with head coaches, will choose the most appropriate supplier.

3. The Athletic Director will forward the purchase order to the district office.

4. When the equipment or materials have been received by the coach, he or she will notify the Athletic Director of the quality of the order.

5. Please remember that the purchase of equipment without the appropriate purchase order may result in your paying for the material.

6. Please direct questions and concerns to the office of the Athletic Director.

Policy books are nothing more than decisions made before the fact; they prevent ADs from "reinventing the wheel" every time a decision has to be made—in this instance, one regarding the purchase of team supplies. Many of the forms in this book will enable you to develop a policy book.

DEVELOPING A FILING SYSTEM

A filing system is relatively easy for most athletic directors. Our system consists simply of files for each sport. Such files should include:

- Copies of coaches' evaluations.
- Any memos received from the coaches in that sport within the past two years.
- Copies of preliminary and finalized budget requests.
- Bids from manufacturers/suppliers.
- Purchase orders.
- Schedules—past, current, and future.
- Team rosters.
- Award winners.
- Copies of work requests.
- End-of-season reports.

You will no doubt require additional files for personal and professionally related activities. A system that incorporates the following headings provides for appropriate filing and referral:

- Athletic Staff
- Booster Club
- Budget
- Coaching Candidates
- Coaching Evaluations
- Coaching Positions
- Forms
- Handbooks
- State High School Association
- Incoming Freshmen Parents' Night
- Inventory
- Leadership Conference (or other specific conferences)
- Payroll
- Photography
- Rentals
- Summer School
- Warranties

LONG-RANGE PLANNING FOR MAJOR ITEMS

A rotational system for the purchase of major items is most practical. It offers the predictability athletic directors require to maintain their sanity. Nothing is more frustrating to us or draining on the budget than three or four requests for unanticipated major costs. For that reason, we encourage coaches to *plan ahead*—to anticipate significant expenses and to expect to satisfy them during their turn in the rotation. The form provided in Figure 5-18 can be used to maintain such a rotational process.

Estimating the Transportation Budget

Transportation costs eat up a major portion of the total athletic budget. The amount of money required for transportation depends on the distances between your school and others in your conference, and on your schedule for the year. The best way to estimate the transportation budget is to use a form similar to the one in Figure 5-19. It should list the distances between your school and the schools you will be visiting during the current year, and compute total costs by applying a formula that involves bus use, meals, and any costs for overnight accommodations.

In some schools, this task is unnecessary. The athletic director simply notifies the administrator responsible for transportation accounts and requests travel on specified dates. Normally, an amount is determined based upon the needs of the previous year, including a modest increase, usually 4 percent to 5 percent. Be careful to use this amount only for travel, because it usually comes from the Transportation Fund levy, which may not be transferred into education funds.

DETERMINING COACHES' SALARIES

Athletic directors are usually freed from the responsibility of determining coaches' salaries. These kinds of decisions are made at the district level—normally, however, with input from the athletic director and others involved in the salary process. In schools with union contracts, even in those that use teacher committees to collaborate with district administrators, coaches' salaries are negotiated and usually are compared with those of neighboring districts to determine equitable figures.

Usually, coaches' salaries are arranged within separate categories—the top categories paying the largest salaries. The categories are most often determined according to the length of the season, the number of athletes, and the amount of "nonschool" time required for practice or competition. Some athletic directors will even admit that salaries are based on whether the sport is considered major or minor. This distinction, however, is often criticized in many schools.

Figure 5-20 provides a typical breakdown of coaching assignments and their respective categories. Generally, the lower the category number, the higher the salary. In addition, each category also contains several steps that reflect the experience levels of coaches in each category. The more experience, the higher the salary within each category.

The number of categories, the amount of salary within each one, and the number of steps within each category are dependent on the financial strength of the district. Athletic directors usually enter into the process only on an input basis. They may also be asked to share financial information from previous years to identify the cash flow and financial self-sufficiency within the department.

Figure 5-18
Major Equipment/Uniform Rotation

Sport	*Equipment*	*Uniforms*	*Warm-ups*
Girls Basketball	*	1994	1990*
Boys Basketball	*	1991*	1992
Track and Field	1990*	1991*	1990
Girls Cross Country	1991	1991*	1992
Girls Golf	1991	1992	1995
Boys Golf	1991	1993	1995
Boys Cross Country	1991	1996	1993
Boys Soccer	1992	1996	1993
Girls Soccer	1992	1995	1993
Wrestling	1992	1990	1995
Boys Tennis	1993	1992	1996
Girls Tennis	1993	1992	1994
Football	1993	1995	1990*
Boys Swimming	1994	yearly	1996
Girls Swimming	1994	yearly	1995
Girls Gymnastics	1994	1994	1992
Baseball	1995	1993	1991*
Softball	1995	1996	1992
Boys Gymnastics	1995	1995	1993
Girls Volleyball	1996	1994	1993
Boys Volleyball	1996	1993	1996
Training Room	1996	—	—

*Next on Rotation Schedule.

Figure 5-19
Approximate Transportation Costs

Sport ____________________ Year ____________________

Mileage	Contest $ Amount	Return $ Amount
01 – 25 Miles	$	$
26 – 50 Miles	$	$
51 – 75 Miles	$	$
76 – 100 Miles	$	$
101 – 200 Miles	$	$
201 – 300 Miles	$	$
301 – Over	$	$
Overnight	$ Amount + room and board	
Other—Car, Van	$	$

Sport—Baseball **Year** ____________________

Away Contests = 13

1 @ 0 – 25 Miles $____________

6 @ 26 – 50 Miles $____________

4 @ 51 – 75 Miles $____________

2 @ 76 – 100 Miles $____________

1 @ 301 + Overnight $____________

Total Contests *Total Transportation Cost*

13 $____________

Figure 5-20
Compensation for Differential Responsibilities

Category IA:

Head Varsity Track—B & G Combined

Category I:

Head Varsity Basketball—B
Head Varsity Football
Head Varsity Basketball—G

Category II:

Head Varsity Baseball
Head Varsity Soccer—B
Head Varsity Soccer—G
Head Varsity Swimming—G
Head Varsity Wrestling
Head Varsity Softball

Category III:

Head Varsity Cross Country—B
Head Varsity Cross Country—G
Head Varsity Gymnastics—B
Head Varsity Gymnastics—G
Head Varsity Volleyball—B
Head Varsity Volleyball—G
Football—Head Freshman
Football—Head Sophomore
Asst. Football—Varsity (3)
Asst. Basketball—B (4)
Asst. Basketball—G (4)
Asst. Track—B & G Combined (6)

Category IV:

Head Varsity Badminton
Head Varsity Golf—B
Head Varsity Golf—G
Head Varsity Tennis—G
Head Varsity Tennis—B
Assistant Baseball (4)
Assistant Football (3)
Assistant Soccer—B (4)
Assistant Soccer—G (4)
Assistant Swimming—B (3)
Assistant Swimming—G (3)
Wrestling (3)

Category V:

Asst. Cross Country—G (1)
Asst. Cross Country—B (1)
Asst. Gymnastics—B (2)
Asst. Gymnastics—G (2)
Asst. Volleyball—G (2)
Asst. Volleyball—B (2)

Category VI:

Asst. Tennis—B (1)
Asst. Tennis—G (1)
Asst. Golf—B (1)
Asst. Golf—G (1)
Asst. Badminton (2)

Salary as Secondary

Salary really is secondary to the other benefits to be derived from coaching. Ask any experienced coach if he or she went into the business to become rich. Not a chance! Coaching, especially in junior high schools and secondary schools, promises rewards far in excess of a check at the end of the season. Don't get us wrong; the check is nice, but it will never be the primary reason why people go into coaching.

Coaches enjoy their jobs because of associations with young athletes, with one another, and with a sport they have grown to love. The satisfaction, even the recognition they derive from these associations is invariably more important than money. If you studied educational administration, you'll recall that Douglas McGregor, one of the field's prominent theorists, indicated decades ago that persons in organizations desire a sense of achievement and autonomy over money and benefits.

If you accept his premise, you have an organizational barometer to determine the degree of coaching satisfaction within your athletic department. In other words, to the extent that coaches desire money over accomplishment, you have an indication of how happy coaches are with their job responsibilities and the operation of the program. If money is their overriding concern, something's wrong within the program.

W. Edwards Deming, the father of Total Quality Management, suggests that most of the problems within organizations are systemic; that is, they are the result of dysfunction within the system, not necessarily the people within the system. So when coaches start shouting for more money, you had better analyze the salary schedule for inequities, but consider the possibility that something else has provoked their dissatisfaction.

The most important consideration for athletic directors regarding coaching salaries is helping the district establish an equitable schedule, one that is comparable to that of neighboring districts. Then, if dissatisfaction is evident among the coaches, scrutinize the nature of departmental interrelationships, policies, and opportunities for coaches to be recognized and to achieve their personal and team goals.

WORKING CLOSELY WITH THE BOOSTER CLUB

There are also other ways to supplement the athletic department's budget and to find ways to purchase high-priced items for coaches most in need of them. Sometimes a balance beam or a seven-man sled must be replaced. If the budget is unable to satisfy such a request, a booster club meeting might be the logical place to turn. Most boosters are genuinely concerned about the athletic program and are more than willing to raise money to improve it. They identify with the success of the athletic program by donating their time, money, and, occasionally their experience and advice—hopefully, only when requested!

To encourage their financial support, meet with them in order to answer questions and to provide the kind of specific information outlined in Figure 5-21. Meet with the coach making the request to secure his or her preliminary input, then make copies of the completed form to share with boosters during the meeting. Boosters appreciate this kind of information, primarily because it identifies the particulars of the need and expedites the decision process.

LET'S WRAP IT UP

Overseeing the budget is one of the primary responsibilities of athletic directors, especially if they want to keep their bosses happy. Staying within the parameters of the school's budget may not guarantee a red-hot sports program, but it assures warm smiles from the school's administration. The athletic director who is interested in moving up the organizational ladder is well advised to watch the budget carefully. This piece of advice does, however, involve a word of caution.

You can curry administrative favor by reducing annual expenditures and promoting a belt-tightening mentality within the department, but most coaches will tighten just so far before they strip off their belts and swing them at anyone with a hand on the purse strings. And no one can blame them, unless, of course, the district is strapped financially, in which case a healthy dose of reality is the best medicine. Such reality is best provided by sharing budgetary facts and figures with coaches and engaging them in departmental planning activities.

"Best practice" for athletic directors, therefore, as with all effective administrators, involves an honest and reasonable approach to budget planning and accountability. On the one hand, you must stay within the guidelines as prescribed by the total school budget. Such "fiscal exertion" is recognized and often rewarded by school principals. On the other hand, a good athletic director is the intermediary between the coaches and the administration, and must have the skills to satisfy the needs of both.

This balancing act can challenge the skills of the Flying Wallendas! Like the Wallendas, ADs watch out for colleagues while they guarantee their own survival. They refine such skills through experience. The smart ones develop the skills early in their careers by acknowledging their responsibilities to the school's administration *and* to their coaches and athletes, and they develop processes that enable them to know what to do—when they don't know what to do! Famed educator Art Costa indicates that this is an attribute of intelligent people. And athletic directors are intelligent people; otherwise they wouldn't be so successful handling such a wide range of often-conflicting responsibilities. Certainly, the magnitude and frustration of your job as athletic director causes you at times to question your sanity as well as your intelligence, but when you "trust to process" and have the self-confidence to engage coaches in decision-making activities, you discover that good things happen to everyone in the department, including *you*.

Finally, you instill confidence in administrators when you bring a sense of closure to the budgetary process by comparing current or projected budgets to past budgets. Figure 5-22 provides a sample copy of annual budgets by fiscal year (FY). It's generally a good idea to share such information with the school's administration at the end of the school year when positive closure is important to everyone.

Perhaps the most important point to remember in this section, however, is the need to engage head coaches in the budgetary process. The synergy created by a collaborative approach to departmental planning will extend to relationships within the department and reflect well on your leadership ability. Most important, the planning and positive relationships will result in a successful program and a rewarding experience for your student athletes.

Figure 5-21
Request to the Booster Club

As you probably know, the _____________ High School Athletic Department is provided with an annual budget that guarantees the safety of each of our athletes and seeks to promote their appearance and athletic performance. In spite of the generosity of the budget, occasionally we find ourselves unable to meet the equipment needs of all our coaches and athletes. At these times, if the need is great enough, we seek assistance elsewhere. The Booster Club is, perhaps, our school's most reliable source of such assistance. For that reason we come to you with the following request:

THE SPECIFICS OF THE NEED:

HOW IT WILL BENEFIT OUR STUDENT ATHLETES:

COMMENTS FROM THE COACH:

Please see any attached sheets for additional information.

Figure 5-22
Sample Annual Budgets

Athletic Budgets (by Cost) FY 93–96

Category	FY 93	FY 94	FY 95	FY 96
General Athletics	16685.00	15750.00	16685.00	12990.00
Training Room	7600.00	7600.00	7600.00	7816.00
Badminton	3180.00	2780.00	2480.00	2203.00
Baseball	6200.00	5725.00	6000.00	2737.00
B Basketball	5350.00	6300.00	4000.00	5886.00
G Basketball	4770.00	3920.00	6400.00	7099.00
B Cross Country	1900.00	775.00	250.00	1359.00
G Cross Country	350.00	1415.00	1330.00	757.00
Football	18350.00	15300.00	17075.00	16928.00
B Golf	2900.00	2615.00	2615.00	2486.00
G Golf	2400.00	2350.00	3275.00	2688.00
B Gymnastics	1920.00	3575.00	1775.00	2283.00
G Gymnastics	3160.00	1775.00	2450.00	1551.00
B Soccer	5875.00	3425.00	7250.00	3781.00
G Soccer	4050.00	6700.00	2450.00	6791.00
Softball	4185.00	4160.00	3835.00	6214.00
B Swimming	2650.00	3190.00	2750.00	2062.00
G Swimming	2390.00	3105.00	2585.00	2510.00
B Tennis	1460.00	1195.00	1400.00	2222.00
G Tennis	1370.00	1700.00	1455.00	876.00
Track and Field	6320.00	6700.00	5700.00	5247.00
B Volleyball	2860.00	2900.00	3100.00	3123.00
G Volleyball	3150.00	3675.00	3860.00	3816.00
Wrestling	3820.00	3420.00	3675.00	3433.00
Security	2500.00	2800.00	2800.00	2885.00
Total	115395.00	112850.00	115250.00	109743.00
Transportation				
Boys	35000.00	36000.00	50000.00	50000.00
Girls	22000.00	22000.00	35000.00	35000.00
Total	57000.00	58000.00	85000.00	85000.00

Printed with permission from Glenbrook High School.

SECTION SIX

The Athletic Director as a School Administrator

First, a quick story:

Several years ago, Mike helped a group of building administrators struggle through an exploration of higher order thought process and questioning technique in the classroom. Each of the ideas was experiencing varying stages of conceptual metamorphosis and was challenging the understanding of even the most experienced department heads in the room. Still in the "trend stage," the concepts, at least in the minds of this group of administrators, were rooted more in the abstract of their discussion than in the concrete of their practice.

At one stage in the discussion, they were all searching for courses or learning experiences in their departments to serve as illustrations of higher order thought process in the classroom. A couple mentioned their Advanced Placement courses; one or two suggested literature classes and science labs. Most were having problems illustrating the one class that consistently engaged students in higher order thought process. At that point, Mike suggested that the meeting adjourn and that everyone accompany him to football practice.

Needless to say, his suggestion provoked a shocked reaction, so Mike explained his reasons. Fortunately, most of the people in the room were at the end of their intellectual tether, so they agreed to go with him, hoping as much for a needed reprieve as an example of higher order thought process. Mike led the administrators from the building to the practice field, where the football team was preparing its offensive game plan.

The first-string offensive linemen were standing on the line of scrimmage, and the defensive prep team was lining up in a variety of defensive alignments at the coach's command. Each time they lined up in a different defensive formation, the coach barked out a new offensive play and told the linemen to point to the defensive player they would block. He then asked them to explain the reasons for their decisions. He would then change the defensive formation but keep the same offensive play and again ask the linemen to indicate which defensive player they would block.

Whenever the defense changed its alignment, he asked the same questions, eventually pointing out similarities and differences in the defensive formations and the necessary adjustments to be made by the offensive linemen if they hoped to block the play effectively. As the practice progressed, each department head nodded in Mike's direction as if to say, "I see what you mean!" The drill illustrated higher order thought process at its best.

The offensive linemen had to identify the defensive formation confronting them (memory and comprehension level thinking), choose from among several different ways to block it (application level thinking), and understand the total range of interrelated responsibilities of each lineman to execute each blocking scheme (synthesis level thinking). Finally, they had to assess quickly which blocking scheme would be most effective and tell the coach (evaluation level thinking).

These kinds of experiences consistently prove to coaches, and—on this day—to most of the administrators in this particular school, that athletic competition is no longer forced by tradition to occupy the lowest rung on education's academic ladder. Such competition engages young athletes in a level of thought process that can be as challenging as any Advanced Placement course, and does it within a format of modality learning that most classroom teachers can only imagine. Athletes hear, see, and do every skill that is required of them, and they are expected to analyze and evaluate a variety of situations during almost every moment of competition.

THE ATHLETIC DIRECTOR AS DEPARTMENT SPOKESPERSON

Because athletic directors have frequent contact with a range of people inside and outside the building, their primary job is to serve as advocates of the total athletic program and to share realities like those above with significant persons in the school and community. Given the current media focus on interscholastic and intercollegiate athletic abuses, coaches at all levels are being criticized for their preoccupation with winning and their apparent disregard for the educational needs of their athletes.

Much of this criticism is deserved, especially in some college sports programs. It is inappropriate, however, for a vast majority of coaches, particularly those on the junior high school and secondary school levels. Our experience has proven consistently that most coaches really care about young athletes and that coaches are powerful influences on the positive development of teenagers. As important, they assist young athletes with levels of intellectual development that most adults in our society fail to associate with athletic competition. Share this information often with parents and others in the community.

Once most parents are convinced that the local sports program is important for their children for a variety of reasons, they will impress upon the community the total educational value of athletic competition. Too often, athletic competition is regarded as the province of mindless "animals" with strong bodies and weak minds. Unfortunately, such a perception is true for some athletes. For most, however, athletics is an opportunity not only to showcase physical ability but to develop and display intellectual power.

To emphasize an oft-repeated observation: "The day of the dumb athlete is gone." We doubt that the day ever existed. Athletic competition always has been strenuous, both physically and mentally—and particularly today, when competitive strategy is as sophisticated as it has ever been. Football players don't choose from among ten to twelve blocking schemes on the line of scrimmage in order to run an "inside belly tackle trap at 5" versus a stunting gap-stack 44 and deserve the title "Dimwit."

Higher order thought process is as evident in athletics as in any Advanced Placement classroom. You must share this fact with fellow administrators and teachers in the building and with persons in the community. When you do, you dispel popular misconceptions about the intelligence and integrity of coaches and athletes, and you sell the athletic program to parents and community members who begin to regard it as an essential complement to the school's academic program.

Start with Goal Statements

Well-conceived goal statements for the athletic program are the logical starting place for such a sharing of information. The fifteen statements in Figure 6-1 were developed by District 225 in Illinois and provide excellent examples of statements that promote academics as well as athletics, and that emphasize the values that generally are so important to the community. These particular goal statements are very important to the coaches at Glenbrook South, because they helped develop them.

The collaborative development of the athletic department's goals is very important if coaches are to "own" and commit to them in their daily behavior. Use the goals in Figure 6-1, therefore, as a starting point, perhaps as something to think about, as coaches work cooperatively to identify their departmental philosophy and goal statements. They may even decide to borrow one or more of the statements. That's all right, too. The point is, coaches and athletic directors require a mutually acceptable starting point to help promote the school's athletic program.

Extracurricular Activities and the Future Success of Students

Well-conceived goals provide that starting point, and the realization that involvement in extracurricular activities reflects and promotes the future success of junior high school and secondary school students adds to it. Current research has done a good job of documenting and emphasizing the importance of extracurricular activities. Some of us are still uncertain as to whether the relationship between sports and the future success of young people is a causal or a parallel phenomenon. In other words, is future success the result of athletic participation or of the inherent drive that normally characterizes most athletes?

Figure 6-1
Goal Statements

All of the athletic programs offer unique situations outside of the classroom—but within the high school environment, where life is played out, not simulated. The purposes to be achieved from the Interscholastic Athletic and the Intramural Programs are as follows:

1. To provide students with the opportunity to engage in competitive activities and to come to understand that the word "compete" is derived from Latin words meaning "to strive together."
2. To provide students with the opportunity to experience self-discipline, sacrifice, and dedication as means of achieving goals.
3. To provide students with the opportunity to exemplify good sportsmanship as a means for learning good citizenship.
4. To provide students with the opportunity to experience working as a member of a team in order to achieve a goal, and, in the process, learn that cooperation and competition are not mutually exclusive concepts.
5. To provide students with the opportunity to experience both winning and losing. Students should come to understand that losing provides opportunities to learn, setting the stage for future winning, and that winning is not as important as an end result, as it is as a feedback indicator that you're probably doing a pretty good job as individuals and as a team.
6. To demonstrate to students that real, lasting satisfaction comes not so much from "winning" per sè as from doing the job to the best of your ability.
7. To demonstrate to students that as individuals they are capable of achieving more than they think they are capable of achieving.
8. To provide students with the opportunity to engage in competitive experiences in an acceptable manner.
9. To provide students with the opportunity to experience a feeling of self-worth and to develop self-confidence.
10. To provide students with the opportunity for experience in problem solving and decision making.
11. To provide students with the opportunity to engage in organized activities with other students whose backgrounds and academic abilities may be dissimilar from their own.
12. To provide students with the opportunity to learn new skills beyond those acquired in physical education classes and to improve upon those already acquired.
13. To provide students with the opportunity to understand and practice the principles of sound health, safety, and physical fitness.
14. To provide students with the opportunity to develop the ability and desire to use their time effectively.
15. To provide students with the opportunity to have a positive rallying point for the school in order to help them develop school loyalty and a sense of participation in a larger whole.

Printed with permission from Glenbrook High School.

Although the jury is still out on that point, most coaches and athletic directors are convinced that athletic participation promotes self-discipline, an improved self-concept, and a healthy aggressiveness that leads to athletic and academic success in school and to the character development that assures personal, social, and career success later in life. You must do all you can to share these realities with the community in order to enhance the self-perceptions of coaches and to encourage the student participation that is so necessary to the success of the athletic program and to the positive development of participating students.

Standing for Something

Be the first in the athletic program to "stand for something," to represent a personal and professional code that guides you through your daily responsibilities and that enables you to model purposeful behavior. Such a code is provided in Figure 6-2 and was developed by the Professional Development Committee of the National Interscholastic Athletic Administrators Association. Frame it and hang it conspicuously in your office to remind yourself and others of your commitment to the purposes of interscholastic athletics.

Rather than detail each of the ten principles, we ask that you notice that they refer to the personal philosophies and value systems as well as the procedural responsibilities of athletic directors. It's not enough to simply oversee the school's athletic program, just as it's insufficient that coaches simply emphasize fundamentals and strategy with their athletes during practice sessions and contests. You must model in your daily behavior the sportsmanship and personal conduct that are so important to coaches and young athletes—and you must do this during the execution of each of your responsibilities, which are outlined here.

THE FUNCTIONS AND TASKS OF ATHLETIC DIRECTORS

Sharing the Program Philosophy

The philosophy of athletics promotes student commitment to an important activity, self-discipline, good citizenship, team membership, the search for personal excellence, self-worth, improved decision making, and a commitment to the principles of good health and fitness. Because such principles are so important to young people and to their parents, they should be publicized throughout the school and community.

A current body of research indicates that young athletes are more involved in drinking, drug use, unprotected sex, and violent behavior than their nonathletic schoolmates. This research is startling and has done much to cause parents and others in society to question the value of athletic participation. Much of this research comes as no surprise to those of us who have devoted years of our lives to athletics. We learned long ago that the natural aggressiveness of athletes sometimes leads to antisocial behavior and to self-destructive abuse of alcohol and other drugs.

Figure 6-2
Code of Ethics

The Interscholastic Athletic Administrator as an Educational Leader:

1. Develops and maintains a comprehensive athletic program which seeks the highest development of all participants, and which respects the individual dignity of every athlete.

2. Considers the well-being of the entire student body as fundamental in all decisions and actions.

3. Supports the principle of due process and protects the civil and human rights of all individuals.

4. Organizes, directs, and promotes an interscholastic athletic program that is an integral part of the total educational program.

5. Cooperates with the staff and school administration in establishing, implementing, and supporting school policies.

6. Acts impartially in the execution of basic policies, and the enforcement of the conference, league, and state high school association rules and regulations.

7. Fulfills professional responsibilities with honesty and integrity.

8. Upholds the honor of the profession in all relations with students, colleagues, coaches, administrators, and the general public.

9. Improves the professional status and effectiveness of the interscholastic athletic administrator through participation in local, state, and national in-service programs.

10. Promotes high standards of ethics, sportsmanship, and personal conduct by encouraging administration, coaches, staff, student athletes, and community to commit to these high standards.

Prepared by the NIAAA Professional Development Committee.
Reprinted with permission from the National Interscholastic Athletic Administrator's Association, P.O. Box 20626, Kansas City, MO 64195.

We also learned, however, that athletic participation subjects young people to a daily regimen that promotes self-discipline and commitment to a cause that has genuine importance in their lives. Such a regimen, especially when controlled by a coach who exercises profound influence on the lives of his or her athletes, results in the emotional, social, and intellectual growth of young athletes and validates the sports program within the community and school.

You must share this message with a wide range of people. Fortunately, a number of opportunities are available within the school and community:

- *Building Administrator Meetings*—In most schools, athletic directors routinely participate in the weekly meetings that involve department heads and the school's administration in program planning. Such meetings provide a continuing forum for you to promote the athletic program as a critical element in the total educational mission of the school. This ongoing contact among department heads also enables you to plan collaboratively with other departments as new teachers/coaches are hired by the school.

  If you are not routinely involved in building administrators' meetings, you should borrow generously from this section to recommend such involvement. Use the format suggested in Figure 6-3 to draft such a recommendation.
- *Booster Club Meetings*—Most schools have booster clubs that promote the involvement of interested parents in the activities of the athletic department. While booster clubs provide opportunities for self-serving parents to influence program decisions (particularly those that affect their children) the athletic director who remains alert to such possibilities can avoid them. If you are alert, you can ensure a booster club that understands the scope of its responsibilities and works closely with you and the coaches to promote the best interests of the athletic department.
- *Advisory Councils*—Many athletic directors develop parental advisory councils, consisting of five to seven members, for input into important departmental decisions. Such councils can also provide help with publicity, fund raising, and communication activities.
- *Local Service and Fraternal Organizations*—Organizations like the Rotary, Lions, the League of Women Voters, and the Optimists' Club are always on the lookout for speakers for luncheons and other meetings. You can provide a valuable resource for such organizations—especially if you're accompanied by coaches—and, in the process, can help publicize the philosophy and activities of the athletic program. Use the sample letter in Figure 6-4 to communicate your availability to such organizations and to establish the kinds of relationships that result in substantial community support for the athletic program.
- *Local News Media*—Sharing information with the local news media can sometimes be a full-time job, but it pays substantial dividends if used wisely. Newspapers and television programs are constantly searching for newsworthy information, something a little out of the ordinary to pique the interest of sports fans. Every school has its stories to share with the local media. Some involve the significant accomplishments of athletes or coaches; others involve human interest stories that provide unique insights into athletic competition.

Often, these stories circulate only within the school; they rarely find their way into the community and surrounding areas. The public relations forms in Section Seven will enable you to receive information from coaches, parents, and athletes about newsworthy events and to share such information with the media. You should also schedule periodic meetings with the managing editors of newspapers and television and radio stations to establish a process for sharing such information. Such meetings establish the relationships with media people that can result in extensive and generous coverage of the athletic program.

- *Conference Meetings*—The conference in which your school is a member can do much to promote athletics within the surrounding area. Because conference activities involve not only athletic directors but school superintendents and principals, most conferences have substantial clout within local political and media organizations. Be sure to use such political strength when circumstances warrant it.
- *State and National Athletic Associations*—You are well advised to establish membership and eventually to seek office in one or more state and national athletic organizations. Such organizations provide valuable contacts for help and advice and a broader forum for the promotion of your program and general philosophy.

Promoting Student Participation

The athletic director and coaches may be the head of a successful athletic program, but young athletes are its arms and legs, and probably its heart and soul. A primary responsibility of athletic directors and coaches, therefore, is to promote student participation and, once students are involved, to do everything necessary to assure their eligibility. The more closely you and your coaches work together to encourage young people to join one or more athletic teams, the more successful the entire program will be.

The old dictum "there's enough to go around" is generally true of most junior high and secondary schools. Some of them enjoy participation rates as high as 75 percent of the entire student body. In such schools—particularly when coaches establish positive relationships with their athletes by promoting solid fundamentals, up-to-date strategy, and genuine concern about them as young people—the entire program can be successful.

The process for securing the successful involvement of students in the athletic program consists of the following four steps:

- *Paint a Bright Picture*—Join forces with the coaching staff to get into your feeder schools to explain the athletic program and to invite students to participate. Be careful to keep the picture sufficiently bright. Young people may thrill to the thought of a Vince Lombardi half-time speech; they may even be intrigued by traditions of physical pain "for the good of the team." But when confronted with the harsh realities of the dog days of late summer and the prospect of sweating in the sun when their friends are still rolling in the surf, many students fail to share a coach's vision of team sacrifice.

Figure 6-3
Involvement in Weekly Administrative Meetings Memo

Athletic Department

TO: Building Principal

FROM: Athletic Director

RE: Involvement in weekly administrative meetings

DATE:

I am writing to let you know that I would like to volunteer my time and presence at the weekly building administrative meetings. These meetings provide a forum for me as an athletic director to gather important information to share with my athletic colleagues, an opportunity to plan and work cooperatively with the academic departments, and a chance to promote the athletic program and its important components to other members of the administrative team.

To provide a well-rounded education to the student athlete at this school, I hope you will consider my involvement in the school's administrative team.

I look forward to hearing from you on this matter.

Figure 6-4
Sample Letter to Community Organization

Athletic Department

Club President
Club Name
Address
City, State, ZIP

Date

Dear Club President,

Frequently, clubs like yours look for talented and enlightened speakers for your meetings and luncheons. I am happy to let you know that our high school athletic department would be a valuable resource for your organization.

The athletic department would be willing to cover procedural responsibilities, and sportsmanship programs, share competition schedules, or bring along members of the coaching staff to provide an overview of their particular program. Perhaps our outstanding student athletes could share their positive experiences in the program.

We are looking to your organization for continued community support and want to continue the positive relationship between your association and our athletic program. We would be happy to discuss with you at your convenience the opportunity for the athletic department to speak at your meetings.

If you are interested, please give us a call at the athletic department.

Respectfully,

Athletic Director
School
Address
City, State, ZIP
Phone

During these introductory meetings to the athletic program, therefore, coaches must be encouraged to save their pep talks for the big game and their demands for self-sacrifice for future practice sessions. Visits to feeder schools to invite students to participate in the school's athletic program must promote good times, friendships, and the invitation to belong to a successful program. Youngsters like to "belong." We all like to belong, as long as we feel safe in the process. That's why it's a good idea to distribute the information in Figure 6-5 to students and parents during these introductory meetings.

Current studies indicate that athletic participation is dropping off in many schools because young athletes simply are not enjoying time spent in practice, even in competition. Yes, we know—since when is practice supposed to be fun? Practice is the time for hard work and the almost mindless repetition of fundamental skills to engage the body's memory and improve performance. *Competition* is fun, especially when all that hard work in practice results in satisfying performances, and maybe even victory.

Many of today's preteens and teens seem unaware of this aspect of athletic competition. They want to win and to enjoy the recognition that accompanies superior performance, but they seem unwilling to commit to the hard work that results in such performance. They are interested in athletic competition but unable, for whatever reason, to make the individual sacrifice that results in team accomplishment.

Good coaches can change such behaviors by introducing young athletes to the merits of hard work and to the satisfaction of commitment, teamwork, and self-discipline. Such lessons take time and depend on strong interpersonal relationships, an experience that satisfies the ego and social needs of young athletes, and rewarding and enjoyable activities during the season. These lessons are not learned overnight—certainly not during the introductory meeting to the school's athletic program.

- Maintaining the Family Concept—After the entering students have been invited to participate, they must be welcomed into the school's athletic family. This step involves a preliminary meeting to explain the Athletic Code (see Figure 1-4, p. 9); the school's eligibility requirements (Figure 6-6); and information regarding physicals (Figure 6-7), emergency notification, insurance considerations, and consent forms (see Figure 6-8). See Section Eight for a further discussion from a legal perspective and for reproducibles.

This step involves much more than paperwork, however. It is the orientation experience for the young athletes and their parents, and must introduce them not only to the expectations of the school but to the realities of athletic competition. That's why it's often a good idea to include one or more speakers in the meeting who can talk about athletic competition from a variety of different angles. Young athletes and their parents need to understand the realities of eligibility requirements, the time demands of practice and contests, the importance of academics, the emotional demands of competition or of being "cut" from a team, the difficulty of balancing athletics and academics, and the program's behavioral expectations of its athletes. This is the time when good speakers put athletic competition in its proper perspective, emphasizing the primacy of academics and the importance of individual excellence over winning at all costs.

Figure 6-5
Introductory Meeting Letter

Athletic Department

Date

Dear Parents of Prospective Fall Athletes:

Welcome to interscholastic athletics at __________ high school. Before the season gets underway, we ask that you attend a short athletic meeting in which we will discuss the athletic code of conduct, eligibility, scholastic endeavors, and the trainers role. Immediately following the meeting, there will be a short breakout session with the head coach from your son's or daughter's sport. Parents need to sign an information form at the end of the meeting (only one parent need attend with the athlete but we encourage both parents/guardians to attend the meeting).

Your encouragement and support of Glenbrook South Athletics have always been the secret to our success. We ask you to continue that support by attending this important program with your son or daughter. The evening is scheduled to begin at (time) P.M. on (date/year). Athletes will not be able to participate in competition without attendance at a code of conduct meeting by parent and athlete. We look forward to seeing you and your son/daughter on (date/year) at (time) P.M. We believe you will find this program very beneficial.

Sincerely,

Athletic Director
School

Fall Sports

Football	Boys Cross Country
Girls Cross Country	Boys Golf
Girls Golf	Boys Soccer
Girls Swimming and Diving	Boys Soccer
Girls Tennis	

Figure 6-6
Eligibility Requirements

Illinois High School Association

(For 1995-96 School Year)
(Revised 3/1/95)

Athletic Eligibility Rules

When you become a member of an interscholastic athletic team at your high school, you will find that both your school and the IHSA will have rules you must follow in order to be eligible for interscholastic sports participation. The IHSA's rules have been adopted by the high schools which are members of IHSA as part of the Association's constitution and by-laws. They must be followed as minimum standards for all interscholastic athletic competition in any member high school. Your high school may have additional requirements, but they may not be less stringent than these statewide minimums.

The principal of your school is responsible to certify the eligibility of all students representing the school in interscholastic athletics. Any question concerning your athletic eligibility should be referred to your principal, who has a complete copy of all IHSA eligibility rules, including the Association's due process procedure. If your principal has questions or wishes assistance in answering your questions, contact should be made to the IHSA Office.

Information contained here highlights only the most important features of the IHSA by-laws regarding interscholastic athletic eligibility. It is designed to make you aware of **major** requirements you must meet to be eligible to compete in interscholastic athletics. You will lose eligibility for interscholastic athletics if you violate IHSA by-laws. Therefore, it is extremely important that you review this material with your parents, your coaches, your athletic director and your principal to thoroughly understand the IHSA eligibility by-laws and how they relate to you.

Attendance

1. You may represent only the school you attend. Participation on a cooperative team of which your school is a member is acceptable.
2. You must be enrolled and attending classes in your high school no later than the beginning of the 11th school day of the semester.
3. If you attend school for ten (10) or more days during any one semester, it will count as one of the eight (8) semesters of high school attendance during which you may possibly have athletic eligibility.
4. If you have a lapse in school connection for ten (10) or more consecutive school days during a semester, you are subject to ineligibility for the rest of the semester. The specific terms of your extended absence must be reviewed by the Executive Director to determine if it is "lapse in school connection or not".

Scholastic Standing

1. You must pass twenty (20) credit hours of high school work per week. Generally, twenty (20) credit hours is the equivalent of four (4) "full credit" courses.
2. You must have passed and received credit toward graduation for twenty (20) credit hours of high school work for the entire previous semester to be eligible at all during the ensuing semester.

Residence

1. Your eligibility is dependent on the residence of your parents, not your own residence. You may be eligible if you attend the public high school in the district in which both of your parents live. If you attend a private or parochial school, you may be eligible when you enroll and attend high school for the first time as a ninth (9th) grade student, regardless of where your parents live.
2. If you have attended the same high school for your entire high school career and your parents move from the district or community traditionally served by your school after you have completed the eleventh (11th) grade, you may remain in attendance at that school, upon approval of the local Board of Education, and be eligible in regard to residence for the twelfth (12th) grade.
3. If you do not reside with both your biological parents, your eligibility may be subject to special provisions. Check with your principal to be sure you are eligible before you participate.

Transfer

1. If you transfer from a high school in one school district to a high school in another school district, you will be ineligible for up to one year unless:
   a. Your parents move into the district into which you transfer;
   b. Your transfer is from a private/parochial school to your home public high school, you are entering a public high school for the first time, and the principals of both your former and the new school agree there is no evidence of violation of the IHSA recruiting rules.
2. If you transfer from one public school to another, in a district which has two or more high schools under the same board of education, you will be ineligible for up to one year unless: (1) your parents move from the attendance area of the school you are leaving and into the attendance area of the school to which you transfer, or (2) you are ruled eligible by the IHSA Executive Director under the special factors provided in the IHSA eligibility by-laws. **Note**: If you transfer schools and your parents do not move, be sure the principal of your new school obtains a written ruling on your eligibility before you play in a contest.
3. If you transfer because you are emancipated, an orphan, from a broken home, from a single parent family or have had reassignment of your legal guardianship by action of the court, you are ineligible until the IHSA Executive Director rules on your eligibility. Be sure the principal of your new school obtains a written ruling on your eligibility before you play in a contest.
4. If you transfer within the first ten (10) school days of a semester, you will be eligible immediately if you comply with all eligibility rules. However, if you transfer after the start of the eleventh (11th) day of the semester, you will automatically be ineligible for thirty (30) days, beginning with the date of your transfer.
5. If you transfer schools and your transfer does not comply with IHSA by-law requirements, you will be ineligible for a **maximum** of one year. The specific length of your ineligibility must be determined by the IHSA Executive Director.

Participation Limitations

1. After you enroll in ninth (9th) grade, you may be eligible for no more than the first eight (8) semesters you attend school. If you attend school for ten (10) or more days in a semester, that counts as a semester of attendance. You are not guaranteed eight semesters of eligibility, but that is the maximum number of semesters of high school attendance during which you may have eligibility.
2. Your 7th and 8th semesters of high school attendance must be consecutive.
3. After you enroll in ninth (9th) grade, you may be eligible for no more than four (4) years of competition in any sport. You are not guaranteed four (4) years of competition, but that is the maximum amount of competition you may have.

Age

1. You will become ineligible on the date you become twenty (20) years of age, unless your twentieth (20th) birthday occurs during a sport season. In that case, you will become ineligible in regard to age at the beginning of the sport season during which you will turn twenty (20).

Use of Players

1. You may not appear at a contest in the uniform of your school while you are ineligible. This means that you may not dress or sit on the bench if you are not eligible to play. Also, you may not compete as an "exhibition" contestant if you are not eligible.

Participating Under a False Name

1. If you compete under a name other than your own, your principal will immediately suspend you from further competition and you and any other person(s) who contributed to the violation of this by-law will be subject to penalties.

Physical Examination

1. You must annually have placed on file with your principal a certificate of physical fitness, signed by a licensed physician, in order to practice or participate. Your physical examination each year is good for only one (1) year from the date of the exam. The physician's report must be on file with your high school principal.

Athletic Eligibility Rules—Continued

Amateur Status

1. If you win or place in actual competition, you may accept a medal or trophy for that accomplishment, without limit to its cost.
2. For participating in competition in an interscholastic sport, or for athletic honors or recognition in a sport, you may receive any type of award (except cash, check or legal tender) that does not exceed $20 fair market value. There is no limitation on the value of your school letter.
3. The amateur rule does not prohibit you from being paid to referee, receiving pay for teaching lessons or coaching in a little kids league, etc. It only applies to your own competition in an athletic contest.
4. If you violate the amateur rule, you become ineligible in the sport in which you violate. You must be reinstated by the Executive Director before you may compete again.

Recruiting of Athletes

1. The rules prohibit recruiting of high school students for athletics. If you are solicited to enroll in or transfer to a school to participate in athletics, you are being illegally recruited and your eligibility is in jeopardy.
2. You will lose your eligibility if you enroll in or transfer to a school in response to recruiting efforts by any person or group of persons, connected with or not connected with the school, related to athletic participation.
3. You will lose your eligibility if you receive special benefits or privileges as a prospective student-athlete which are not uniformly made available to all students who attend your school.
4. You may not receive an "athletic scholarship" or any other special benefit from your school, provided because you participate in athletics.
5. It is a violation for any student-athlete to receive or be offered remuneration or any special inducement which is not made available to all applicants who apply to or enroll in the school.
   Special inducement includes, but is not limited to:
   a. Offer or acceptance of money or other valuable consideration such as free or reduced tuition during the regular year or summer school by anyone connected with the school.
   b. Offer or acceptance of room, board or clothing or financial allotment for clothing.
   c. Offer or acceptance of pay for work that is not performed or that is in excess of the amount regularly paid for such service.
   d. Offer or acceptance of free transportation by any school connected person.
   e. Offer or acceptance of a residence with any school connected person.
   f. Offer or acceptance of any privilege not afforded to non-athletes.
   g. Offer or acceptance of free or reduced rent for parents.
   h. Offer or acceptance of payment of moving expenses of parents or assistance with the moving of parents.
   i. Offer or acceptance of employment of parent(s) in order to entice the family to move to a certain community if someone connected with the school makes the offer.
   j. Offer or acceptance of help in securing a college athletic scholarship.
6. It is also a violation to induce or attempt to induce or encourage any prospective student to attend any member school for the purpose of participating in athletics, even when special remuneration or inducement is not given. Please remember that you may not be offered or receive **any benefit, service, privilege or opportunity** which is not also provided or made available to all prospective students at that school.

School Team Sports Seasons

1. Each sport conducted by IHSA member schools has a starting and ending date. Your school may not organize a team, begin practice or participate in contests in a given sport until the authorized starting date. Your school may not continue to practice or participate in contests after the authorized ending date. This means that:
   a. You may not participate on a non-school team coached by any member of your school's coaching staff unless it meets specific criteria established by the IHSA Board of Directors.
   b. No school coach may require you to participate in an out-of-season sport program as a requirement for being a member of a school team.
2. Violation of the sport season by-laws will result in penalty to you and/or to your school's coaching personnel.

Playing in Non-School Competition

1. During the time you are participating on a school team in a sport at your high school, you may neither play on a non-school team nor compete in non-school competition as an individual in that same sport.
2. If you participate in non-school competition during a sport season and subsequently wish to join the school team in the same sport, you will not be eligible.
3. If you are trying out for or competing as a representative of the United States in recognized national or international competition during your high school's sport season in the same sport, you must obtain approval from the IHSA Office. Your principal must initiate the request for approval in writing prior to any such participation.
4. You may try out for a non-school team while you are on your school's team in that same sport, but you may not practice, receive instruction, participate in workouts, or participate in competition with a non-school team in that same sport until you cease being a member of your school's team. You cease being a member of your school's team when the team(s) of which you are a member terminates for the school year.
5. You will become ineligible if you play on any junior college, college or university team during your high school career.

All-Star Participation

1. After you have completed your high school eligibility for football, basketball, soccer or volleyball, you may participate in one (1) all-star contest in any of these sports and still play for other school teams, provided:
   a. the high school season in that sport has been completed;
   b. the all-star contest has been approved by the IHSA.

   You may lose your eligibility for other interscholastic sports if you play in all-star competition in any of these sports under any other conditions.
2. You are not restricted from participating in all-star competition in sports other than football, basketball soccer or volleyball, except that you may not do so during the school season for the sport.

Coaching Schools

1. A coaching school is defined as "any program sponsored by an organization or individual which provides instruction in sports theory and skills to groups of persons." The term "groups of persons" is defined as more than two (2) students from any school.
2. During the school year, you may not attend a coaching school or clinic for any interscholastic sport.
3. You may attend a coaching school, camp or clinic during the summer (that period between the close of school in the spring and the opening of school in the fall) within the following criteria:
   a. You may not attend a coaching school, camp or clinic for any fall sport(s) after July 31.
   b. You may not attend a coaching school, camp or clinic for any winter or spring sport(s) after the day your school begins in the fall.

Misbehavior During Contests

1. If you violate the ethics of competition or the principles of good sportsmanship, you may be barred from interscholastic athletic contests, either as a participant or spectator or both.
2. If you are ejected from a contest for unsportsmanlike conduct, you will be ineligible for your team's next contest. You are also subject to other penalties.
3. Any other person(s) found to be in violation of the ethics of competition or principles of good sportsmanship may also be barred from interscholastic athletic contests.

Figure 6-7
Interscholastic Athletic Medical and Parent Consent Form

To the Parents: Both sides of this form must be completed before your son/daughter can participate in Interscholastic Athletic practices or contests. Your cooperation is appreciated.

Athletic Director

TO BE COMPLETED BY THE STUDENT Name of Sport ______________________

Name ______________________ I.D. # ________ Year in School — 1 2 3 4
Last, First—Please Print Circle One

Birth Date __________ Place of Birth-County __________________ State __________

School Attended Last Year ______________________________ Sex: M F
Circle One

Name of Physician ______________________ Physicians Phone Number __________

Physician's Address ______________________________ Town ______________

I hereby apply to participate in Interscholastic Athletics at ____________ High School. I agree to abide by the Constitution, Rules, and Bylaws of the Illinois High School Association and the ____________ high school Code of Conduct.

____
Student's Signature

TO BE COMPLETED BY THE PHYSICIAN

Name of the Student/Patient ______________________ Height ______ Weight ______

Disease History: Allergies ______________________________

Seizures ______________________________

Comments: ______________________________

____

Athletics Allowed:

All Sports ____	Football ____	Soccer ____
Badminton ____	Golf ____	Tennis ____
Baseball ____	Gymnastics ____	Track ____
Basketball ____	Softball ____	Volleyball ____
Cross Country ____	Swimming ____	Wrestling ____

I hereby certify that I have examined the above named student and there appears to be no medical reason why he/she is not physically able to compete in supervised athletic activities checked above at the school.

Date of Actual Physical ______________ Doctor's Signature ______________________
Please use hand stamp with Signature

Physicals more than one year old are not acceptable in accordance with IHSA Bylaws.

Figure 6-8
Parent Consent Form for Participation in Interscholastic Athletics

TO BE COMPLETED BY THE PARENT/GUARDIAN

Student's Name: ______________________________

Address: ______________________________ City: ______________

I, (We) as parent(s), understand that the school district has made available an accident insurance program in which my child may enroll and that the program is optional and limited to the coverage specified in the brochure. I (We) realize that there is a possibility that a child may suffer injury, including permanent paralysis or death, as a result of participation in athletic activities.

I, (We) further understand that the school district disclaims any financial responsibility for the costs of medical treatment, hospitals, ambulances or paramedics, etc. arising out of or by virtue of an injury to my (our) child while participating in such interscholastic competition or preparation therefore.

My, (Our) above named child has my (our) approval to participate in the following interscholastic sports. (Please use an X).

All Sports	_____	Football	_____	Soccer	_____
Badminton	_____	Golf	_____	Tennis	_____
Baseball	_____	Gymnastics	_____	Track	_____
Basketball	_____	Softball	_____	Volleyball	_____
Cross Country	_____	Swimming	_____	Wrestling	_____

I, (We) are aware of the opportunity to view the film "Informed Consent" which is available at the school offices should I (we) wish to view it, upon request. I further acknowledge that before my child can participate in such school-sponsored sport(s) this consent must be executed by me (us) and filed at the school, together with the results of a physical examination indicating that my child is physically fit to participate in such school sponsored activities.

______________________________ ______________________________
Date Name—Parent or Guardian—Please Print

______________________________ ______________________________
Telephone Number Name—Parent or Guardian—Signature

Some schools also use the meeting to inform parents and their children of athletic study halls required for athletes who are performing below academic standards. Such schools receive weekly eligibility reports from teachers, some of which identify students who are either ineligible or performing poorly in class. Athletic directors can then inform coaches of player ineligibility or the assignment of the player to the athletic study hall, which usually begins thirty to forty-five minutes before school and engages the athlete with one or more members of the National Honor Society, who have volunteered their time to work with the athletes.

Such study halls usually receive rave reviews from parents and others in the community. The study halls affirm the athletic department's commitment to the academic success of its athletes. Schools with such study halls maintain the eligibility of many young athletes who otherwise might not be able to play as juniors or seniors. They also acknowledge the realities of the NCAA's Bylaw 14.3, which prevents young athletes from playing in college if they have failed to meet eligibility requirements in high school.

If your school has no such program, consider developing one, then be sure to get as much publicity as possible about its positive influence on young athletes. Remember the four steps to effective PR: Do something good, then tell everyone, tell everyone, and tell everyone. Use the form in Figure 6-9, from Mike's recent book, *Advising Student Athletes Through the College Recruitment Process*, to get started. Parents will be much more inclined to encourage their children to risk the physical demands of athletics if the program also accommodates the demands of academics.

- *Planning for the Future*—The third step in assuring the successful involvement of students in the athletic program involves planning for the next level of competition. If you are the athletic director in a junior high school, your athletes and their parents must understand the academic and athletic expectations of the high school program. They will benefit from a large-group meeting with you and one or more of the school's counselors to discuss achievement test results, educational program planning, and the related demands of athletic competition. This is also the time to mention the high school's, and—if different—the state's, eligibility requirements and the dates of introductory and orientation meetings planned by the high school.

If you are a high school athletic director, your athletes and their parents must understand the provisions of the NCAA's Bylaw 14.3 (Proposition 48), the processes and expectations of the Clearinghouse, and a variety of related information about the extraordinary competition for scholarships as well as the unlikelihood of professional careers. See Section Eight for more information on NCAA and legal issues.

- *Keeping in Touch*—This final step affirms your interest in the school's athletes as something other than "pawns of the game." Certainly, your coaches are the primary persons to maintain contact with athletes after graduation, but you should be the driving force behind their good intentions. This is not to say that coaches must maintain ongoing communication with every athlete; it means simply that junior high school coaches should discuss former athletes with high school coaches and that high school coaches should routinely send letters to former players in college to assess their satisfaction with the college program.

Figure 6-9
REFERRAL FORM—Athletic Study Hall

Athletic Department

TO: Classroom Teachers

Please use this form to refer student athletes for remedial work to the Athletic Study Hall. Once assigned, the student will receive tutorial help to gain a better understanding of the subject matter and assistance with the completion of incomplete work. Please fill out the form completely. Someone will be in touch with you shortly after you deliver the form to discuss the specifics of the student's needs.

Thanks for your help.

Student's Name: ______________________________

Date of Referral: ______________________________

Please list incomplete work, including tests, quizzes, and homework:

In one or two sentences, please describe the student's classroom behavior:

Grade to date: _____ (Please deliver the form to the *Athletic Dept.)*

For Athletic Study Hall Use:

DATE STUDENT ASSIGNED TO STUDY HALL: ______________

DATE STUDENT RELEASED FROM STUDY HALL: ___________

COMMENTS:

Figure 6-10 provides a letter you might share with your coaches to make such communication easier for them. If your coaches decide to use such a letter, encourage them to file the return letters from their former players in order to have information on specific college programs to use with future high school athletes. Such information is very helpful when meeting with athletes and their parents to discuss college planning and to make final decisions regarding scholarship offers.

Let's conclude this section on promoting student participation by indicating that the best way to engage students in the athletic program is to ensure their enjoyment of the experience and their likelihood of success. The old dictum "success breeds success" probably is most evident in the world of sports. Young athletes—or for that matter, all of us—want to be involved in winning programs. Such involvement satisfies our desires for accomplishment and recognition—and the best way to guarantee a winning program is to attract dedicated athletes. The process, therefore, is self-renewing.

Coordinating Coaching Activities

Section Two of this book discussed the process of working with coaches. This subsection takes a closer look at the actual responsibilities of athletic directors in their day-to-day relationships with coaches. If the responsibilities are performed competently and sensitively, the relationships with coaches will be positive. Perhaps the best way to assure such relationships is to follow a simple piece of advice offered by prominent educator Daniel Griffiths several decades ago.

Griffiths advised administrators to restrict their decisions to the processes by which decisions are made and to make very few terminal decisions. Such a process orientation results in better decisions, more power for the administrator, and positive relationships with the staff. The increased synergy of the cooperative involvement of everyone in the department results in the improved decisions, and the increased trust among everyone creates increased power for the athletic director.

Coaches have considerable power to use with their athletes and many of the parents in the community. They also have considerable power to *give*, and they tend to give it to people they trust. The athletic director, therefore, who engages his or her staff in departmental decision making promotes their autonomy as professionals, expresses trust in their professional competencies, and, in turn, receives their support. Such support translates into personal and professional power.

Griffiths went so far as to indicate that the administrator who has to make most or all of the decisions for the staff is overseeing a dysfunctional program! Restricting decisions to the processes by which they are made, however, is no easy task, particularly if you are an ex-coach and inclined to run the athletic program like a practice session. Griffiths advised against making such decisions. He believed, as we do, that if coaches are involved in making program decisions, they will be more inclined to abide by them and eventually to commit to them. Quite simply, this means that good athletic directors bite their lower lips a lot and promote widespread decision making within the department.

A veteran athletic director shared this important piece of advice with anyone starting in the field: "Never pass up the opportunity to keep your mouth shut!" He then went on to indicate that during his first year on the job, he spent too much time talking in meetings and everywhere else in the school trying to convince anyone who would listen that he *deserved* to be the athletic director.

Figure 6-10
Letter to Former Athletes in College

Athletic Department

Date

Athlete's Name
Address
City, State ZIP

Dear ______________________:

It's time for a voice from the past! I was sitting here wondering how things were going for you in college and decided to drop you this note. Frankly, I'm wondering if the experience with your studies and your sport is everything you expected it to be. Can you answer a couple of quick questions for me?

1. Are relationships with the coaching staff satisfying and productive, about as you expected?
   Better _______ As expected _______ Worse _______
   Comments:

2. Are you enjoying your sport as much as you expected?
   Better _______ As expected _______ Worse _______
   Comments:

3. Does the sport leave as much time as expected for your studies?
   Better _______ As expected _______ Worse _______
   Comments:

4. Are your studies about as hard as you expected?
   Better _______ As expected _______ Worse _______
   Comments:

5. If you had it to do all over again, would you decide on the same school?
   Yes _______ No _______
   Why or why not?

6. Based on your experiences so far, what one piece of advice would you give future athletes:
   regarding your particular school:

   regarding college athletics in general:

THANKS for the help. Your advice will come in handy for future athletes in your old high school. All the best of luck to you—and stay in touch!

(Coach's Name)

He concluded the observation with, "I wish someone had slapped me in the face. I have since learned to ask the right questions and stop trying to come up with all the answers. The right questions tap into the strengths of my staff, promote their involvement, and result in better commitment from them. It's nice to see them committed, instead of feeling *I should be committed!*"

Overseeing the decisional process, therefore, is energizing for coaches and satisfying for athletic directors. When good athletic directors complement this process orientation with high visibility, they establish themselves as key members of the athletic family. High visibility requires you to attend as many contests and meets as possible. A succession of even the most exciting basketball and field hockey games can start to wear on the most enthusiastic athletic director, but, as John Wayne once said, "It goes with the badge!"

- *Promoting a First-Class Operation*—George Kelly, the long-time coaching legend at the University of Notre Dame, once told us that once you get young athletes to act like winners, they *will* be winners. Research supports his belief. Psychological studies consistently reveal that changes in behavior can precede changes in values and attitudes. For years, teachers have assumed that the attitudes of students must be adjusted before their behavior will change. To the contrary, research indicates that once behavior changes, attitudes will often follow.

  One of your primary responsibilities, therefore, is to encourage coaches to expect their athletes to behave like ladies and gentlemen. The easiest way to promote such an expectation is to require that athletes dress appropriately for contests. Figure 6-11 provides a reminder, taken from the Student Athlete Handbook, to share with coaches early each year. As you work together to promote appropriate behavior on the part of your athletes, you'll also promote winning attitudes within the program.
- *Keeping Coaches on the Same Page*—One of your most important responsibilities is to ensure that all coaches understand the rules, regulations, and policies governing the total athletic program. This includes the coaches' handbook, the Athletic Code governing student behavior, and many of the rules and regulations expected by the NCAA and other regulatory organizations.

  To assure that all coaches understand and have access to policy statements, you should discuss the Coaches' Handbook and any related materials during the first meeting of the year. Then, to be sure that coaches remain updated on all relevant information regarding interscholastic and intercollegiate athletics, you should provide updates of any changing NCAA legislation, new conference or state association information, or modified program policies. See Figure 6-12 for a form to use to provide such updated information to coaches and others in the building.
- *Sharing Information with the Administration*—Many administrators may be forward-thinking and innovative regarding curriculum and instructional practice, but most of them cherish predictability within the school. Rarely have we met a school principal who likes surprises—and no one can blame them. Running a school with hundreds of students—maybe thousands —and scores of teachers can sometimes challenge the resources of even the most flexible administrator.

Keep the principal informed of significant events in the athletic program, including changes in NCAA legislation that may have legal implications for the school. Many of these communications should be shared in writing in order to document them; use the form in Figure 6-12. Of course, the sensitive nature of some departmental issues precludes sharing them in writing. Such issues should be discussed with the administration behind closed doors.

- *Resolving Conflict*—This brings us to the resolution of problems within the department. The kinds of issues that must be shared behind closed doors probably have profound legal implications for the school. They must be handled carefully, probably in consultation with district attorneys. The kinds of issues we are discussing in this subsection deal with the conflicts that occur inevitably among persons who interact on a daily basis.

  These kinds of conflicts usually don't have to be shared with the administration. Most often, they resemble family squabbles, spats between departmental brothers and sisters that must not be brought to the attention of administrative parents. In such instances, athletic directors are big brothers or sisters who help resolve such problems before they become larger issues. One particular strategy has worked well for us over the years.

  Before we mention it, let's acknowledge that you won't have to scour the department for problems. Most conflicts invariably find their way to your office door, usually in a flurry of activity. Most require immediate attention—some few a delayed reaction to provide time for parties to cool down. Almost always, however, such conflicts involve divergent opinions, which sometimes can have far-reaching consequences. Experience suggests that the best strategy for resolving such issues involves shared values.

  Most coaches enter the profession for similar reasons. They enjoy the world of athletic competition, and they like working with young people. The combination of the two can make for some mighty powerful values, and those values can represent a common ground for all parties to stand on while discussing problems, whatever they may be. Once shared values are used to find a mutually satisfying solution to the problem, everyone is a winner. The key is to use the values as a starting point, then promote a dialogue that seeks a common solution, not a victory of one coach over the other.

  A good example of this strategy can be found in the coaching career of John Wooden, the coaching legend at UCLA. Coach Wooden had established a team policy restricting facial hair of any kind—or for that matter, anything that would distinguish one player from others on his team. Wooden believed that basketball teams should look and act like teams and not collections of individuals doing their own thing.

  The policy was based on the value that athletes must learn team commitment, mutual cooperation, and a subordination of self for the good of the other players. Clearly it worked for Wooden and his program. His accumulation of National Championships and the number of players who remain dedicated to him speak volumes of the success of his values and team expectations.

Figure 6-11
Student Athlete Handbook

Appropriate Dress

Each athlete is responsible to dress appropriately while attending away competitions. The wearing of inappropriate attire could result in removal from team competition on the specific day infraction occurs. See your coach or athletic director if you are concerned about specific attire. Please take pride in your appearance and your team.

Equipment

Each athlete is responsible for each item of equipment issued to him or her. Lost or stolen equipment must be paid for at the replacement rate cost. An athlete will not be allowed to participate in the next season sport or will not be allowed to receive his or her awards, grades, or diploma until the borrowed equipment has been returned.

Transportation

The high school provides transportation to and from all athletic contests. All athletes are required to use school transportation. Athletes may not participate in any away contest if they use alternate transportation without prior verbal permission from the coach.

The athletic department realizes that extenuating circumstances do occur. Athletes must secure verbal approval from the coach and the coach needs written notification from the parent, in advance of contests, of transportation change.

Under no circumstances are students allowed to drive or ride with anyone other than parents to or from athletic contests.

Figure 6-12
Sample Update of NCAA Legislation

Athletic Department

TO:

FROM: Athletic Director

RE: NCAA Updates for Student Athletes

DATE:

As previously discussed, the NCAA has established a central clearinghouse to certify eligibility for athletes who will be attending a Division I or II institution. The following is important information that you will need to make available to your athletes who plan on participating in athletics on the collegiate level:

NCAA Changes for 1996 Graduating Class

1) 13 Core Courses Required:
   3 English
   3 Math
   2 Nat/Phys Science
   2 Add'l from above
   2 Soc. Science
   2 Add'l from above
   or For. Lang., Philoso,
   Non-doct. religion

2) NCAA Test Scores Required:
   Sliding Scale of Core GPA, SAT or ACT:
   —Minimum of 2.000 Core GPA/21 ACT/900 SAT
   —2.500 or Above Core GPA/17 ACT/700 SAT

3) Registration Process:
   Submission of NCAA Clearinghouse student release form
   $18.00 registration fee
   Counselor gets yellow/pink copy and sends yellow form along with a copy of student's transcripts to the clearinghouse.
   Final transcripts must be sent to clearinghouse upon graduation.

NCAA pamphlets are available in the athletic office or guidance office. If you have any questions, please see the college career guidance counselor, athletic director or call the NCAA at the National Office.

Well, prior to one of his National Championship games in the NCAA tournament, one of his players, a highly talented but thoroughly committed free spirit, began sporting some facial hair. The assistant coaches noticed it and began squabbling among themselves about the implications of losing such a valuable player just prior to a National Championship game. Some suggested that the staff just disregard the player's face, which (excuse the pun) was bristling with potential problems.

Others suggested simply talking to him to see if he might "get with the program" and shave off the offending hair. Wooden asked his staff to consider the reasons behind the team policy. After some discussion, everyone eventually agreed that team membership and individual commitment to a common cause were more important than the uncommon expression of one's free spirit. Coach Wooden thanked his staff and congratulated them on achieving consensus, then stated that he would talk to the player.

He summoned the player into his office and said that he believed strongly in personal values, and that he would never try to come between a young man and his beliefs. He asked the player if this expression of uniqueness was important to him. The player responded, yes, it was, so Wooden acknowledged the young man's decision and indicated that he wouldn't try to stop him. He then concluded the conversation with, "We'll certainly miss you in the championship game, but you have to do what you think is right."

Needless to say, the player saw the error of his ways, shaved his face, and made his usual outstanding contribution to yet another UCLA National Championship. In the process, John Wooden reaffirmed the values that made his teams so successful, demonstrated that the good of the program is more important than the personal expression of any one player, and reflected the kind of courage that established his reputation at UCLA. More important, he demonstrated to his coaching staff and to at least one of his players that commonly shared values are the glue in most professional and social interactions and that they can be used to resolve differing opinions.

- *Serving as the Liaison for the Booster Club*—We've already indicated that commonly shared values are also important to guide relationships with parents and other members of the booster club. We've emphasized, for example, the need to achieve consensus on policy statements early in the school year in order to avoid conflicts as the year progresses. Similarly, you would be wise to serve as the liaison between coaches and the booster club—as the intermediary who screens contacts between them and controls the process by which funds for departmental needs are requested.

  Coaches who attend booster club meetings at their own discretion risk the potential abuse of booster club generosity and expose themselves to the subtle manipulation of unprincipled members of the club. "Give a little; expect a little" is the operative philosophy of some parents. Have your coaches fill out the form in Figure 6-13 to indicate their desire to request funds or to solicit help from the booster club. It provides documentation of the request, the reasons for the request, and its eventual disposition. File each request, whether approved or disapproved. Such a record is helpful for future reference.

- *Being a Tournament Manager*—As athletic director, you are also responsible for all tournaments and play-off contests. You must invite participating schools as appropriate (see the invitation in Figure 6-14), hire supervisors, oversee concessions, coordinate the schedule, arrange facilities, control the distribution of passes, arrange for media coverage, oversee any financial guarantees (see the letter in Figure 6-15), maintain security, arrange for officials, purchase and perhaps distribute awards, and then find the time to handle special circumstances such as inclement weather and unexpectedly large crowds.

  As daunting as this may seem, the processes you establish to handle each aspect of the responsibility can make the job considerably easier for you. A clear advantage of the responsibility is that tournaments can provide "carrot money" to supplement the departmental budget. Some schools incorporate tournament expenditures into their annual budgets, then use the profits to defray added expenses during the year. Tournament profits can add up to sizable sums of money and can come in handy to pay for important pieces of equipment that break unexpectedly.

Evaluating the Effectiveness of the Program

Mike often reminds the students in his educational administration classes that evaluation is a form of measurement. In essence, evaluation measures the current situation. It describes what *is* and, when used by the right person, provides an analysis of the discrepancy between *what is* and *what should be*. It is important to recognize that it provides only an indication of needed growth, not a guarantee of such growth. This is an important concept for administrators because it suggests the need for follow-up activities to promote growth. The concept applies equally to the evaluation of the athletic program and to the coaches within it. In the farming analogy earlier in the book, if evaluation stimulated growth, farmers would be carrying measuring tapes in their overalls and saving a whole lot of money on fertilizer.

Speaking of fertilizer, athletic directors who pad annual reports with positive if inaccurate comments about athletics may keep the principal happy, but operating that way does little to provide for the continuing improvement of the program. The only way to assure improvement within the program is to conduct periodic needs assessments within the department, then make efforts, in conjunction with the coaches, to meet those needs. Figures 6-16 through 6-19 provide forms for conducting a needs assessment.

Conduct an assessment at the end of each school year. The process is simple, and it provides a nice yearly summary for coaches. Notice how the process assesses the professional growth needs of coaches as well as the equipment and resources needs of the program. It has the potential to improve the competencies of coaches as well as the operation of the program. The topics in Figure 6-18 are left blank so that you can use it as a reproducible. You can no doubt imagine the breadth of topics coaches will identify in Figure 6-17.

Figure 6-13
Booster Club Requests Form

Athletic Department

TO: Head Coaching Staff
FROM: Athletic Director
RE: Booster Club Requests
DATE:

As you are aware, it is the desire of our Booster Club members to help solicit funds for any special items that you feel are important for the success of your program.

Please document in the appropriate space below your item, the reasons for the request and the date of the last item you received from Booster Club.

Please see the sample below. Forms not returned will alert the athletic director that you are not requesting any items from Booster Club this year.

Sample

Request: Stationary Bike

Reason: Large amount of rehabilitation is necessary for the student athletes at the high school. One bike in the training will not allow all the student athletes to complete their rehabilitation.

Last Item: Ice Machine

Date Rcvd: Fall 1993

Booster Club Request

Request: ______________________________

Reason: ______________________________

____

____

Last Item: ______________________________

Date Received: ______________________________

Signature: ______________________________ Sport:

Please return form to athletic office no later than (date).

Figure 6-14
Tournament Invitation

Athletic Department

TO: Participating Schools

FROM: Athletic Director

RE: Volleyball Tournament Invitation

DATE:

NO. OF PAGES: 1

____________________High School is looking for two schools to participate in
(School name)
a 2-day Girls' Volleyball Tournament. Please note the following information:

Location: ____________________High School Gymnasium
(School name)

Date:

Times: Friday—5:00 P.M. Saturday—9:00 A.M.

Tournament Cost: $100.00

If interested, please call the athletic director or fax letter of interest.

Figure 6-15
Financial Guarantees Letter

Athletic Department

TO: ______________________ School
(School name)

FROM: Athletic Director

RE: Boys' Soccer Tournament Costs

DATE:

NO. OF
PAGES: 1

According to our records, we have not received payment for your participation in our fall soccer tournament. Please check your records to determine date of payment. If payment has not been made, please remit a check for the amount of $_______.

Any questions, please call the athletic department at _________________________.
(Phone number)

Thank you for your assistance in this matter.

Figure 6-16
Identification of Topics

One of the values of our athletic department is our desire to continually improve our program and our skills as coaches. The end of each year signals the opportunity for each of us to identify our professional needs and to outline an in-service format for next year which will provide the information and the practice we need to make our athletic program even better than it is this year. Please take a few moments to think about topics that might constitute the substance of next year's professional growth program. In essence, what do we need institutionally and personally to make our athletic department more effective?

You probably have a topic or topics that are important to you as a member of this department. I would like to know what they are so that we can work together to accommodate them in order to make you, our parents, and, most of all, our kids more comfortable with our department's programs and processes.

Please take a moment to list your preferences in the space provided:

Figure 6-17
Categorization of Topics

First of all, thanks for sharing the topics that you feel need our collective attention. They cover a range of responsibilities within the Athletic Department. For that reason, I have listed the responses of the entire department within the following categories and have identified in parentheses following each topic the number of coaches who selected it. Please survey each list, give them some thought, and decide if any more should be added to the list.

You may have given additional thought to the original request for information, or you may have discussed possible topics with one or more coaches. Jot them down in the space provided within the appropriate categories and return the list to me by ___(date)___.

1. Administration

2. Facilities and Equipment

3. Coaching Technique

4. Strategy

5. Scheduling and Organizational

Thanks for your help!

Figure 6-18
Topic Selection

Thanks for your help with this final list. All the topics you have identified are listed within each category. To select the topic that you would like to study next year, please put a "1" next to the one that is most interesting to you and a "2" next to the one that is next most interesting. We will do our best to honor your request. If we can't we will be in touch to discuss alternatives with you.

1. Administration

2. Facilities and Equipment

3. Coaching Technique

4. Strategy

5. Scheduling and Organizational

Thanks for taking the time to do this.

Figure 6-19
Identification of Consultants

Now that we have identified the topics we want to study next year, we should consider the names of persons who can help us. Please give me the names of consultants or others who might be able to meet with your group to lead you in the study of your topic. They may be inside or outside the building. If outside, I will contact them to determine their fees and availability. If everything works out, I will indicate that someone from your group will be calling to arrange a meeting schedule. I remind you to arrange for at least three meetings, with a 6- to 8-week period of time between each meeting to provide for some practice time.

Please provide the name of your group and the name or names of suggested consultants:

Name of group:

Name(s) of consultant(s):

Again, thanks for your help. I'll be in touch.

A Final Word About the Process

1. This format is not the only needs assessment format that works. It is helpful to the extent that it seeks the input of coaches and engages them in an in-service and professional growth "package" that is relevant, and provides them with some sense of ownership. It is ongoing throughout the school year, and avoids the "one-shot" deals that are so common in most schools. It also provides an obvious link with coaching technique and provides opportunities for coaches to engage in collegial activities. Other considerations are listed in items 2 through 4.
2. Following a review of coaches' evaluations within the past year, you must identify the topics that recur and provide for study as well. If, for example, a significant number of coaches demonstrate problems with motivation or team discipline, it should be a topic for possible in-service next year. If you have facilitated the coaches' self-evaluation in postobservation conferences, the staff should be able to identify topics before you have to!
3. All of this presupposes a preliminary meeting with the entire department to outline the purposes and procedures of the process. Such a meeting also provides the opportunity to express your awareness that such a process involves decentralized decision making at its best, and that the department is dependent upon coach input for improvement.
4. The money for consultants can be written into the budget in consultation with other school or district personnel, or it can be secured with any of several grants available through the state or federal governments. "Grantsmanship" is a growing art for athletic directors!

Coordinating Facilities with Others in the Building and Community

The local school is the hub of community activity for a variety of reasons. The staff, often in conjunction with significant segments of the student body, offers a variety of programs: informational, discussion-oriented, sports-related, or musically or dramatically entertaining. Oftentimes, community groups provide similar kinds of activities, or simply use the school's facilities to promote private activities. Such widespread use of facilities and equipment suggests a significant coordinating responsibility for someone in the building, usually the athletic director.

The task is simplified by making your office accessible to the school and community and by using a form that outlines the expectations of the school system. The reproducible in Figure 6-20 accommodates such a need. Duplicate it and make it available in conspicuous areas of the building or in your office.

Figure 6-20
Community Rental Requests

_______________high school will allow access to the gymnasium space
(School name)
when not in use by the high school. Those individuals/groups wishing to rent the facilities must meet the following requirements:

1. *All individuals/group must reside in District #__________.*
2. *All individuals/group must have at least $1 million dollar insurance hold harmless agreement that name District #__________ as insured.*
3. *These individuals/group must agree to and adhere to the attached rental fees and maintenance fees listed in contract.*

If the above requirements are met, the individuals/group may submit in writing the dates of requested use of the facilities. The athletic director will notify the party involved by phone or written letter regarding acceptance of the requested dates.

Working with Other Departments to Determine Player Eligibility

No matter how well conceived or reasonable your school's eligibility requirements are, they will fail to promote academic awareness among student athletes if classroom teachers and others disregard the notification process. Keep the process simple and provide frequent reminders of the need for notification. Athletic directors, like others in positions of authority, must guard against the establishment of processes that punish school personnel for trying to do their jobs conscientiously.

Some special education departments, for example, require a variety of forms from teachers who identify students with potential learning interferences. Similarly, many athletic departments expect classroom teachers to fill out a variety of forms to identify not only ineligible students but the reasons for their ineligibility. The result is an addition of paperwork teachers would just as soon avoid. Because their proper performance, in effect, is punished by the organization, they tend to avoid the entire process; they simply fail to identify ineligible students or to promote their improved academic performance.

These problems can be avoided by using Figure 6-21, the Academic Eligibility Compliance Memo. It is brief yet comprehensive and simplifies the procedure for teachers, who can identify students needing some kind of academic intervention without burdening themselves with unwanted paperwork. Most important, the process works, and it provides information that is useful if you and your school decide to incorporate athletic study halls, as was discussed earlier in this section.

THE AD AND SCHOOL SPIRIT

School spirit is far more than screaming and shouting at officials, cheering when an opponent is injured, or waving frantically at opposing players as they attempt free throws. In fact, these are excellent examples of what students and parents should *not* be doing during athletic contests. School spirit is not only an expression of spectator support but added evidence of the self-discipline and respect for an opponent that should be displayed by participants during the contest. It is a reflection of personal as well as school pride, an opportunity for students and parents to display the courtesy and good breeding that are so important in most school communities.

You can promote such spirit by modeling appropriate behavior during contests and expecting nothing less than respectful behavior from students and members of the community. As with any form of gang activity in schools, athletic directors, coaches, and administrators must exercise "zero tolerance" for abusive or overtly disrespectful behavior. They do so by publicizing the school's expectations and detailing the consequences of violations. The reproducible in Figure 6-22 provides an excellent example for your use. It is reprinted with the permission of the Illinois High School Association.

Figure 6-21
Academic Eligibility Compliance Memo

Athletic Department

TO: Academic Teachers

FROM: Athletic Director

RE: State Academic Eligibility Compliance

DATE:

In order to comply with the State High School Association's weekly academic eligibility standards, we must enlist your assistance.

Please note on the following page(s), the student athletes currently enrolled in your course(s). If, at any time during the semester, one of these students enrolled in your class is failing, please photocopy this list and forward it to the athletic department.

Upon receipt of this note, we will notify the coach and the student athlete of his or her ineligibility for at least one week. Failure to improve upon the failing grade will result in a continual suspension from competition.

We appreciate your continued support of the athletic program. With the above procedures, we hope that both departments can help improve the athlete academically.

Thank you in advance for your assistance.

State Academic Eligibility Compliance

Course: Instructor's Name:

Athlete's Name	I.D. #	Grade	Sport	Coach
Name	1256		Swimming	Name
Name			Volleyball	Name
Name			Soccer	Name
Name			Tennis	Name
Name			Volleyball	Name
Name			Football	Name
Name			Golf	Name
Name			Golf	Name
Name			Football	Name
Name			Soccer	Name
Name			Tennis	Name
Name			Cross Country	Name
Name			Cross Country	Name

Figure 6-22
Sample Publication of Expectations

Sport A Winning Attitude

The Coach...
1. Inspires in his/her athletes a love for the game and the desire to win.
2. Teaches them that it is better to lose fairly than to win unfairly.
3. Leads players and spectators to respect officials by setting a good example.
4. Is the type of person he/she wants his/her athletes to be.

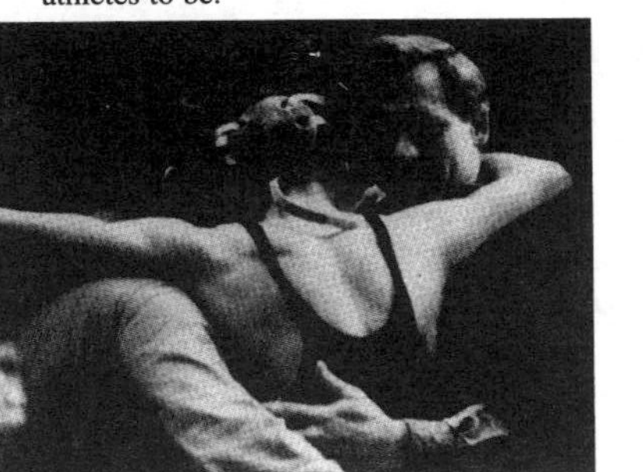

The Official...
1. Knows the rules.
2. Is fair and firm in all decisions. Calls them as he/she sees them.
3. Treats players and coaches courteously and demands the same treatment.
4. Knows the game is for the athletes, and lets them have the spotlight.

DON'T FORGET TO LET US KNOW WHEN...

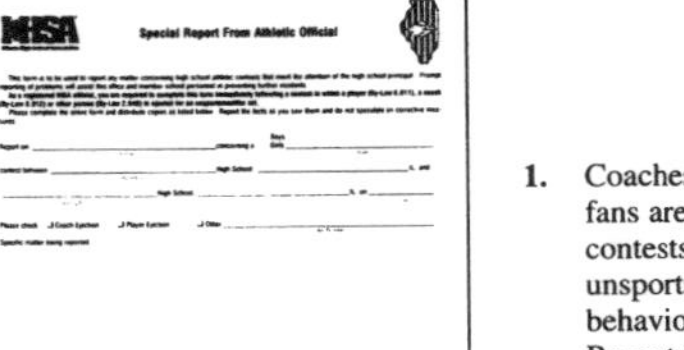
IHSA Special Report From Athletic Official

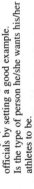

1. Coaches, players, or fans are ejected from contests for unsportsmanlike behavior. (Special Report Form From Athletic Official)

IHSA MEMBER SCHOOL SPECIAL REPORT FORM

2. Officials fail to perform their responsibilities in a professional manner. (IHSA Member School Special Report Form)

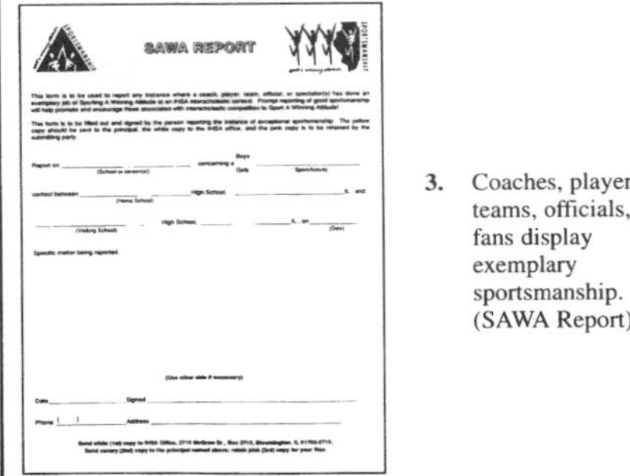
SAWA REPORT

3. Coaches, players, teams, officials, or fans display exemplary sportsmanship. (SAWA Report)

IHSA®

Illinois High School Association

For Coaches & Officials

SPORTSMANSHIP MISSION STATEMENT

Good sportsmanship is the attitude and behavior that exemplifies positive support for the interscholastic programs of IHSA member schools, as well as for the individuals who participate in such programs. People involved in all facets of the interscholastic program are expected to demonstrate respect for others and display good sportsmanship.

Published by:
Illinois High School Association
2715 McGraw Drive, P.O. Box 2715
Bloomington, Illinois 61702-2715
Phone: (309) 663-6377
Fax: (309) 663-7479

Figure 6-22, continued
Sample Publication of Expectations

Coaches and Officials - Keys to Good Sportsmanship

One of the goals of interscholastic competition is to teach important values while enriching the educational experience of the young men and women who participate. Good sportsmanship is certainly one of those important values, and as a result, promoting good sportsmanship is clearly one of our highest priorities.

We also believe coaches and officials play key roles in teaching and promoting good sportsmanship. This brochure contains a brief summary of sportsmanship expectations for both coaches and officials. By following these guidelines coaches and officials can enhance the lifelong lessons that are being taught in the interscholastic classroom. We urge you to read it carefully and hope you will remember to SPORT A WINNING ATTITUDE when coaching or officiating interscholastic contests in IHSA member schools.

Behavior Expectations

OF THE COACH. . .

- Exemplify the highest moral character, behavior and leadership, adhering to strong ethical and integrity standards.

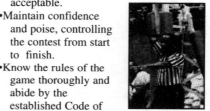

- Respect the integrity and personality of the individual athlete.
- Abide by and teach the rules of the game in letter and in spirit.
- Set a good example for players and spectators to follow - please refrain from arguments in front of players and spectators; no gestures which indicate an official or opposing coach does not know what he or she is doing or talking about; no throwing of any object in disgust. Shake hands with the officials and the opposing coaches before and after the contest in full view of the public.
- Respect the integrity and judgement of game officials. The officials are doing their best to help promote athletics and the student/athlete. Treating them with respect, even if you disagree with their judgement, will only make a positive impression of you and your team in the eyes of all people at the event.
- Display modesty in victory and graciousness in defeat in public and in meeting/talking with the media. Please confine your remarks to game statistics and to the performance of your team.
- Teach sportsmanship and reward your players that are good sports.
- Be no party to the use of profanity or obscene language, or improper actions.

OF OFFICIALS...

- Accept your role in an unassuming manner. Showboating and over-officiating are not acceptable.

- Maintain confidence and poise, controlling the contest from start to finish.
- Know the rules of the game thoroughly and abide by the established Code of Ethics.
- Publicly shake hands with coaches of both teams before the contest.
- Never exhibit emotions or argue with participants and coaches when enforcing rules.

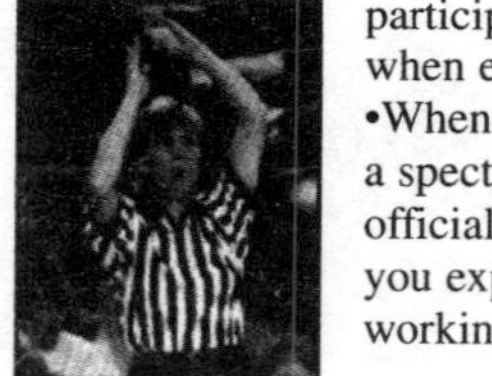

- When watching a game as a spectator, give the officials the same respect you expect to receive when working a contest.

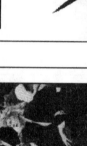

ADDITIONAL RESPONSIBILITIES

Athletic directors have a range of additional administrative responsibilities. They must:

- Organize and submit reports to state and conference regulatory bodies.
- Develop eligibility lists for contests and enforce state and conference requirements.
- Arrange for the ancillary personnel to conduct contests.
- Coordinate all related events such as awards banquets, pep rallies, and fund-raising activities.
- Provide for the purchase and maintenance of equipment.
- Oversee the establishment of policies, for example, awards criteria and cutting procedures.
- Prepare team rosters.
- Establish entry lists and operating procedures for tournaments and play-off contests.
- Perform other responsibilities as determined by the Principal.

LET'S WRAP IT UP

The responsibilities listed above are detailed in the appropriate sections elsewhere in this book. Here, let's just reemphasize how important it is for you to oversee the decisional activities of your programs, and to avoid making all the final decisions. Overseeing the decisional process necessarily engages other members of the department in planning activities and promotes ownership of departmental decisions among coaches.

Such a process orientation is contrary to the predispositions of many athletic directors, most of whom as coaches learned to make quick decisions. One principal was heard to comment recently: "I don't want some wimp in that position who's afraid to make a decision." We wondered if the flipside of that comment suggested that he wanted coaches who *were* wimps—supersensitive toadies unable to do anything without the approval of the athletic director. We hope not.

The school that wants strong coaches with the backbone and the character to promote self-discipline and positive values among hundreds of headstrong teenagers wants athletic directors and other administrators who encourage a sense of autonomy and commitment in coaches and teachers. Engaging them in the department's decisional activities is a necessary step in the right direction.

SECTION SEVEN

Maintaining Effective Publicity

First, a quick story:

One of the daughters of a colleague was an outstanding basketball player. She was the highest scorer in the largest county in the state during each of her last two years in high school, competing against players who were among the best in the state. In fact, by the end of her high school career, she had established school records in scoring and rebounding that are still the standards of performance for young basketball players in her hometown.

Although she received local newspaper coverage from admiring sportswriters, she was virtually unrecognized in neighboring areas, particularly in the city only a few miles away. Her coach rarely sent press releases to any of the media, choosing instead to avoid dissension and jealousy among the other girls on the team. Although he compiled cumulative records, he never used the information to promote statewide recognition of her accomplishments.

She never realized that she had been the highest scorer in the history of girls' basketball in her county until another girl broke her record several years later. Even more unfortunate, she received only one or two scholarship offers to play in college—both offers from local schools. If her father had not been a coach and familiar with the college recruiting process, she might have gone completely unrecognized by some of the larger schools in the country.

Fortunately, he made several contacts, shared videotapes with college coaches, sent some of the local press releases and all of her statistics, and she ultimately received a scholarship to a school that had a fine basketball program and an excellent reputation for her intended major. In fact, she earned a starting position only two games into her freshman season, became one of the leading scorers in the conference, and was selected as her team's Best Defensive Player at the end of the year.

She ultimately graduated from college, decided to go into education, and is now coaching at a nearby school. She indicated to us just the other day that one of the first things she did as a coach was establish, as she put it, a "media pipeline" throughout the state to assure her girls the kind of coverage they deserve.

How many young athletes out there fail to receive the kind of recognition they deserve because coaches are unfamiliar with the "media pipelines" available to them? More to the point, how many coaches believe that such media coverage is unrelated to their job responsibilities? And how many of them fail to provide the recognition that is well deserved by many young athletes and that ultimately promotes their own programs?

Successful athletic programs have always acknowledged the mutual dependency that exists between coaches and athletes. Athletes depend on their coaches for a knowledge of fundamentals, effective strategy, and acknowledgment of their efforts and accomplishments. Such acknowledgment comes in the form of assistance with the family's decisions to promote the continuation of a sport on the college level, with or without a scholarship, and of media recognition that publicizes team and individual accomplishments.

Coaches depend on their athletes for their very existence. There would be no sports team without groups of young people who choose to commit themselves to coaches and to one another in order to realize mutually desirable goals. Young people are most inclined to make such commitments when they anticipate an experience that satisfies their ego and social needs and recognizes their accomplishments.

The term "PR," therefore, represents "press releases," as well as "public relations"; the two are interrelated. Press releases provide the information on player, coach, and team accomplishments, and the resulting improved public relations benefit the program as well as the athletes within it. As our country's most prominent social institution, education thrives on public relations—and coaches, like everyone else in schools, must recognize the power of effective communication both inside and outside the local community.

Our athletes benefit from the kind of media attention that only coaches can provide, and our athletic programs benefit from the kinds of athletes that only coaches and media attention can attract. A primary responsibility of athletic directors, then, is to assure a conscientious approach to PR among coaches and to model effective PR within the athletic department.

An effective starting point is to use a form like the sample in Figure 7-1 to maintain a list of the area newspapers, the first and last names of contact personnel, and their addresses. You might add a fifth column to include their phone and fax numbers in the event you require immediate coverage on an important news item. Share this form with others in the department to make their PR jobs easier, and to impress upon them the importance of frequent press releases.

Figure 7-1
Sample Listing of Area Newspapers

Title	LName	FName	Address	City ST Zip
Evanston Review		Sports Editor	1569 Sherman Ave	Evanston, IL 60201
Northbrook Star		Sports Editor	1344 Shermer Rd.	Northbrook, IL 60062
Highland Park News		Sports Editor	444 Central Ave	Highland Park, IL 60035
Libertyville Review		Sports Editor	414 N. Seymour Ave.	Mundelein, IL 60060
Deerfield Review		Sports Editor	400 Lake Cook Rd.	Deerfield, IL 60015
Barrington Courier Rev.		Sports Editor	200 James St.	Barrington, IL 60010
Prep Sports Editor Sun	Bell	Taylor	401 N. Wabash	Chicago, IL 60601
Sports Dept.	City News Bureau		35 E. Wacker Dr.	Chicago, IL 60601
Sports Editor Pioneer P	Edison	Jim	130 Prospect	Park Ridge, IL 60068
Reporter	Erickson	Randy	4941 N. Michigan	Chicago, IL 60630
Chicago Prep Sports Tr	Knue	George	435 N. Michigan	Chicago, IL 60611
Des Planes Suburban	McCardle	Jim	1000 Executive Way	Des Planes, IL 60016
Bugle Newspapers	Miller	Diane	8746 N. Shermer	Niles, IL 60648
Pioneer Press	Muret	Don	130 S. Prospect	Park Ridge, IL 60068
Daily Herald	Stengle	Marty	217 W. Campbell	Arlington Hts., IL 60004
Sports Writer	Swiderski	Gregg	2702 St. James	Rolling Meadow, IL 60008
Lerner Papers	Anderson	Steve	8135 River Dr.	Morton Grove, IL 60053

EFFECTIVE PR AND THE COACHING STAFF

Coaches contribute to effective PR by assuring the following activities:

- Report scores to local media outlets. The coach's most obvious responsibility in the PR process is to report the scores of just-completed contests. Head coaches can delegate the task to assistant coaches or team managers, but reporting must be done by telephone to assure immediate coverage.

  The immediacy of such reporting can be not only inconvenient but downright disconcerting at times to many coaches. Winning coaches reach for the phone as if it were the last chicken wing on the platter, but losing coaches regard phone calls to newspapers as just another trumpet blaring their misfortune. They're about as eager to make phone calls as to watch last week's game film.

  Give coaches the memo in Figure 7-2, to remind them of their responsibility. They'll appreciate the suggestion that they assign the task to another coach or to the team manager, who may be less affected by unwelcome reminders of disappointing seasons in local papers. Be sure, too, that you read the papers after every contest to see that coaches are, in fact, reporting their scores.

- Share significant information with local media. The most immediate concern, score reporting, is only one aspect of maintaining contact with local papers. Sometimes team or individual performances involve statistics that warrant feature articles. Coaches must be willing to promote the kinds of relationships with local sportswriters, therefore, that enable them to pick up the phone and share information—and to get the kind of coverage that may result in photographs and interviewing sessions with athletes.

- Assure reporting within the school. Students and teachers in the coach's school appreciate inside information regarding team and individual performances. Coaches should report scores, along with team and individual accomplishments, in the school's daily announcements as well as the school newspaper. Reporters for the school newspaper enjoy meeting with coaches at regular times during the week to discuss past as well as upcoming contests.

- Announce team and individual awards throughout the school. Some coaches invite the entire school and local community to join the coaches, the athletes, and their parents in the celebration of a completed sports season. Awards Night, particularly if it involves stimulating guest speakers, is an excellent time to spread the word throughout the school that a particular sport provides a wholesome and satisfying experience for a wide range of student athletes.

  Attendance at the sports banquet is frequently restricted to the athletes and their parents, but if only a few others attend, you can help publicize the merits of involvement in the sport. See Figure 7-3 for a reproducible that can be used to invite the general student and parent populations to the banquet. You may have to charge the parents of nonathletes for the meal, but if the banquet speaker is well publicized, a minimal fee should not be a problem.

Figure 7-2
Memo to Coaches Regarding Media Information

Athletic Department

TO: Head Coaching Staff

FROM: Athletic Director

RE: Student Athlete Media Information

DATE:

A reminder that the head coach of each sport is responsible for reporting to the press contest scores and significant contributions after each competition.

If you are unable to fill this responsibility yourself, please assign this task to an assistant coach or team manager. The task must be completed after each competition on the varsity level.

Listed below are the necessary telephone or fax numbers for your convenience:

Name of Paper ______________________________

Phone No. ______________________

Fax No. ______________________

Figure 7-3
Invitation to a Sports Award Banquet

Athletic Department

Dear School and Community Members,

_________________High School cordially invites you to attend the fall sports award banquet held in the auditorium at 7:30 P.M. on __________________.

A motivational guest speaker will be in attendance, and special team and individual awards will be presented for each fall sport.

Please join us in honoring our student athletes, and in celebrating a memorable fall sports season. We look forward to seeing you on __________________. For additional information, please call the Athletic Office.

Sincerely,

Athletic Director

Fall Sports

Football
Boys Cross Country
Girls Volleyball
Boys Soccer
Girls Golf

Girls Cross Country
Girls Swimming
Girls Tennis
Boys Golf

- Meet with parents regularly. Many coaches conduct weekend meetings with parents to discuss past contests and to give insights into the team's performance. Parents enjoy such meetings. They get to know the coaching staff better, and they gain insights into strategy and technique that promote a better understanding of subsequent contests. Such meetings also provide a logical transition into informal sessions at the end of the season when parents, players, and coaches can discuss the student's athletic and educational future. In addition, these meetings establish the kinds of relationships with parents that result in improved emotional and financial support of the athletic program.
- Provide workshops for local coaches and clinics for young athletes. We were approached several years ago by a junior high school principal who wondered why high school coaches don't invite junior high coaches to accompany them on scouting trips and to meet with them during planning sessions for upcoming contests. We asked ourselves the same question, and the result of that question was a much closer relationship between high school and junior high coaches and mutual experiences that improved the knowledge and understanding of everyone.

One of the high school coaches even developed a series of workshops offered during the summer. Area coaches in his sport were able to meet for several weeks during the summer to discuss strategy, fundamentals, player motivation, and team discipline. Everyone benefited—especially the athletes, who experienced a consistency of fundamental skills, strategy, and treatment that improved their performance as they moved from one level of competition to the next.

The coaches even worked together during the summer months to develop clinics for the athletes. Junior high school coaches enjoyed the experience of working once again with former players, now in high school. High school coaches benefited by meeting junior high players and encouraging them to participate in high school. The attendance at clinics increased; young athletes wanted to meet high school coaches, and older athletes were able to renew acquaintances with former coaches.

The Letter in Figure 7-4 can be sent with appropriate materials regarding such clinics, to promote cooperation among coaches from varying educational levels in the community and to encourage a wide range of young athletes to attend. No single activity does more to promote positive PR for the athletic program in the community.

EFFECTIVE PR AND THE ATHLETIC DIRECTOR

The athletic director's responsibilities regarding PR must complement the coaches' responsibilities and provide the synergy that results in support of the athletic program throughout the community. Athletic directors must engage in the following activities:

- Oversee the maintenance of bulletin boards in the school. Some coaches aggressively resist maintaining bulletin boards for their sports—until they observe widespread student and parent interest in the display. Newspaper clippings, notices of upcoming contests, announcements of individual and team accomplishments, team rosters, photographs of recent contests, school records in the sport, notices of awards won, and catchy phrases do much to attract attention and, ultimately, to generate interest in the sport.

Figure 7-4
Student Invitation to a Conference

Athletic Department

Date

Dear Student Athlete,

Congratulations on being selected to represent the Athletic Department at the Fourth Annual Central Suburban League Leadership Conference on Tuesday, November 7, from 5:00 P.M. to 9:30 P.M. and Wednesday, November 8, from 7:30 A.M. to 3:30 P.M.

Enclosed you will find an informational pamphlet and registration form. Please review this information, fill out the registration form, and return it to the Athletic office *no later than Friday, September 22.*

The Leadership Conference is an excellent opportunity to participate in problem-solving activities and team-building opportunities for leadership.

We look forward to your participation in the Conference. We will provide more information for you regarding bus times, etc., when you turn in your registration form at the Athletic Office.

Respectfully,

Athletic Director

Encourage your coaches to maintain a bulletin board throughout their respective seasons. Appropriately situated in the PE and athletic department corridors, such bulletin boards do more than most coaches realize to recognize the accomplishments of the team and players, to attract attention to the sport, and to promote athletic programs.

- Develop and maintain "Walls of Fame." Like bulletin board displays, Walls of Fame recognize the efforts and accomplishments of former athletes and coaches and promote interest in the merits of the sports program. Some schools display the pictures of former athletes who achieved All-State or All-American honors. Normally, such displays are located near the gym or in the school lobby.

  Such displays are especially effective when they are expanded to include the noteworthy distinctions of *current student athletes*—those players who maintain high grade point averages and who are recognized by conference and statewide organizations for their academic as well as their athletic accomplishments. Such an expanded policy supports the claim of the athletic department that academics is more important than athletics. It serves as visual documentation of your school's commitment to a total educational experience for student athletes. The Wall of Fame is also the appropriate place for the pictures of coaches who contribute significantly to the success of the athletic program. Such contributions need not be limited to winning records and Hall of Fame honors. Recognition is also appropriate for coaches who dedicate themselves to the academic and athletic needs of the school's athletes by writing articles and books, presenting frequently at conventions or workshops, developing useful materials for the school's athletes, or devoting decades of their lives to the well-being of young people.

  The school that recognizes and honors such coaching accomplishments confirms its claims that people don't have to achieve enviable win-loss records to realize greatness in the coaching profession. More appropriately, the coach who has only moderate success "in the arena" but who touches the lives of student athletes in significant other ways is deserving of *at least* as much recognition as the coach who wins most of his or her contests. If we are to be consistent with our professed values, we must recognize these coaches, too. Use the form in Figure 7-5 to encourage students, teachers, and parents to recommend coaches for such an honor.

- Distribute periodic press releases to local newspapers, and radio and TV stations. Large schools sometimes pay teachers a stipend to write summaries of the school's weekly contests and forward them to the local media. Smaller schools often leave this task to athletic directors, many of whom share it with one or more students from the school newspaper. However they are accomplished, weekly or periodic press releases summarizing the goings-on in the athletic department provide excellent public relations between the school and community.

- Share significant events with the local media. If the process for developing weekly or periodic press releases identifies revealing quotes from athletes or coaches, or uncovers appealing human interest stories, such releases should be expanded into feature articles for the local media. Unless you have access to particularly gifted student writers, such stories should be written by someone in the athletic department, or shared over the phone with newspaper editors who can write the copy themselves.

Figure 7-5
Honorarium Form

Athletic Department

List below the significant accomplishments of student athletes, head coaches, assistant coaches or supervisory personnel who you feel have made major contributions to the athletic department:

Name of Individual ______________________ Date ______________

Position or Responsibility ________________________________
(athlete, coach, announcer, etc.)

Narrative:

Signature: ____________________________

Please keep one copy for your records and forward original to the Athletic Office.

Reminders within the athletic department are necessary if you hope to receive all the stories with human interest potential—some of which relate only incidentally to contest statistics and summaries. Circulate the reproducible in Figure 7-6 throughout the department periodically to encourage coaches and athletes to provide information regarding potential stories.

- Establish positive relationships with local newspaper and radio people. The sports editor who shared lunch with you for a couple of hours a few weeks ago is the person most likely to accept your ideas for a feature article on the school's new soccer program. At the very least, he or she will give you a sense of direction regarding the newspaper's priorities for feature articles. Often, sports editors who know you well will call to ask if you have any stories that might make good features.

  Many times, your efforts to maintain good public relations will result in friendships that transcend the job and the need for PR. New athletic directors, especially, are encouraged to contact sports editors and other media persons in the community to organize lunch dates or other kinds of meetings to initiate relationships. If you are a veteran athletic director, pick up the phone and arrange a meeting that will maintain such relationships. The time is well spent.

  An element in these relationships is to do all you can to make their jobs easier. Send them copies of team rosters at the start of each sports season, perhaps action shots of some of the stand-out athletes in the school. It's also wise to send them lists of the coach's names and their phone numbers at school—even an indication of the best times to contact them.

  Finally, remember that the sports editors of the school newspaper, radio station, or television station can help with the athletic department's public relations efforts. You compliment student officers and enhance their sense of purpose when you invite them to weekly meetings to discuss the happenings in the athletic department. Invite them for a brief breakfast meeting, provide rolls and milk, and share important information with them. School media reach surprisingly large numbers of people, not only in the school but in the community.

- Distribute a newsletter within the school to share information about the athletic department. Newsletters—even if they aren't read as enthusiastically as you might hope—remind the school that the athletic department is alive and well, and that it is a vital part of the school program. When you write a newsletter, be sure to include the following information:

  —Scores of all recent contests

  —Noteworthy accomplishments of athletes and coaches.

  —Significant adjustments in the program, such as the addition or deletion of sports

  —Dates, times, and places of upcoming contests

  —A "thank-you" section to recognize the contributions of teachers, administrators, or students regarding some facet of the program

Figure 7-6
Press Information—Significant Contributions

Athletic Department

Please list any information, stories, articles, or quotations that will provide positive press information from the athletic department; human interest stories, positive team/individual statistics or coaching/student athlete honors and awards should be included.

This information will aid the athletic department in providing the media with press releases of positive news articles for the community. No information will be released to the press without prior permission from the individual(s) involved.

Name of Individual ______________________________ Date ____________________

Position or Responsibility ____
(athlete, coach, announcer, etc.)

Narrative:

Signature of individual submitting information: ____________________________________

Please keep one copy for your records and forward original to the Athletic Office.

The school newsletter should be purposefully short. You don't want to devote hours of your time each week to the development of a lengthy report that may not be of great interest to the majority of teachers and students. In addition, if the newsletter is longer than one or two pages, only the most loyal fans will read it. The purpose of the newsletter is to promote support of the athletic program and to encourage students and teachers to attend upcoming contests.

- Distribute a newsletter within the community; it should be distributed quarterly and provide a somewhat different focus. You will still want to report the current records of teams; acknowledge the accomplishments of athletes and coaches; announce the dates, times, and locations of upcoming contests; and discuss adjustments in the program, but the thank-you section should be replaced by the following subheadings:

  —Notes about and from the booster club—Acknowledgment of recent contributions from the booster club, information about elections of new officers, and a message from the club president do much to promote community support of the club's activities and to recognize the work of its members.

  —NCAA updates—Information about recent changes in NCAA legislation is not only interesting but critical for many parents, particularly for those who expect or hope to help their student athletes explore opportunities to continue playing a sport in college. It's probably safe to say that many parents, perhaps most, are still unfamiliar with or confused about Bylaw 14.3 (Proposition 48). This subsection of the newsletter, therefore, can promote an improved understanding of such things as eligibility requirements so that parents are better informed when they meet with counselors and other school personnel to discuss post-junior high or -secondary school decisions.

  —Important dates and activities—This section should announce the starting dates of upcoming seasons and explain steps that must be taken by athletes and their parents to join a team. This is the time to mention the need for physicals, parent permission slips, emergency notification cards, insurance forms, and all the other materials that students must complete before being permitted by the school to participate in a sport.

  —A word from the AD—An informal message to the community about the place of interscholastic sports in the lives of students, the gratitude of the athletic department for the community's continuing support, the effects of recent NCAA legislation, or a reaction to one or more hot topics in the media makes for an interesting conclusion to the newsletter.

  The community newsletter can be longer than the school newsletter. Most parents, especially those of young athletes, are intrigued by information about the NCAA or the athletic director's reactions to controversial topics in the media. Most will take the time to read the newsletter, so sufficient time should be devoted to it to guarantee its readability. You may want to use desktop publishing to assure a well-designed and appealing format.

- Distribute schedules of all contests. You might review the information in Section Three—specifically Figure 3-3, p. 67.

- Distribute all information received from conference, state, and national regulatory organizations. Rules changes will constitute the largest body of such information, but regulatory organizations also distribute statistics and news items regarding the nature of state or national athletic competition. Such information can be incorporated into school or community newsletters, or distributed to coaches by using the Information Form in Figure 7-7.

DEVELOPING ACCEPTABLE PRESS RELEASES

A long-time friend of ours and a very successful businessman was convinced that "presentation is half the sell job." Years of experience taught him that an attractive appearance sells products. Our experience has taught us much the same thing. In a society stumbling over the clutter created by our love of "things," no one can deny the appeal of an attractive appearance.

Athletic directors soon learn that presentation affects everything from program promotions to press releases. An attractive appearance enables good press releases to find their way into feature articles. Keep the following principles in mind, therefore, when organizing and sending press releases to the local media:

- Formatting Press Releases—Most newspapers and other media are accustomed to receiving press releases in a specified form. Figure 7-8 illustrates the basic press release. In Figure 7-9, the separate sections of the release are appropriately labeled. First of all, notice that the release does not include a headline. The paper will create a headline, if needed. Most school releases are incorporated into columns and do not require headlines. The release, however, does include a heading which most journalists refer to as the "slug." In this case, the slug is "New Coaches" and provides a reference point for editors when they format it.

  Underneath the slug, the form indicates the suggested release date of the information. This section usually indicates "For immediate release," as on Figure 7-9, but it may specify a future date. The release then includes the name of the athletic director, the address of the school, and the phone and fax numbers of the athletic department. The actual copy follows, and the press release is concluded with the word "end" or a series of pound signs as illustrated in the figure.

  Only one side of the sheet should be used, and the copy should be double-spaced. If multiple pages are involved, they should be mailed loose or paper-clipped, never stapled. Some newspapers scan the copy they receive to transfer it to office computers, and stapled materials interfere with this process. This scanning process suggests something else about press releases.

- Composing Press Releases—Because newspapers often scan releases and transfer them immediately into copy, well-written and presentable press releases are often used in their entirety. Organize them carefully, or have someone on the staff develop them. An English teacher on the coaching staff can come in mighty handy at such times. When newspapers use the entire press release, they are less likely to misinterpret or misrepresent the information you have provided.

A well-constructed press release adheres to the following standards:

—It is, first of all, always truthful. Never misrepresent facts in order to enhance the program's image with the reading public. Our occasional zeal to make someone or something look good can result in just one misrepresentation that can ruin our credibility for a long time. Most newspapers are good enough at manipulating the truth without any help from us. Once they discover that we do it, too, they tend to disregard much of what we send them.

—Similarly, always cite and document relevant statistics and facts as clearly as possible. When opinions are cited, quote the source.

—Attract attention to the release by relating the important facts and information as soon as possible. The first several sentences should reflect the journalist's love of "who, what, when, where, how, and why." The answers to each of these questions should be stated in concise and relatively short but lively sentences.

—Sentences containing unfamiliar or unusual names, complicated figures, or highly esoteric terminology should be short and simply stated. The purpose of the release is to communicate to the public, not to confuse people with needlessly complicated sentences. Paragraphs should also be short, and they should be presented in a descending order of importance. Bear with us, but the speaker's dictum is equally appropriate for the development of good press releases: "Tell them what you're going to say. Say it. Then tell them what you said." The only reason this piece of advice is so hackneyed is that it's so true.

—Inform the reader of the main point of the story as soon as possible. English teachers call it the *thesis statement* or the *topic sentence*. The statement involves one, two, or three sentences early in the press release that indicate its main focus. Support the statement with all relevant and specific information, then conclude the release with a summary statement that concisely and creatively restates its focus (see Figure 7-9).

—Be sure to use the full names of persons and avoid the use of initials unless you first specify what they represent. For example, early in the release refer to the "National Collegiate Athletic Association (NCAA)," and each time thereafter to the "NCAA."

- Distributing press releases—Most staff writers are working feverishly on deadlines one or two days before the paper is to "go to press." If the local paper, therefore, is published weekly, always try to get press releases to the *sports editor* or the *city desk* at least three or four days prior to its distribution. If it is published daily, mail the releases as soon as possible after they are completed, or, if time is a problem, deliver them personally to the paper.
- Finally, include photographs only if you have developed some prior arrangement with the newspaper. Generally, newspapers prefer photographs taken by staff photographers and will usually arrange to have one available to you if you call the sports editor well ahead of time. You might also call the sports editor to express your willingness to share some photos, if you have some particularly good ones. Keep in mind, however, that newspapers tend to prefer black-and-white photos and are usually uninterested in "talking heads" or group shots.

Figure 7-7
Sample Athletic Department Information Form

Athletic Department

IHSA BYLAW 6.012

The IHSA Sportsmanship bylaw 6.012. Any coach ejected from a contest for unsportsmanlike conduct shall be ineligible for the next interscholastic contest at any level, in addition to other penalties the IHSA or the school may assess.

Please remember that two bylaws are in effect for the school year—6.012 is for coaches and by-law 6.011 for athletes. Specific guidelines for dealing with violations have been set. Anyone with questions regarding the above rules should see the athletic director.

BOOSTER CLUB APPAREL

The booster club is selling jerseys and windbreakers and other various items. Help support the school athletic teams and the boosters. See the letter included for details.

FALL SPORT RULES INTERPRETATION MEETINGS

Remember that attendance is mandatory at a rules interpretation meeting for your specific sports. Please check the bulletin board in the athletic office or the attached sheet for the time and date that is best for you to attend. Failure to attend a required rules meeting could result in team dismissal from the state series.

DINNER DANCE DATE

The increasingly popular Booster Club Spring Dinner Dance will be held at the city hotel again this year. Last year this affair was a huge success and raised a large amount of money for the athletic department. This function, the golf outing, and membership dues are three of the major fundraising projects of the booster club. The place to be on (date) in the ballroom of the hotel in the city.

Plan to attend this outstanding event from 6:30 to midnight. We will have food, music, dancing, raffle tables, door prizes, silent auctions, and good times. Mark your calendar now!

Figure 7-8
Press Release

Press Release

TO: Community *Newspaper*,

Release Date:

Athletic Director
Address
City, State, Zip
Phone:
Fax:

Figure 7-9
Sample Completed Press Release

Press Release

New Coaches (Slug)

TO: The Pittfield *Review,* the *News Sun,* the Chicago *Tribune*

For Immediate Release (Release date)

Name
Address
City, State, Zip
Phone:
Fax:

Pittfield High School would like to welcome three new coaches to the athletic program for the current school year. Mike Penrod will be a varsity assistant in football this year. Mike is a graduate of Kansas State University, served as a graduate assistant for them a year later, and will be joining the Pittfield teaching staff in the PE department. Greg Royer will also be a varsity assistant in football, is a graduate of Northwestern University, having played middle linebacker, and will be teaching English and speech.

Lou Adler, a former All-Conference high jumper at Ohio State University, will be the new head track coach, and will be teaching psychology and sociology in the social studies department with John Gasfield. All three coaches came highly recommended to the athletic department and are welcomed additions to the staff. Please be sure to welcome them to the Pittfield community.

MAINTAINING A FLOW OF INFORMATION TO ADMINISTRATORS

The school and the community are interested in a flow of information from the athletic department because of their interest in the program. The school's administration shares that interest, but requires periodic updates of significant happenings for other reasons as well. We have indicated already that principals and superintendents don't like to be surprised. The smart athletic director, therefore, regularly shares information with them—preferably in a monthly report. Following are a few examples:

- Student participation—Share periodic reports on the numbers of students participating during each sports season. A great deal of money is invested in the athletic budget, and administrators expect periodic dividend reports. Principals recognize that a popular athletic program is almost as effective in attracting residents to the community as the academic reputation of the school. They like to share this kind of information, therefore, at Rotary luncheons and evening meetings with the Parent Advisory Council.
- Coaching full-time equivalents (FTE)—FTE allocations are a continuing concern of administrators. New jobs have to be filled, and, occasionally, old jobs have to be eliminated. Both affect the school budget and the quality of services offered to the student body and the community. Status reports of changing coaching allocations, therefore, are critical if the administration is to provide the financial support needed to sustain viable programs. Occasionally, assessments will be conducted within a department to determine such needs. More often, like the swamp full of alligators, assessments are unnecessary because problems will surprise you by nipping you in potentially embarrassing places.
- Win-loss records and championships—The monthly or annual report to the administration is your "State of the Department" report. It should include the win-loss records of all the teams that have participated to date and the specifics of any championships won. Because of their ongoing contact with the community, administrators must be kept updated on the performance levels of teams and individuals within the athletic program. Parents like to talk about the school's sports program—and particularly about their own children's accomplishments.

  The administrator who is familiar with such accomplishments helps sell the school and the program to the community. Nancy routinely shares championship plaques with her principal for display in his office or on the walls of the main office. The principal enjoys receiving them, and also enjoys discussing them with visitors to the school—many of whom are parents.
- Special accomplishments—Principals also like to be informed of special honors received by athletes and coaches in order to send them personal notes of congratulation. Coaches often receive recognition from the state for particularly successful seasons, lifetime accomplishments, or special contributions; athletes receive all-conference and all-state recognition, both for their athletic and their academic accomplishments. A note from the principal immediately following such recognition promotes positive relationships in the school; therefore, the principal must receive notice of such accomplishments immediately, not in the next monthly report.

- Facilities and equipment—It seems that facilities and equipment, even in relatively new schools, require frequent repair or replacement. Although the budget is the appropriate planning document for such concerns, it doesn't hurt to promote support by alerting administrators to potential needs. The monthly or annual reports are the logical places to solicit such help.
- Status of budget—The monthly report is also the logical place to inform the administration of the status of the departmental budget. Principals love to hear that the athletic department is doing well financially. They may not be as pleased to hear about unexpected expenditures, but immediate notification of such expenses softens the blow at the end of the year and often encourages a more generous response during future budget discussions.

Figure 7-10 provides a blank copy of a monthly report format. Use it as a guide to maintain a flow of communication between the athletic department and the school's administration.

KEEPING HALLS OF FAME WITHIN REACH

Coaches deserve Hall of Fame recognition for a variety of reasons, not the least of which is their continuing contribution to the needs of young athletes. Outstanding win-loss records create interesting newspaper copy, but a lifetime of genuine concern for student athletes creates values, self-esteem, and a sense of commitment in future generations. Our schools and communities are quick to recognize winning programs—and thus continually reemphasize the importance of winning.

They confirm in the minds of young athletes the already blatant expectation that the only genuine satisfaction of athletic participation is "beating the other guy." The values of participation and the joy of developing a "will to win" are lost in a mindless preoccupation with winning. Coaches who promote such expectations, no matter how successful their teams, do little to foster positive social and personal values in their athletes. They are, unfortunately, the ones who often receive the Hall of Fame recognition.

Coaches who devote their lives to student athletes and to the good of the community receive Hall of Fame recognition much less often. They are the unsung heroes who profoundly influence young people and make genuine contributions to their schools and communities. They, too, deserve nominations for Hall of Fame recognition. Halls of Fame may not recognize them as readily as they do winning coaches, but, by nominating them, you have affirmed to the individual coach and to everyone in the department the athletic values that have meaning for you.

Use the form in Figure 7-11 to inform coaches of recent nominations and save the Halls of Fame list in Figure 7-12 for future reference. It contains the names, addresses, and phone numbers of national coaching Halls of Fame. Remember also that each state has a Hall of Fame for each sport; so do most major metropolitan areas in the country. Look up the addresses and phone numbers of state and city Halls of Fame as well. Coaches deserve the recognition, and they will appreciate your willingness to seek it for them.

Finally, use the nomination form in Figure 7-13 to nominate athletes and coaches for recognition on your "Wall of Fame." Such recognition may not involve the national or statewide focus that some coaches and athletes might deserve, but it acknowledges their contributions to the school and provides continuing recognition for them.

Figure 7-10
Monthly Budget Report

Athletic Department

Sport	*Monthly Balance*	*Sport*	*Monthly Balance*
Badminton	____________	Baseball	____________
Boys Basketball	____________	Girls Basketball	____________
Boys Cross Country	____________	Girls Cross Country	____________
Football	____________	Boys Golf	____________
Girls Golf	____________	Boys Gymnastics	____________
Girls Gymnastics	____________	Softball	____________
Boys Swimming	____________	Girls Swimming	____________
Boys Soccer	____________	Girls Soccer	____________
Boys Tennis	____________	Girls Tennis	____________
Boys Track and Field	____________	Girls Track and Field	____________
Boys Volleyball	____________	Girls Volleyball	____________
Wrestling	____________	Other	____________
Transportation	____________	Repair	____________
Training Room	____________	Security	____________

Monthly Concerns: ____

____

Athletic Director
Signature ______________________________ Date ________________

Keep one copy for athletic office budget files and submit original with cover page to building principal.

Figure 7-11
Hall of Fame Nominations Memo

Athletic Department

TO: Coaching Staff

FROM: Athletic Director

RE: Hall of Fame Nominations

DATE:

The following individuals have been nominated to this year's Hall of Fame for their unique contributions to sports. Please join me in extending congratulations for their outstanding contributions at this high school and around the state.

Name	*Sport*	*Hall of Fame Nomination*
1		
2		

The above individual(s) join the accomplished list of coaches who already hold the distinction of Hall of Fame Inductees

Past Hall of Fame Inductees

Name	*Sport*	*Year of Induction*
1		
2		
3		
4		
5		
6		
7		
8		

Figure 7-12
National Associations and Halls of Fame

American Baseball Coaches Association
108 S. University Ave., Suite 3
Mount Pleasant, MI 48858-2327

Naismith Memorial Basketball Hall of Fame
1150 W. Columbus Ave.
P.O. Box 179
Springfield, MA 01101

National Football Foundation and Hall of Fame
Bell Tower Bldg.
1865 Palmer Ave.
Larchmont, NY 10538

United State Golf Association
P.O. Box 708
Far Hills, NJ 07931

National Association of Collegiate Gymnastics Coaches
Southern Connecticut State University
Department of Physical Education
501 Crescent St.
New Haven, CT 06515

National Soccer Coaches Association of America
4220 Shawnee Mission Pky., Suite 105B
Fariway, KS 66205

National Softball Association
P.O. Box 23403
Lexington, KY 40523

National Interscholastic Swimming Coaches Association
Glenbrook South High School
4000 W. Lake Ave.
Glenview, IL 60025

International Tennis Hall of Fame
100 Park Ave., 10th Floor
New York, NY 10017

National Athletic Trainers Association
2952 Stemmons Fwy., Suite, 2000
Dallas, TX 75247-6103

American Volleyball Coaches Association
1227 Lake Plaza Dr., Suite B
Colorado Springs, CO 80906

National Wrestling Coaches Association
Iowa State University
10 State Gymnasium
Ames, IA 50011

Figure 7-13
Wall of Fame Nominations

Athletic Department

Name of Nominee:

Name of Nominator:

Date:

Please list all relevant reasons for this nomination. Narrative descriptions are particularly helpful:

LET'S WRAP IT UP

That coaches and young athletes deserve recognition for their dedication and accomplishments is evident. No one can argue that we all require a sense of accomplishment in our lives. Consistently recognizing the *right* accomplishments, however—the kind that promote not only a sense of self-esteem but a commitment to the good of the community—is one of the most important roles we, as athletic directors, perform.

Consider, for example, the sample letters from the school principal in Figures 7-14 and 7-15. They acknowledge the contributions of student athletes who have performed well in the classroom and who have committed themselves to the athletic program by participating in three sports. These are valuable young people in our schools. Also valuable are the athletes who exhibit the kind of sportsmanship that honors themselves and the school. Figure 7-16, the High School Sportsmanship Award, recognizes their contributions. Use it in your school to recognize and promote the kind of behavior that is so important to a "classy" operation.

Press releases, public relations, and all forms of recognition are critical elements in our job responsibilities, but they are only tools. Use them correctly to acknowledge the accomplishments of young people, to improve relationships within the department, and to promote the fundamental values of athletic participation and the good of the community.

Figure 7-14
Letter of Congratulations to a Student Athlete

Athletic Department

Dear Three-Sport Athlete,

Congratulations on completing a year of high school as one of an elite group of athletes who have competed in three sports. To accomplish an endeavor of this magnitude is indeed a great feat, especially during this time of academic and sport performance pressures.

Enclosed you will find a token of gratitude from us. It is paid for and supported by our booster club. We know you will wear this patch proudly.

We appreciate your continued dedication and hope that you will continue to represent our school in such a positive way.

Congratulations!

Sincerely,

School Principal

Figure 7-15
Letter to a Scholar-Athlete

Athletic Department

Dear CSL Scholar-Athlete:

Congratulations on completing an excellent year at ____________high school as an elite athlete who has competed in sports while maintaining an excellent academic record. To accomplish an endeavor of this magnitude is indeed a great achievement.

The criteria for the CSL Scholar-Athlete Award are:

1. You must be a senior varsity letter winner.
2. You must have a minimum of two sports seasons of interscholastic competition in the same sport.
3. You must have a "B" average in all high school work based on six semesters for fall sports and seven semesters for winter and spring sports.

Enclosed you will find a token of gratitude from ____________high school, which is monetarily supported by the booster club. We know you will wear this patch proudly.

Again, congratulations! We appreciate your support of our school's athletic program.

Sincerely,

School Principal

Figure 7-16
High School Sportsmanship Award

High School Sportsmanship Award

This is to certify that

is hereby recognized for exhibiting outstanding sportsmanship

1. Gained an understanding and appreciation for the rules of the contest.
2. Exercised representative behavior at all times.
3. Recognized and appreciated skilled performances regardless of affiliation.
4. Exhibited respect for the officials.
5. Displayed openly a respect for the opponent at all times.
6. Displayed pride in your actions at every opportunity.

_______________ *School Principal*

_______________ *Athletic Director*

SECTION EIGHT

Keeping on Top of Legal Issues

First, a general story:

When Proposition 48 was first enacted by the Annual Convention of the National Collegiate Athletic Association (NCAA) in the early to mid-1980s, it confused a lot of people, including school people. It is now called Bylaw 14.3 and is quite a bit older, but its original intent and its specific requirements are still misunderstood by teachers, counselors, administrators, and even coaches. Among other things, what has resulted in communities across the country is a series of lawsuits seeking compensation from school systems for poor advice regarding NCAA eligibility requirements.

In the process, the NCAA has discovered that our legal system is a knife that cuts both ways. Over the past several years, almost since the inception of Prop 48, parents, students, and school personnel have inundated them with questions and concerns about the academic eligibility of students with learning disabilities. Most of the questions involved the apparent inability of such students to satisfy the NCAA's core requirements, specifically the thirteen academic units that represent college preparatory courses.

One case in particular concerning a high school swimmer in Illinois aroused sports fans across the country. Eventually the questions and the widespread publicity they provoked gave way to a Department of Justice investigation into possible discrimination. Specifically, the Department of Justice sought to determine whether Bylaw 14.3 was being applied unfairly and was therefore violating the Americans With Disabilities Act (ADA).

The NCAA's response, well before major lawsuits became an issue, was to allow all prospective athletes, regardless of their disability status, to make school-paid recruiting visits before meeting all of the academic standards of

Bylaw 14.3. They also sought to allow students with learning disabilities to take summer school classes after graduation to meet eligibility requirements prior to enrollment in college. Such concessions involve some good news and some bad news for students and school professionals.

The good news is that students with learning disabilities are now provided a broader interpretation of academic eligibility and have been guaranteed a process that accommodates their learning needs. The bad news is that school counselors, coaches, and other school personnel must be familiar with these adjustments—as well as all the others that are inevitable within the next few years—to advise student athletes and their parents through the college preparation and recruitment processes.

The continued reluctance or inability of some high school counselors and coaches to understand the changing requirements of the NCAA and other regulatory organizations will result in sizable numbers of young athletes' missing out on playing a sport in college. Not only will the athletes suffer lost opportunity, but their parents will search long and hard for someone to blame and, in some instances, to hang out to dry inside a local courtroom.

Public opinion, molded by media influences, can blame the alleged impersonality of the NCAA just so long before fair-thinking adults realize that the unwillingness or the inability of school personnel to keep updated on eligibility requirements is the primary culprit, certainly the most immediate and accessible. Schools, therefore, must be constantly aware of the need to provide important information to counselors and coaches and to anticipate the legal consequences inherent in almost everything we do as members of an athletic department. See Figure 1-9, p. 19, for a sample of NCAA requirements.

Mike received a call recently from a high school coach who was concerned that the Clearinghouse refused to accept two social studies courses for a senior athlete who had just received a scholarship offer to a major university. The coach was alternately worried that the boy was likely to lose the scholarship and angry that the Clearinghouse would refuse to accept the word of the school's principal, who was "a just and honorable man."

Mike asked him if the school had mailed its Form 48-H early in the school year to secure approval from the Clearinghouse for courses expected to meet the requirements of Bylaw 14.3. The coach responded that the school had never had an NCAA Division I or II athlete in the past and that the principal and athletic director simply had forgotten to mail the form to the Clearinghouse. Mike's first reaction to the coach was that the principal goofed!

He and the rest of the school's administration were trying to convince the Clearinghouse of the validity of their academic courses long after the horse had gotten out of the barn. Unfortunately, the principal was discovering that horses are handled more easily when they're in the barn and that parents are quick to seek legal counsel when principals and athletic directors fail to perform important aspects of their jobs.

Now, instead of basking in the sunshine of their accomplishments with one of their athletes, they're trying to "beat the rap" in court. Too bad—and very easily avoidable.

Awareness of eligibility requirements is but one problem that bristles with such legal implications. On a day-to-day basis, we as coaches and athletic directors find ourselves in a veritable briar patch of potential legal issues. They cling to our sweatpants before and during practice, and they draw blood when we walk irresponsibly through practice sessions or contests. As athletic director, you are the person most responsible for alerting coaches to such hazards and for assuring that everyone—coaches and players alike—enjoys the athletic experiences without getting hurt.

"Getting hurt" can happen in a variety of ways, only a portion of which is physical. Coaches can be humiliated in front of their colleagues; some can be censured or dismissed without just cause. Young women—players or coaches—can be victims of sexual harassment. Athletes can be forced to play on debilitating injuries or receive incompetent treatment for injuries received during practice or competition.

Coaches can engage young athletes in potentially harmful activities before they have the fundamental skills to perform them. Athletes of either sex can be denied opportunities to participate in certain sports. Athletes can receive serious injuries from horseplay before practice when coaches fail to supervise properly. Coaches who are unable to teach proper fundamentals can cause serious injury to young athletes. Any one of an avalanche of specific requirements governing the eligibility and participation of athletes can be violated due to ignorance or unconcern.

All these issues can result in serious legal complications for the athletic department and the school. Students can receive debilitating injuries or discriminatory treatment; coaches can receive inappropriate administrative supervision; and resulting lawsuits can consume huge blocks of administrative and coaching time and result, nonetheless, in settlements that run into the thousands, even millions, of dollars. With so many litigious gremlins lurking behind practice equipment and around every corner of the athletic department, it's a wonder that anyone decides to engage in school sports.

ATHLETICS AND THE LAW

For the last several decades, the justice system has determined the direction of education more than any other single influence in this country. From segregation to skirt length, everything that happens in schools has come under the scrutiny of lawyers and judges. While this phenomenon has promoted some sense of social balance in our country, it also has caused a lot of nervous tics in those of us who work with students and parents on a daily basis.

Educators might reasonably assume that any of their decisions designed to promote the normative values of the school system will be acceptable to parents and students. After all, the law asks simply that we be reasonable. The general standard applied to most of us is easy enough: "Would a reasonable person have acted as you did under similar circumstances?" That seems fair—and certainly uncomplicated enough to permit a wide range of acceptable decisions and behaviors.

Well, you and I know that we may make a wide range of decisions, particularly in athletics, but that their acceptability is rarely uncomplicated. The concept of reasonableness is subject to a multiplicity of interpretations. Persons who are affected by our decisions evaluate them through their own individual frames of reference and, as might be expected, react very subjectively to them. In many instances, so do court systems.

Perhaps one of the most important considerations for anyone involved in education, let alone athletics, is this capriciousness of the law. Consider the many cases involving athletic injuries and alleged incompetence on the part of coaches that are decided in favor of the athlete and subsequently overturned on appeal—or vice versa! Some, when appealed, have even been thrown out of court for insufficient cause.

Another complication involves the way we make decisions. Only occasionally do we consider the legal consequences of a decision. Most often, we act in good faith and expect that those affected by the decision will understand our reasons for making it. If only life were that simple! A further complication involves the unpredictability of young athletes and the reality that the decisions of coaches involve not only possible unreasonableness but potential injury—sometimes significant injury.

Fortunately, the law has anticipated such concerns for coaches. Two factors tend to favor coaches accused of negligent behavior: assumption of risk and contributory negligence. Assumption of risk means that athletes and their parents understand that a certain activity involves potential injury, and the athlete *assumes the risk* anyway. Contributory negligence means that the athlete in some way, probably through his own negligent behavior, has *contributed* to the injury that resulted.

Regardless of an athlete's inclination to take risks or to act carelessly, however, coaches are on shaky legal ground when they fail to provide proper instruction or supervision for all athletes during practice or competition. Football players, for example, in the heat of a game, may decide to use spearing tactics they learned watching the pros. Such techniques can result in serious head injuries. If young athletes are not warned that such tactics are potentially dangerous, their coaches are potentially liable for any damages that might result.

We can hear your reactions now: "Do you mean to tell me that if I spend hours drilling youngsters on proper technique and, for one reason or another, they choose to do something stupid, it's my fault?" In a word—yes. More pointedly, you are *potentially* liable if you fail to instruct athletes about the consequences of improper technique or careless execution. It can happen in any sport. Football is not the only one that involves potential serious injury.

The same is true of sliding head first in baseball, intentionally fouling in basketball, head butting in wrestling, or any number of tactics designed to create an apparently necessary, if dangerous, competitive edge. Such tactics must be minimized with appropriate instruction. General principles like "align the spine" in football must be shared with young athletes in order to assure proper technique during the development of fundamental skills.

Other responsibilities are equally important if coaches are to avoid legal problems. Some of the characteristics that athletic directors must guarantee within the athletic program are outlined here.

Provide a Secure Environment

Players must feel safe when they attend contests or practice sessions. They and their parents must believe in the competence of the coach and his or her concern for their safety. They must understand that blatant intimidation—from coaches or teammates—gives way to cooperation, sensitivity, and concern for the emotional as well as the physical well-being of athletes.

Abraham Maslow told us years ago that human beings are unable to feel a sense of belonging until they feel safe and secure in their relationships with others. What that means for coaches is that athletes are unable to commit to program goals and feel a sense of team commitment until they feel safe every time they come to practice or a contest.

Provide Appropriate Supervision

Good supervision means much more than getting out to practice early or watching the locker room at the end of the day. It involves everything that happens in between—in essence, the full scope of coaching responsibilities when they are "in loco parentis." Like an "all-seeing" parent, a coach must *be aware of* as much as possible during contests or practices. Are athletes mismatched during drills? Are groups of them ganging up on one player during scrimmages?

Does an athlete appear to be playing hurt but unwilling to mention it for any of a variety of reasons? Is an assistant coach coming down too hard on a player? Are any of the athletes using improper and potentially dangerous tactics on other players during scrimmages or contests? Is the whole team simply too tired to continue scrimmaging without possible injury? Are any of the coaches demanding performance from athletes who are obviously unable to deliver? Are the conditioning drills at the end of practice, especially when they are punishments for poor performance, too strenuous for some or all of the players?

These kinds of questions relate to good supervision. They relate to the quality of the experience young athletes can expect when they play a sport, and they suggest significant legal implications whenever they are disregarded. Your job is to assure that these questions remain foremost in the minds of coaches during practices and contests. Above all, legal reprisals are less important than the safety of young athletes when emphasizing the importance of good supervision.

We can't go around inspecting every decision or coaching behavior through a built-in legal lens. Anyone who would do that is more concerned about the safety of the organization than of the students within it. We can do without those kinds of people. Certainly, an awareness of legal issues is important, but a sensitivity to the needs of students is more important. When we work with competent coaches who genuinely care about young athletes and promote their well-being, we have to worry about litigation only marginally.

The criterion of reasonableness suggests that coaches are expected to be adult in their relationships with young athletes and to understand and reflect in their behavior the purpose and nature of their involvement in sports. If they focus on winning as just *one* of the outcomes of their interaction with young athletes—and at times the least important—they will be more inclined to be reasonable in their associations with parents and community members, their athletes, and fellow coaches.

Your primary job is to promote such predispositions. Mike taught educational administration and supervision at the graduate level in a local university for over twenty years. When asked the question, "What is the number-one responsibility of school principals?" he invariably responded: "To sustain a focus on the normative values of the school." The same is true of athletic directors, whose primary job is to sustain a focus on the normative values of the department—namely those statements of philosophy contained in Figure 6-1, p. 162.

Too often, the budget, facilities and equipment, squabbles among personnel, the need for more coaches, inadequate faculty support, and questionable relationships with the administration or the parent community are like those alligators nipping at our hind ends, when our original intention was to drain the swamp! They represent the more pressing problems, but many of those problems are symptomatic of a much larger issue—the inability of the department to focus on the fundamental reasons for its existence. If we as athletic directors promote a focus on the fundamental values of athletic participation, we discover that poor community relationships, intradepartmental squabbles, and, yes—even the budget—become less problematic.

LOOKING AT THE BIG PICTURE FIRST

What else do smart athletic directors do to assure the safety of players and coaches and to avoid the legal tangle that threatens the survival of some sports in schools? They anticipate problems by engaging some or all of the department in planning activities that focus on the reasonable treatment of athletes and coaches. Such planning should result in policy statements that promote good decision making.

That's what a policy book is—an accumulation of well-thought-out, pre-determined decisions. Good administrators don't reinvent the wheel every time a decision has to be made. They anticipate situations and circumstances by developing policies that make such decisions for them and, more important, that inform school personnel of likely decisions well before they ask for them.

Whether you are a veteran or a neophyte, you must spend time early each year developing or revising your department's policy book. Especially relevant for purposes of this section are policies outlining the expectations and responsibilities of coaches and the job descriptions of head coaches, assistant coaches, and athletic trainers.

Figure 8-1 provides a sample statement regarding the department's expectations of coaches. Notice that the statement does not refer to win-loss records or past athletic accomplishments. Although television and newspapers focus almost exclusively on winning seasons and game and career statistics, most athletic departments—particularly in junior high and secondary schools—agree that the primary contribution of coaches in all sports is to develop character, self-discipline, self-esteem, and a sense of teamwork in young athletes.

These are the qualities that reach meaningfully into the lives of young people by promoting sensitivity to the needs of others, a social conscience, and a work ethic that leads to a positive self-concept and an intelligent orientation to the future. Coaches promote such behaviors in athletes by providing leadership and promoting self-discipline among athletes, by constantly improving their own professional competencies, and by acknowledging the responsibilities they have to athletes, parents, the school, and other coaches in the school and area.

Figure 8-1
Athletic Policy Statement

Athletic Department

Interscholastic sports at our high school form part of a diverse extracurricular activities program. The activities are regarded as vital parts of the total educational offerings of our school. The sound development of the physical capacities of youth complements and enhances the intellectual, emotional, and social development of every young man and woman. These opportunities are useful tools in the achievement of the goals of a comprehensive education.

Our school's dedication to excellence extends to our competitive athletic program. In this endeavor, the Interscholastic Athletic program serves as one of the extensions of the classroom, which attempts to meet certain district student goals through experiential learning opportunities and can only enhance and reinforce the learning that occurs within the classroom.

Printed with permission from the Glenbrook North High School athletic handbook.

The statement in Figure 8-1 was developed by Glenbrook North High School and provides an annual focus for everyone in the athletic department. It doesn't sit unnoticed in a departmental policy book that gathers successive layers of dust with each passing year. It is resurrected at the beginning of each year and used to answer important questions within the department:

- Is this statement still a true reflection of how we are expected to behave as coaches in our school?
- Are the messages you receive from the administration or the parent community in the course of a school year consistent with the intent of this statement?
- Do you feel that the circumstances of contemporary sport require changes in the statement?
- Is this statement still a true reflection of your philosophy as a coach in this school?
- Can you live with—and by—this statement, use it as a reasonable standard of your professional behavior, and ultimately be evaluated by it each year?

The answers to such questions promote a periodic reevaluation of the department's coaching philosophy, result in a consensus of what is important within the department, and provide a format for the annual evaluation of head coaches by the athletic director. Annual evaluations become reasonable appraisals of coaching performance when coaches have the opportunity to question and occasionally change the criteria by which they are judged.

Use the form in Figure 8-2 at the beginning of each school year, therefore, to ask each head coach to think about the policy statement and to provide a written reaction prior to your first meeting. Once you receive the forms, develop a composite of their reactions, and redistribute it to the coaches, asking them to think about the ideas of their colleagues in order to discuss them during the meeting and make possible changes in the statement.

This process makes for some very interesting and productive discussions. As important as the general philosophy of the actual statement may be to each of the coaches, its impact on their yearly evaluations is especially meaningful to them. Once they have accepted the fact that it is used to determine their effectiveness as head coaches, they will look it over very carefully, and the discussions it provokes will refamiliarize them each year with their responsibilities and help identify any departmental or organizational interferences that keep them from meeting the expectations.

The Big Picture and Assistant Coaches and Trainers

Because the statement applies to all coaches, it is also used by head coaches to evaluate their assistants. The annual review of the statement, therefore, not only influences the focus of their own evaluations but provides the framework for judging the effectiveness of their assistants. As a rule, the athletic director evaluates the head coaches and head coaches evaluate each of their assistants.

In addition to the general statement of coaching philosophy, your job description for assistant coaches will provide further information for them to consider when evaluating colleagues. Have your head coaches review the descriptions of assistant coaches to assure that they are developing comprehensive evaluations. The job description for head coaches shown in Figures 2-1 and 2-2, pp. 37 and 38, can be easily modified to use for assistant coaches.

We suggest the following process:

- Have head coaches evaluate their assistants first, close to the end of the season. Have them use the form in Figure 8-3 to write the evaluations. It provides the standardized format you'll need to review each of the evaluations before you write evaluations for the head coaches. After all, the depth and insight of their evaluations suggests something about their ability to lead others and to provide a vision for each of their programs.
- Review each of the evaluations and discuss them with the head coach(es) as needed. Some adjustments may be required in the wording before they are given to each of the assistants.
- After you have reviewed and discussed their evaluations of each assistant, write evaluations for each head coach as soon as possible following the conclusion of their seasons. Don't wait to write evaluations for all head coaches at the end of the school year. The task will be too time consuming and may threaten your ability to write comprehensive, well-thought-out descriptions of their coaching abilities.
- Give the evaluation to the coach and schedule a meeting to discuss it later. His or her preliminary review of the evaluation provides substance for the follow-up meeting and suggests a specific focus for the discussion. If the coach agrees with the evaluation, the meeting can focus on future goals and professional growth activities. If he or she disagrees with the evaluation—well, you have a lot to talk about.

The head coach, of course, should handle the evaluations of his or her assistants in much the same way. The process of reviewing the evaluations prior to a short meeting invests the process with a level of importance that has potential to improve the quality of coaching in the department. Most head coaches, however, will have their own process, and, if it works for them, it's probably best to leave it alone. In that case, you might require them to meet with first- or second-year coaches to discuss evaluations and to outline future expectations. Such a process is unnecessary with veteran assistants.

ATHLETIC TRAINERS

If your school is blessed with the services of a good athletic trainer, you have been smiled upon by the God of Sport. A competent athletic trainer helps prevent injuries, provides immediate treatment for injuries during practice or contests, assesses players' readiness to return to competition, promotes an awareness of safety principles among coaches and players, and provides valuable public relations within the community. Because athletic trainers are so vital within the program, they must be provided relative autonomy in their relationships with coaches.

Coaches, even the most charismatic and dynamic old warhorses in the stable, must never be allowed to second-guess or question the trainer's diagnosis or treatment plan. If the trainer stipulates that a particular athlete is unable to return to competition, the issue should be closed until he or she gives the athlete permission to return to practice or competition.

Figure 8-2
Coaching Expectations

Athletic Department

To: Head Coaching Staff

From: Athletic Director

Date:

Instructions: Please use this form to suggest modifications to the policy statement regarding coaching expectations. The policy is attached. Please review the statement, then record your observations on this form and return it to me by (date). I will develop a composite of all the coaches' comments and give it to you prior to our meeting on (date). At that time, we will discuss the policy statement and suggest whatever changes we feel are appropriate. Remember, any actual changes in the statement must be approved by the principal. Thanks.

Figure 8-3
Assistant Coach Evaluation

INSTRUCTIONS: Use the following form to write an expository evaluation of your assistant coaches. Be sure to use the policy regarding Coaching Expectations to provide the framework and the specific standards for the evaluation. Please keep in mind that your comments identify both the strengths and the weaknesses of the coach and should be used to promote his or her professional growth as a member of this department. Thanks for taking the time to do this very important task.

Coach's Name: ______________________________

Head Coach: ________________________________

Sport: ______________________________________

Following is a descriptive analysis of the above-named coach's contribution to our current season:

Any violations of such a policy should provoke an immediate meeting between the athletic director and the violator. The athletic trainer's job is too important to permit alternative diagnoses or treatment plans within the department. Perhaps share the job description in Figure 8-4 with the coaches in the department to assure their understanding of the trainer's responsibilities. Then, use the form to evaluate the trainer at the end of each school year.

DEALING WITH ACCIDENTS AND INJURIES

Trainers are invaluable at practice or contests when athletes are injured. Most important, athletes receive the kind of immediate diagnosis and treatment they require to promote healing and to prevent further aggravation of the injury. Less critical, but important for the rest of the staff, coaches are relieved of possible misdiagnoses and potential legal complications. They also can continue the practice session, confident that the injured athlete is in good hands.

No matter how quickly the athletic trainer responds to injuries that occur during practice, coaches invariably must provide some kind of preliminary treatment. They must check for vital signs if the player is unconscious, or look for parts of the body that appear to be broken. Excessive bleeding must be controlled, and unconscious athletes must be assumed to have injuries to the spinal column.

Coaches, particularly head coaches, must have at least a rudimentary knowledge of first aid so that injured athletes are properly cared for until the trainer or other medical personnel can diagnose and treat the injury. A policy like the one in Figure 8-5 should be provided to all coaches to guarantee a uniform response to injuries during practice or contests.

In addition, accident reports like the one in Figure 8-6 should be available in the athletic department, and required from coaches after each injury. If your school enjoys the services of an athletic trainer, he or she can fill it out; otherwise, coaches should fill it out and submit it to the athletic director. Appropriate documentation is essential in case a parent, guardian, or someone else questions or challenges the coach's or school's response to an athletic injury.

Additional Considerations

- A reminder: Make sure each athlete has a current physical exam and parental (guardian) permission card on file.
- Coaches must make every effort to prevent injuries by promoting good physical conditioning, including off-season strength training programs if young athletes are not involved in other sports.
- When athletes are injured, treatment plans must always follow the requirements of the school or family doctor and should *never* include methods that are beyond the competencies of trainers or coaches.
- Drugs of any kind must never be administered by school personnel.
- Student trainers, if the school has them, must always be properly supervised by the athletic trainer, especially when assisting with injuries.

- Finally, coaches must be expected to check equipment periodically to assure safety. That includes practice equipment such as blocking sleds and pitching machines as well as football and batting helmets.

The desire to enhance the performance of athletes and to win contests must never jeopardize the physical or the emotional well-being of young athletes. Clearly, the fundamental goal of any contest is to win. We must learn, however, that the victory is never worth the loss of our own integrity or personal pride. Coaches must teach such lessons to young athletes, and athletic directors must assure that the lessons are continuing as well as consistent.

SHARING INFORMATION WITH THE RIGHT PEOPLE

If knowledge is power, information is energy. Information stimulates thought processes and promotes understanding. A school, particularly, must guarantee a positive and continuing flow of information to each of its constituencies to promote their understanding of school policy and of the many requirements mandated by regulatory organizations like the NCAA. A general meeting at the beginning of each school year involving athletes and parents provides opportunities for the athletic department to share and discuss relevant information and to open the door to continuing communication throughout the school year.

Health and Injury Issues

Initial agenda items for such a meeting usually involve parent permission slips, materials regarding physical exams, and health insurance information. Figures 4-3 and 4-4 in Section Four, pp. 103 and 105, of this book already have provided the permission slips, and Figure 1-4, p. 9, has outlined the Athletic Code. Refer to Figure 8-7 for information regarding physical exams and Figure 8-8 for information about, and examples of, the health insurance program. These items constitute the nitty-gritty of the early-year meeting and generally require the immediate attention of parents.

Eligibility Issues

Figure 8-9, from Mike's *Advising Student Athletes Through the College Recruitment Process* (Prentice Hall, 1996), provides information regarding eligibility requirements for both the NCAA and the National Association of Intercollegiate Athletics (NAIA). Notice that the pertinent information about specific requirements has been left blank on the form. This has been done for two reasons.

One, the NCAA and the NAIA change their eligibility requirements periodically. Recently, given continuing debate and the NCAA's constant struggle to refine Bylaw 14.3, the bylaw has changed almost yearly. Schools are advised, therefore, to leave the form blank rather than change it each year. Two, encouraging young athletes and their parents to write down the specifics of the eligibility requirements engages them in the actual processing of the information.

We promote modality learning in our classrooms; we might as well use it in our large-group meetings! The parent who writes down the number of academic units required of young athletes is more likely to remember it when registration time rolls around. The same is true of the young athlete who writes down the grade point average required of students interested in playing a sport on the college level. If for some reason, they failed to hear the specifics when they were mentioned in the meeting, they will also be more likely to approach their coach after the meeting to review them.

Figure 6-12, p. 182, can be used during the year to inform athletes, parents, coaches, and others about changes in NCAA legislation. For example, the NCAA has made changes in eligibility requirements regarding students with learning disabilities. You should circulate such information as soon as the legislation is enacted by the NCAA convention.

This kind of information is relevant for players and parents, especially those who may be directly affected by any changes, no matter how slight, in NCAA bylaws. It also is important for coaches, counselors, and building administrators, who are expected to know the legislation and to advise athletes and their parents accordingly. Share this form routinely with everyone to assure their understanding of rules changes. You'll look good in the process.

Contacting the NCAA and Other Regulatory Organizations

Athletic directors and coaches should feel free to contact the NCAA whenever they have questions or concerns about NCAA bylaws, or require information about actual or rumored changes in policies. The counselors in Legislative Services are very helpful and provide valuable information to coaches, counselors, school administrators, and even parents and students. To contact the NCAA, write or call the National Collegiate Athletic Association. See the addresses listed in Figure 8-10.

The National Association of Intercollegiate Athletics (NAIA) is the governing body of a significant number of colleges and universities in the United States. Although the schools represented in the NAIA are less competitive than the NCAA Division I colleges and universities, they nonetheless represent outstanding schools, and they provide thousands of young athletes the opportunity to continue playing their sports in college and to receive an excellent education. To contact the NAIA, write or call the National Association of Intercollegiate Athletics (Figure 8-10).

Finally, junior college has always been a realistic option for a significant number of young athletes seeking opportunities to play a sport in college. Junior colleges have become especially appropriate for high school students who fail to meet the provisions of Bylaw 14.3 and must seek alternative ways to continue playing beyond high school. The National Junior College Athletic Association (NJCAA) has done a good job of coordinating its policies with those of the NCAA, and enables high school athletes who fail to meet the provisions of Bylaw 14.3 to achieve eligibility and eventually participate in a four-year college. To contact the NJCAA, write or call the National Junior College Athletic Association (Figure 8-10).

Each of these organizations is available to anyone interested in securing information about eligibility, scholarship availability (they all grant scholarships), recruiting procedures, duties of coaches, membership requirements, committee activities, or any of a number of principles and policies. You should feel free to contact the NCAA or any of the other regulatory organizations whenever you have questions about governance procedures. Encourage parents, also, to call or write the appropriate organization for information or advice. Figure 8-10 contains the addresses and phone numbers of each of the organizations and should be shared with parents early in the school year.

Figure 8-4
Certified Athletic Trainer Job Description

Supervisor: Athletic Director

Qualifications: Bachelor's Degree. National Athletic Trainers Association (NATA) certification.

Salary: See attached pay scale. Additional compensation will be made in accordance with the state guidelines.

Benefits: Benefits are the same as the teacher's benefit package.

Hours: The hours must be flexible to ensure proper coverage of all athletic practices and contests while keeping the total hours on duty to a reasonable limit. Hours will be arranged and monitored by the Athletic Director.

Contract: The trainer's contract will extend from the first Monday in August through the last day of the regular school year. The trainer will earn the same number of legal and granted holidays as are given to ten month employees. The trainer will also be granted ten additional vacation days per school year. These vacation days must be approved by the athletic director.

Evaluation: The athletic director will be responsible for at least one written evaluation of the trainer per year. The evaluation is to be submitted through the building principal to the director of personnel.

Major Duties:

1. Maintain and supervise a clean and orderly training room.
2. Insure adequate supplies in medical kits and cabinets.
3. Work with coaches to ensure that all protective equipment is in safe condition.
4. Request, inventory, and supervise the use of all consumable supplies for the training room.
5. Initiate and maintain a Student Trainer Program. Train and supervise the student trainers in the care of athletic injuries.
6. Be responsible for treatment of all minor athletic injuries and conditions.
7. Serve as mediator among student, coach, parent and physician to ensure that prescribed restrictions of activity and treatment are followed.
8. Maintain accurate records of injuries, treatments, and rehabilitation.
9. Maintain all therapeutic equipment used in the rehabilitation of athletes.
10. In case of emergency, provide emergency first aid and arrange transportation to the hospital.
11. Assist with the checking of protective equipment at the time it is issued and encourage athletes to report any equipment in need of repairs.
12. Perform other duties as requested by the athletic director or principal.

Printed with permission from Glenbrook South High School, District #225.

Figure 8-5
Uniform Response to Injuries Policy

DIRECTIONS FOR CALLING PARAMEDICS/AMBULANCE

1. Call paramedics:
   - A. State your name and position.
   - B. Describe nature of injury.
   - C. Describe location of injured athlete.
   - D. Give present phone number.
2. Send responsible person(s) to meet and direct paramedics to injured athlete.
3. Assist paramedics with injury information if needed.

*Outdoor sports practicing on outdoor track, varsity baseball field, west stadium practices field may send an assistant coach or responsible person to summon the paramedics from the fire station. The ambulance may use the gate near the ice rink for the west practice fields.

*When paramedics are summoned to the football stadium they should be instructed to use the stadium access road.

GENERAL EMERGENCY PROCEDURES

ACTIONS TO BE TAKEN

1. Administer necessary and possible first aid.
2. Call paramedics if necessary.
3. Contact parents as soon as possible.
4. Assist emergency personnel by providing any pertinent information about the athlete's injury and medical history.
5. Accompany athlete to hospital if possible.
6. Arrange for transportation from hospital for staff and family of athlete, if necessary.

ATHLETIC INJURY PROCEDURES

General Guidelines:

***REMEMBER - Most Important:* The injured athlete takes priority over everything!**

1. KEEP THE ATHLETE STILL, COMFORTABLE, AND REASSURED.
2. WHEN IN DOUBT, DO NOT MOVE AN INJURED ATHLETE.
3. SEND SOMEONE FOR THE ATHLETIC TRAINER IF ONE IS AVAILABLE.
4. CALL PARAMEDICS IF NECESSARY.
5. NOTIFY PARENTS AS SOON AS POSSIBLE.

1. When Head Athletic Trainer is present:
   - A. Notify Head Athletic Trainer.
   - B. If there is a serious injury and it is obvious that an ambulance will be needed, send assistant coach or student trainer/lab assistant to call paramedics.

Printed with permission from Glenbrook South High School Athletic Training Department.

2. When injury occurs on school grounds and the Head Athletic Trainer is not present:
   A. Administer first aid.
   B. Call ambulance if necessary.
   C. Notify parents of injury.
   D. See that the athlete has transportation home.

3. When team is away and injury occurs:
   A. Consult the Certified Athletic Trainer if one is present. You must follow his or her instructions.
   B. Request assistance of host team coach or athletic director if trainer is not available.
   C. Call ambulance if necessary.
   D. Send an adult and athlete's emergency information with him or her to the hospital. If at all possible, send an assistant coach with the injured athlete.

4. **Notify the Head Athletic Trainer as soon as possible after an athletic injury occurs.**

DO NOT REQUEST THE REMOVAL OF ANY INJURED ATHLETE IF YOU ARE IN DOUBT AS TO HIS OR HER CONDITION, OR WHEN THERE IS A BACK, HEAD, OR NECK INJURY. CALL FOR THE PARAMEDICS.

INJURED ATHLETE AND PARTICIPATION

The welfare of the athlete is of the utmost importance. Decisions of the Certified Athletic Trainer must be considered final. However, the coach and the athletic trainer should communicate to arrive at a sound decision concerning the playing status of the injured athlete. The athletic trainer and coach should communicate regularly with regards to injured athletes.

TRAINING ROOM OPERATION

1. Practices
   A. The training room will be open during the school day from 10:00 A.M. until the end of practice. Earlier openings will be arranged in conjunction with Physical Education/Training Room classes if necessary.
   B. Special practices or changes in original schedules should be submitted in advance to the Athletic Trainer.
   C. During the outdoor seasons, the Athletic Trainer can be contacted by radio from the Athletic Director's offices or by a student trainer/lab assistant in the training room, if the Athletic Trainer is on the fields.
2. Contests
   A. All home games will be covered except when football is away and your team is at home.
   B. The Certified Athletic Trainer will be traveling with the Varsity Football Team.
   C. Any changes in contest schedules should be submitted in writing to the Head Athletic Trainer at least 48 hours in advance.
3. Training Room Facilities and Equipment
   A. Athletes are not allowed in training room without a coach or trainer present.
   B. If a coach opens the training room for the athletes he or she must directly supervise the athletes:
      1. The coach is directly responsible for the neatness and cleanliness of the training room.
      2. **NEVER** leave the training room unattended if you opened the training room.
      3. ONLY THE CERTIFIED ATHLETIC TRAINER IS ALLOWED TO INITIATE TREATMENTS.
   C. First-aid kits, water bottles or coolers, and ice containers are available from the training room. The coaches are responsible for the condition and return of this equipment.
   D. Water bottles should be kept clean and tops should not be removed, in order to prevent the spread of disease and illness.

4. Student Trainers/Lab Assistants
   A. Student Trainers/Lab Assistants are being taught basic injury care; however, the coach must assume all responsibility in case of injury. The student trainer is there to assist you.
   B. Student Trainers/Lab Assistants are trained to tape and treat minor injuries.
   C. When possible, a student trainer will be assigned to work with your team, and possibly travel with them.
   D. Student Trainers/Lab Assistants are not to use the whirlpool or other modalities without permission of the Certified Athletic Trainer and his or her supervision.
   E. Neither coaches nor student trainers are to diagnose injuries and request specific treatment from the training room. These are the responsibilities of the team or attending physician and the Certified Athletic Trainer.

ATHLETIC EMERGENCY INFORMATION CARDS

The Athletic Trainer will distribute emergency cards to each coach at the beginning of their respective seasons. The coach is responsible for having each athlete fill out the card and have it signed by a parent or guardian. When all cards have been returned, give them to the Athletic Trainer. These cards will be kept in the medical kit of that particular sport. These cards will provide the necessary information in case of an emergency. These cards are provided for the protection and safety of the athlete and coach.

USE OF RADIO COMMUNICATION DEVICES

There are presently three portable radios obtainable in the trainer's office and a base-station radio in the Athletic Director's office. The Head Athletic Trainer may be summoned by the use of these radios.

*Radio will be carried by the Head Athletic Trainer during outdoor seasons.

1. Fall practices
   A. Radio with Varsity Football Team
   B. Radio with student trainers in Training Room
2. Fall contests
   A. Radio with soccer team which is playing on main soccer field, when Head Athletic Trainer is on school grounds, but unable to be at the contest.
   B. Indoor sports may use base station in Athletic Director's office to contact athletic trainer.
3. Spring practices
   A. Radio with Girl's Varsity Soccer team
4. Spring contests
   A. Radio on girl's main soccer field
   B. If possible, radio on Main baseball field
   C. If possible, radio on Frosh baseball field
   D. If possible, radio on Varsity softball field

Figure 8-6
High School Student Accident Report

School Name ______________________ Date ______________

Name ______________________ I.D. #__________ Age ______________

Parent or Guardian ______________________ Phone ______________

Address ____

Staff Member Supervising ______________________ Title______________

Accident Date______________________ Time ____________ AM/PM ________

Describe Injury and Body Part ____

DESCRIPTION OF ACCIDENT

Where did accident occur?____

Description of accident by person preparing the report (including activity, equipment, special situations, and contributing factors)

____

____

What would you recommend to prevent a repeat accident? ______________________

____

Student sent to: _______Nurse _______Athletic Trainer _______Not Referred

Prepared by ______________________ Title______________

Administrator Signature______________________

* *

Care provided by Nurse or Athletic Trainer______________________

______________________ Signature______________________

Parent/Guardian contacted: _______Yes _______No Name ______________________

Action Taken

_______Returned to Class _______Sent Home _______Sent to Physician

_______Released to Parent _______Sent to Hospital _______Other, Describe ______________

Additional Information for Athletic Injuries

_______Participant _______Spectator _______Intramural _______Interscholastic

Sport _______ Level_______ Practice_______ Game_______

Field Condition ______________________ Equipment ______________________

Specific Drill Involved ____

Athletic Director's Signature______________________

Printed with Permission from Glenbrook South High School, District #225.

Figure 8-7
Sample Physical Exams Information

Physical Exams

In accordance with the Illinois State High School Association's By-Law 3.070, "Students shall have filed with their high school principal a certificate of physical fitness issued by a licensed physician not more than one year preceding practice or participation in an interscholastic activity."*

Therefore, it is imperative that before any student begins participating in a sport, that there must be a current physical form filed in the athletic administration office.

In addition, a current parent consent certificate must accompany this physical form. The parent/guardian signature is mandated to ensure that parents understand the possibilities of injury to their student athletes.

**Printed with permission from the* Manual for High School Coaches*; published by the Illinois High School Association.*

Figure 8-8
Health Insurance Program Information

ADDITIONAL HEALTH INSURANCE COVERAGE

As you are aware, the high school does not provide medical insurance coverage for any accidental injuries received at practices, or home or away contests. However, the school district has selected an affordable insurance for your family to purchase for coverage for your son/daughter in case of injury.

Attached you will find a brochure provided by (name of company) , that explains vital information regarding student accident insurance. If you choose to take advantage of this insurance plan, please fill out the enrollment application and send it directly to the insurance company.

If you have any questions, please feel free to contact the agent at the address listed below:

Agent Name
Company Name
Address
City, State, ZIP
Phone No.
Fax No.

Remember, the insurance plan is not mandatory for you to purchase. It is only an option that the school district has provided for your student-athlete.

Figure 8-9
Eligibility Requirements for Intercollegiate Sports

DIRECTIONS: The following discussion contains very important information. You **MUST** abide by it if you plan to play a sport in college. *THE BAD NEWS:* If you fall short in any area, you will not be eligible to receive a scholarship, practice, or play in an NCAA Division I or II school during your first year. For that matter, you may **NEVER** play a sport in college if you are declared academically ineligible. *THE GOOD NEWS:* The rules are not hard to follow. If you maintain a decent college-prep program in high school and study to the best of your ability, you will have no problem with the following requirements.

Be sure to write them down as we go along, and ask questions at any time. We're here to make sure you understand the rules.

The NCAA's Bylaw 14.3 (Proposition 48)

1. Graduate from high school.
2. Maintain a grade point average of ____ on a 4.0 scale and earn a composite score of ____ on the ACT or a ____ on the SAT OR earn a lower grade point average but a higher ACT/SAT score. Ask your counselor or coach to see the NCAA "Sliding Scale." It shows the relationship between test scores and grade-point average.
3. Maintain a program of at least ____ academic units (full year courses), including the following:
   - English—4 years
   - Math—2 years
   - Social Studies—2 years
   - Science—2 years
   - Other: __________, __________, __________, __________, __________, __________, __________, __________, __________.

NOTES:

NAIA REQUIREMENTS

The requirements of the National Association of Intercollegiate Athletics (NAIA) are similar to those of the NCAA. The NAIA also awards athletic scholarships and requires its own set of eligibility requirements. Write them down as they are mentioned:

YOU MUST MEET ANY TWO OF THE FOLLOWING THREE REQUIREMENTS:

1. Graduate from the upper half of your high school class.
2. Earn a grade-point average of ____ on a 4.0 scale.
3. Receive a composite score of ____ on the ACT or a score of ____ on the SAT.

For further explanations of some of the specifics of test scores and academic program, see your coach and counselor. You may have a unique situation that requires special consideration. Talk to your coach and counselor anyway, if only to make sure that you are meeting the requirements of either organization.

NOTES:

Figure 8-10
Letter to Parents of Prospective College Athletes

Athletic Department

Dear Parents of Prospective College Athletes, Date

Your son/daughter has expressed interest in participating in athletic activities beyond high school. In addition to the information provided in the attached pamphlets, the following information will be helpful to you and your child in securing answers to questions such as eligibility, scholarship availability, recruiting procedures, principles, and policies.

The National College Athletic Association (NCAA)
6201 College Blvd.
Overland Park, Kansas 66211-2422
Phone—913-339-1906
E-mail—www.ncaa.org

The National Association of Intercollegiate Athletics (NAIA)
6120 South Yale Avenue
Suite 1450
Tulsa, Oklahoma 74136
Phone—918-494-8828

The National Junior College Athletic Association (NJCAA)
P.O. Box 7305
Colorado Springs, Colorado 80933
Phone—719-590-9788

The National College Athletic Association Clearinghouse
2255 North Dubuque Rd.
P.O. Box 4044
Iowa City, Iowa 52243-4044
Phone—319-337-1492

A reminder to mark your calendars for (date), at 7:30 P.M. to join the coaching staff and guest speakers to discuss these regulatory organizations, their requirements for participation in colleges and universities, and the recommended path for your son/daughter to follow.

DEALING WITH DRUGS AND OTHER PROBLEMS

Over the years, coaches establish close relationships with entire families in the community. On that basis, they often contribute to the school's public relations efforts and become essential liaisons among segments of the community. While usually an advantage, such familiarity can cause problems, particularly when coaches forget that their relationships with students and parents are primarily professional.

Coaches must be reminded, therefore, to follow a prescribed protocol for writing letters, making referrals inside and outside the school, and talking with parents on the phone or in person. Such a protocol must always emphasize a descriptive and anecdotal interpretation of student behavior. Written communiqués to school personnel or phone calls to parents regarding questionable student behavior must describe the behavior rather than state opinions or give interpretations.

Figure 8-11 provides an example of a referral to a school counselor regarding the behavior of a basketball player. The coach is obviously concerned that the athlete may have been using drugs, but she makes her point by describing the athlete's behavior rather than interpreting it. Had she stated that the athlete was using drugs, she might have subjected both her school and herself to potential legal problems with the parents.

Consider this case. Just a few years ago, A friend had a young coach burst into her office, apparently claiming to everyone in hearing distance, that "Stanley is high again!" She ushered the coach quickly into her office and asked him for the full story. He indicated that he had told the trainer yesterday that Stanley had come to practice high and that he wanted someone to deal with it. Apparently, he assumed, the trainer hadn't found the time to confront Stanley or to talk to his parents. Our friend sent for the trainer.

The trainer told her and the coach that he had talked to Stanley the previous day, and that Stanley had told him that he was taking a new medication for his asthma. The trainer called the parents to confirm the story and hadn't received their return call yet. He had planned to let the coach know as soon as he heard from the parents. Expecting the coach to react sheepishly, at least apologetically, our friend was surprised when the coach told the trainer to let him know when the parents called, then turned abruptly to leave.

Needless to say, our friend asked him to stay for a moment. When the trainer left the office, she asked the coach to review the incident and to reflect on his reaction to the athlete's behavior. The discussion grew into two more meetings and eventually convinced the coach that his "rush to judgment" could have damaged the young man's reputation and provoked a legal response from the parents.

All ADs experience similar incidents, many that have become full-blown court cases and have resulted in surprisingly large settlements, all because someone shared an uninformed opinion rather than a simple description of one student's behavior. Although contrary to our natural inclination to share our opinions, writing anecdotal or descriptive referrals is relatively easy, and it opens the door to serious dialogue among parents and school professionals who are qualified to interpret student behaviors and to recommend appropriate action. We suggest an occasional inservice, therefore, early in the school year, to introduce coaches to, or remind them about, the need to write descriptive referrals.

Figure 8-11
Sample Anecdotal/Descriptive Memo

TO: Tom Jones
Counseling Department

FR: Louise Adler

RE: Mandy Brown

I thought it wise to contact you regarding a recent incident with Mandy during yesterday's practice. As you may know, Mandy has had some problems at home with her parents' divorce and the illness of her younger brother. I noticed before practice yesterday that Mandy appeared to be unsteady on her feet; I thought at first that she was having some fun with a couple of her teammates, because they all were stifling laughs.

When practice started, however, I noted as well that her speech was slurred. In fact, at one point, she had trouble pronouncing the word "basketball." Again, some of her teammates snickered, so I turned the practice over to my assistant, Jill, and asked Mandy to talk to me in the hall. I asked her at that time if anything was wrong and if she felt OK. She said yes and then became suddenly angry, asking, "Why the hell are you always picking on me?"

As any of her teammates can attest, I don't pick on Mandy and, in fact, am concerned about this most recent behavior. Please talk to her and do whatever you think is appropriate to determine its causes.

Thanks for your help, and contact me if you would like to discuss the situation.

DISCIPLINING ATHLETES

Writing descriptive referrals is part of the larger issue of disciplining student athletes. Having coached for more collective years than we care to admit, we realize that most coaches prefer to handle their own team discipline. Like Coach John Wooden, who shared his concept of discipline with us years ago, we learned that "the bench" is the coach's most effective tool in developing well-disciplined athletes. It deprives athletes of their fundamental need to compete and motivates them to do whatever is necessary to find their way back onto the field or court.

Motivation

Motivation, therefore, is inextricably linked to team discipline. Well-motivated athletes can be self-disciplined athletes, if coaches use the character-shaping tools available to them. As athletic director, you must assure that such tools are used consistently and, when necessary, teach coaches how to use them. One of these tools is motivation.

Unfortunately, most coaches believe that motivation is something "I do to you." They shout and cajole during practice and prepare inspirational pregame and half-time speeches and assume that what "they do" influences "what their athletes do." Sometimes it works. An occasional half-time speech will inspire entire teams to perform well beyond their potential and to realize that moment of sports magic.

Most often, however, motivation is inherent in the athlete. It involves the basic needs that he or she seeks to satisfy each day during practices or contests. To the extent that coaches satisfy their athletes' needs for recognition, achievement, a sense of belonging, and a strong desire to compete—no, competition is not all bad!—they motivate athletes. That motivation promotes self-discipline in them.

"Self" is the operative word. It relates both to motivation and to discipline. Back to that half-time speech. If you spend fifteen minutes during a half-time delivering your Class A speech and the players saunter casually out of the room, have you been motivating them? I don't think so. More likely, you've been talking in someone else's sleep! This is not to say that you can't try occasionally to inspire them, but it is important to distinguish between *motivation* and *inspiration*, just as it is important that coaches distinguish between *self-discipline* and *punishment*.

Punishment

Punishment is the coach's or school's response only when self-discipline breaks down—and then the punishment should be strong enough to prevent future breakdowns. To quote Coach Wooden again: "Make the rules clear and the penalties severe." Only when the consequences of rules violations have teeth in them do some young athletes realize the importance of abiding by them.

Most adolescents are a breed apart. As adults, most of us realize that headstrong, self-indulgent behavior is childish and ultimately benefits no one—not even ourselves. We realize the importance of subordinating ourselves to "the group," whether it be the family, our circle of friends, the school, the society, or our sports programs. For us coaches and athletic directors, "The Program" is all of us, and it is more important than any one of us, including the head coach and the occasional superstar-blue chipper who blesses coaching careers but may expect special treatment.

We must realize that the program is not only our current group of coaches, parents, and young athletes but also future generations of parents and players, who will seek the same benefits of athletic participation that have fascinated and shaped young people for decades in this country. That we maintain the program, therefore, by expecting self-disciplined behavior and by appropriately punishing violators, in spite of occasional threats of litigation, is essential if we are to offer our communities valuable and entertaining experiences for everyone.

We find ourselves performing a delicate balancing act. We realize the importance of self-discipline, and we know that appropriate motivation, as well as reasonable and immediate consequences for misbehavior, help promote it. We also realize that some parents and others in the community will disagree with our decisions to punish violators, particularly when those players help win championships.

We must work together with school personnel to develop reasonable and consistent policies, and to accept help from others—deans, counselors, and teachers—when we apply those policies. Athletic departments can't work in isolation from the rest of the school, no matter how desperately we want to discipline our athletes ourselves. That's not reasonable, especially in a society as complicated as ours.

When we act unreasonably, we invite legal problems. It's probably not quite as simple as that, but it's mighty close, and it's useful for you to keep that in mind. Trust the process, work—"network" seems to be the popular word today—closely and collaboratively with others in the building to handle discipline problems and to develop procedures and policies that promote motivation and self-discipline, but that ultimately protect the future integrity of the athletic program.

LET'S WRAP IT UP

We all understand the importance of "Safety First." We know that it applies to every aspect of the athletic program, from conditioning programs, practice drills, and proper execution to player discipline, parent-coach communication, and the treatment of injuries. Safety First is the catch phrase of reasonable people everywhere, so it must guide the behaviors of coaches, and it must constitute one of the primary responsibilities of an athletic director.

"Safety First" dictates that you consider the needs of coaches before you implement policies that affect them. It suggests that you include coaches in the development of such policies. It reminds you to involve coaches in departmental decision making, particularly when other coaches are added to the staff. It requires that you apply all policies fairly and consistently. In essence, it suggests that you treat your coaches as you would expect to be treated.

"Safety First" also applies to sharing information with parents, athletes, coaches, and others in the school and community. You are on safe ground every time you inform people about changes in NCAA legislation and state or conference rules and regulations. You guarantee your own safety as well as the safety of others when you work with young athletes and their parents to assist them through the college selection and recruiting processes at the end of their high school careers.

You promote "Safety First" among your coaches when you inform them of policies governing the prevention and treatment of athletic injuries. You assure safety when you require coaches to use trainers and other medical personnel to deal with injuries. You promote safety within the department when you remind coaches of policies regarding transportation, the maintenance of equipment, and proper ways to inform parents and school personnel of student misbehavior.

Finally, you provide a safe and secure environment when you encourage athletes to succeed in the classroom and coaches to disregard a win-at-all-costs philosophy of competition. The win-at-all-costs philosophy results in a disregard for athletic policies governing recruiting and eligibility; a senseless preoccupation with winning; the subordination of classroom achievement; the manipulation of players, parents, and the school; and abused and injured players.

All these abuses are potential legal problems. Your task, as athletic director, is to impress on coaches that reasonable people don't do those things. If, for some reason, you fail to make such impressions, someone will do it for you, and everyone will suffer in the process.

SECTION NINE

Considering the Ancillary Issues

First, a quick story:

Timmy wore the thickest-soled sneakers he could buy and still stood barely five feet tall. He was slender, baby-faced, and about as close to shaving as winning a slam dunk competition. Worst of all, he was halfway through his junior year in high school and loved sports with a passion found only in the "athletically challenged." Desperately seeking anything in the real world that corresponded to his ideal self-image, Timmy tried out unsuccessfully for swimming in his freshman year, soccer and wrestling in his junior year, and, most recently, baseball in his junior year.

This recent failure to make a team seemed consistent with unsuccessful attempts to be elected to the Student Council, the Intramural Board of Directors, even to be accepted as a helper in the Early Bird Tutoring Program. Timmy had no place to turn. His parents encouraged him as best they could, but they alternated between helplessness and unfocused anger at their inability to help him. A few coaches in the school felt sorry for him, but they had only so much room on their teams and, although they wanted to help him, could offer only occasional moral support.

Fortunately, the school's athletic director realized the frustrations that Timmy and others like him were experiencing every year, so she decided to act. First, rather than simply post lists of tryout results, she told coaches to meet with athletes who were being cut from a team to explain the reasons and to identify alternative sports or activities for them within the program. She also asked them to be sensitive to the problems of some students and to report the especially delicate issues to her.

Next, she met with the guidance director and told him that she would forward lists of students being cut from teams and ask that he share the lists with counselors to encourage contact with particularly fragile students to try to ease the hurt and to explore the issue further. The guidance director agreed and discussed the process with his staff at the next departmental meeting. They, too, agreed that such a process would help students win the struggle with their identity problems and find satisfying experiences not only now but after graduation.

Timmy's counselor met with him shortly after he was cut from the baseball team. One meeting grew into several, all of them focusing on Timmy's feelings and his intentions for the future. He rejected almost immediately the coach's offer to be a manager for the baseball team. He decided against trying out for a different team or for the swim team again, telling his counselor, "Hey, maybe it's time I accepted the fact that I'm not a jock!"

This was not an easy admission for Timmy, but it opened the door to other activities to explore. Finally, one day the counselor suggested that Timmy consider being a sports reporter for the student newspaper. The paper needed reporters, and Timmy seemed to be the right person for the job. Timmy agreed, met with the faculty sponsor of the newspaper, and spent the remainder of his junior year and all of his senior year writing sports news for the paper.

He was good. His love of sports gave him insights that resulted in interesting perspectives for other students and compliments for him. Timmy still admitted to friends and family that he was "a jock waiting to happen," but he smiled whenever he said it and then promptly rattled off the statistics of the school's most recent contest. He had finally found his niche in school—perhaps not as glamorous as the occasional "blue chipper" that dominated the pages of local papers—but every bit as satisfying.

The last time we saw Tim, he had grown some seven or eight inches, was working as a broker with a Chicago firm, had a house in the suburbs—with three lovely children—and satisfied his continuing love of sports by playing golf whenever his schedule and wife permitted. To this day, he remembers those conversations with his counselor.

Not every young, unfulfilled athlete is as fortunate as Timmy. Many suffer damaged self-images and carry the loss of athletic participation for a good portion of their lives—frustrated and angered by a system that simply won't make room for them. Many find alternative ways to satisfy their need to compete. Some even become Little League coaches, sharing their frustrations by badgering children rather than introducing them to the joys of athletic competition. We've all seen them. The process that helped Tim might not help them, but it's worth a try.

Establish a process in your school by using the reproducible Tryout Policy in Figure 9-1 to set a team selection policy for your department. Discuss it with your staff first to assure that it meets their needs and expectations, then use it each year to remind them of the process. Also, use the form in Figure 9-2 to share with counselors the list of students who have been cut during recent tryouts. We feel confident that these two processes will reflect your department's sensitivity to everyone in your school, not just the coaches and athletes.

Figure 9-1
Tryout Policy

Tryout Policy Philosophy

The high school athletic department is sensitive to the needs of the athletes during the tryout period. It is the school's desire to see that as many student athletes as possible are involved in the program during the athletic season.

Unfortunately, due to facility space, time constraints, numbers of equipment, and additional factors, limitations are placed on sizes of teams for each individual sport.

The athletic department recognizes these concerns and is striving to maximize the options available for student athletes in the athletic arena as participants or supporters of the program.

Tryout Policy Procedures

1. Choosing the members of the various athletic teams is the responsibility of the coach.

2. Before tryouts begin, coaches will provide team information to all candidates and parents of the team at a fall meeting. Such information shall include:
   a. Length of tryout period—a minimum of five days.
   b. Objectives used to select the members of the team.
   c. Number of team members that will be selected and criteria involved in selection—positions needed, etc.
   d. Distribution of practice and competition schedule. The coach will explain the commitment necessary to join team.
   e. Clear notification that tryouts are based on the performance during the selection period. Tryouts are not based on summer participation or coaching camps the athletes participated in previous to selections.

3. Lower level coaches will follow the criteria for selection that have been established for the particular sport. Head coaches will be involved in lower level selections to aid the lower level coaches.

4. When lowering the numbers on teams becomes a necessity, a coach will provide the following opportunities for each player:
   a. Lists or rosters of team membership will not be posted. Each coach will meet with each candidate individually to discuss strengths, weaknesses, and squad membership or reason for nonmembership.
   b. Coach will discuss options or alternatives for those individuals who do not make the team. Such alternatives could include participation in the student activities program or a manager position on the team.
   c. Each athlete must have had an opportunity to perform in at least one intrasquad competition.

Figure 9-2
Students Cut From Teams Memo

Athletic Department

TO: (Guidance Director)

FR: (Your Name)

RE: Students recently cut from (name of team)

DATE:

Attached is the list of students who were cut recently from the __________ team. Please share this information with your counselors to alert them to possible problems with one or more of these students. They know these students as well as anyone in the building and can be of considerable help if one or more of these students should need it in dealing with this kind of rejection. Please feel free to contact me or to have any one of your counselors contact me if I can be of additional help.

WORKING WITH THE CHEERLEADER AND POMPON SQUADS

Sensitivity to others in the school relates not only to athletes or "wannabe athletes" but to other vital components of the athletic program—the cheerleading and pompon squads among the most obvious. Just walk around most schools in midsummer to appreciate the hard work of cheerleaders and the pompon squad. While the school's football and soccer teams are pumping iron, the cheerleaders and pompon squad are sweating over new routines and learning to do them with smiles on their faces!

Establish good working relationships with the faculty sponsors of both squads and maintain an open-door policy with the squad members. The cheerleading and pompon squads are as much a part of the sports program as the highest scorer on the basketball team or the winningest coach in the program. They should be included in most activities, including preseason meetings and postseason banquets, and their sponsors should be involved, whenever possible, in most, if not all, department meetings.

Use the policy statement in Figure 9-3 as a model for your department's booklet. It outlines the sponsor's responsibilities and, like the coaches' job descriptions, provides the substantive criteria for an end-of-the-year evaluation. As with the coaching philosophy and job descriptions, it should be reviewed periodically with faculty sponsors and modified to reflect reasonable and acceptable changes in job responsibilities.

HANDLING THE LITTLE CHORES

Not everything you do as athletic director influences the ebb and flow of human existence. In fact, a large part of your job doesn't even create a ripple in the pond of humanity that surrounds you each day. Ripple or not, they are jobs that have to be done. Following are just a few:

Team Photographs

Each year, team and individual photographs have to be taken for the yearbook, contest programs, and local press releases. Team pictures tend to be a chore for most head coaches. The photograph sessions generally are scheduled just before a scrimmage or practice, and the athletes are about as interested in standing still as in twisting an ankle. In fact, any of us who has organized a photograph session with our teams marvels at General Eisenhower's ability to mobilize an entire army!

Be sensitive to this difficulty, and do whatever is necessary to make the experience as comfortable as possible for coaches and players. Notify coaches well in advance of the scheduled session, and give athletes the time to do their talking and horsing around before the actual photographs are taken.

Sometimes it's also a good idea to pay for one extra picture for each team to permit players to get their contortions and face-making out of the way before the "real" pictures are taken. Such a practice acknowledges the athletes' need for joke time and releases some of their pent-up energy before the photographs are taken. It's also a good idea to have one or more of the booster club members present to assist with picture taking. Some of the players are never really sure of who they are and tend to behave for them!

Figure 9-4 provides a sample memo Nancy uses to notify her coaches of team pictures. Notice that it is shared with coaches two and a half weeks prior to the actual session and that it is accompanied by Figure 9-5—the time schedule for individual teams.

Workshops

Generally, there are a variety of workshops provided for athletes and coaches. They are organized by individual conferences, commercial enterprises, and state or national organizations. It's often a good idea to involve representatives from your school in as many of these workshops or conferences as possible.

Figures 9-6 and 9-7 illustrate and provide examples of sign-up procedures and notification of selection and involvement in one such conference. This particular workshop, a Leadership Workshop for the Central Suburban Conference just outside Chicago, has proven to be a valuable experience for both coaches and athletes. It trains potential student leaders in the athletic program and enables coaches to identify and train members of their teams to assist with current and future leadership responsibilities.

This is but one example of the variety of workshops and conferences available to coaches and athletes. It suggests a significant area of responsibility for athletic directors—one that often goes unrecognized in the school and community. Consequently, it's a good idea to notify the local papers of the names of student athletes who have been selected to participate in such programs. The recognition is important for the students, and it helps inform the parent community of the valuable learning experiences that are available to athletes in your school—yet another selling point for your program.

More About the Booster Club

Let's admit it—involvement with the booster club is sometimes a lot like weeding your garden. You find yourself on your knees once in a while; you often have to be careful to keep your hands clean; you can get burned on occasion; and you have to return to the chore often enough to "keep things looking good." As generous and sensitive as some of the parent volunteers can be, others can be manipulative and self-serving. We need *all* of them, because most members of the booster club are energetic and enthusiastic about sports and, if monitored carefully, provide a potentially valuable service to the athletic program. Do all you can, therefore, to put on a happy face during this love-hate relationship and find parent volunteers who will give unselfishly of their time and expect in return only the satisfaction of performing a service for the young people in their community.

Use the form in Figure 9-8, or one like it, to invite parents early in the school year to join the booster club. Notice the four membership categories, each involving a different level of financial support. Membership involves a season pass for the parents and any pre - high school age children in the family and—in the gold, silver, and bronze categories—recognition in the school's Athletic Calendar or Program.

Figure 9-3
Cheerleading/Poms/Team Mascot Sponsor Job Responsibilities

Purpose

To provide leadership and guidance to the individuals who are participating so that they make wise and effective decisions while instilling school spirit.

Duties and Responsibilities

1. Responsible for team conduct and promotion of respect and sportsmanship.
2. Responsible to lead team by good examples.
3. Responsible for equipment and supplies. Each sponsor will present an inventory at the end of the year to keep accurate counts of equipment.
4. Responsible to see that team members have opportunities for fair and impartial try-outs. Responsible to coordinate and supervise the tryouts.
   a. Sponsors will provide team information to all candidates of the team. Such information shall include length of tryout period, objectives used to select squads, practice and competition schedules, and the commitment necessary to become a member of the team.
   b. Lists or roster of team membership will not be posted. Each sponsor will meet with each candidate individually to discuss strengths, weaknesses, and squad membership or reason for nonmembership.
   c. Sponsor will discuss options or alternatives for those individuals who do not make the team. Such alternatives could include participation in the student activities program or a manager position on the team.
   d. Tryouts are based on the performance during the selection periods. Tryouts are not based on summer participation or coaching camps the individuals participated in prior to selections.
5. Responsible for the coordination of an awards banquet to honor the outstanding team members and their activities.
6. Responsible for any other duties relating to cheerleader/poms as may be directed by the principal or the athletic director.

Figure 9-4
Notification of Team Pictures

Athletic Department

TO: Fall Head Coaches

FROM: Athletic Director

RE: Booster Club Ad Book Pictures and Team Pictures

DATE:

I have scheduled the fall Booster Club Ad Book pictures for (date). Please note the attached schedule which lists the time for your pictures. Two Booster Club members will be accompanying the photographer to aid in obtaining all of the names of your varsity team members for the photograph. These people will come to the area where you are practicing for the picture and would appreciate any help or assistance that you can give them.

Please note the dates and times for fall team and individual pictures. Also attached you will find the order envelopes for the pictures. Please distribute these order envelopes to the individuals on your teams. Team members will need to bring the envelopes with them in order to place orders.

I realize that there is not a good day to have these pictures taken, but I hope by getting these schedules to you at an early date, you can plan your practice schedules around these dates.

Thank you in advance for your cooperation.

Figure 9-5
Sample Picture Schedule

Athletic Department

BOOSTER CLUB PICTURE SCHEDULE

DATE

VARSITY ONLY

BOYS' SOCCER	8:00 A.M.
BOYS' CROSS COUNTRY	8:20 A.M.
GIRLS' CROSS COUNTRY	8:40 A.M.
GIRLS' SWIMMING	9:00 A.M.
GIRLS' TENNIS	9:20 A.M.
GIRLS' VOLLEYBALL	9:40 A.M.
FOOTBALL	10:00 A.M.
BOYS' GOLF	10:30 A.M.
GIRLS' GOLF	10:50 A.M.

Figure 9-6
Workshop Nomination

Athletic Department

TO: Head Coaching Staff

FROM: Athletic Director

RE: Student Leadership Workshop

DATE:

The fourth annual student athlete leadership workshop is scheduled for (date) from 5:30 P.M. to 9:00 P.M. and on (date) from 8:00 A.M. to 3:00 P.M.

We are asking you to nominate two sophomores or two juniors, or a combination, to attend this workshop. Please fill out the bottom portion of this form and return it to the athletic mailbox no later than (date).

The conference committee has decided to move the leadership workshop back to the above date because many of the schools could not obtain a commitment from their coaches as well as their athletes for the summer months. They also decided to involved younger athletes who might have the potential to become leaders, so that they were trained for the following year, instead of seniors who might already have their season over with by the time the leadership workshop was completed.

The conference committee is also looking for coaches who are interested in working with athletes at this workshop. If you are interested, please check the appropriate box below.

Thank you in advance for your cooperation.

(Please return the attached portion to the athletic office no later than ______ date ______)

Name of Athlete: ______________________ Year in School Sophmore Junior

Name of Athlete: ______________________ Year in School Sophmore Junior

_______ Yes, I am interested in assisting with the leadership workshop in the evening of (date) and during the school day of (date). I understand that there will be a short training session for adult leaders that I must attend.

Coach's Name ______________________ Sport ______________________

Figure 9-7
Notification of Conference Selection

Athletic Department

Date

Dear Student Athlete

Congratulations on being selected to represent the athletic department at the fourth annual leadership conference on (date) from 5:00 P.M. to 9:30 P.M. and on (date) from 7:30 A.M. to 3:30 P.M.

Enclosed you will find an information pamphlet and registration form. Please review this information, fill out the registration form and return it to the athletic office no later than (date).

The Leadership Conference is an excellent opportunity to participate in problem-solving and team-building activities for leadership.

We look forward to your participation in the conference. We will provide more information for you regarding bus times, etc., when you turn in your registration form at the athletic office.

Respectfully,

Athletic Director

Figure 9-8
Booster Club Membership Invitation Letter

Athletic Department

Dear Parents: Date

This is your invitation to become members of the high school athletic support organization, the ___(name)___. Our club is composed of moms and dads who want to support the various boys and girls athletic programs at the high school. We are involved as enthusiastic fans and as financial helpers as well. Our fundraising activities help to assure our students of a first class athletic program, including many items that might not otherwise be an affordable expense to the school. A list of some of the equipment that the Booster Club has provided for the athletic programs over the years is attached to this letter. We are very proud of our accomplishments.

BOOSTER CLUB membership is open to all parents of high school students. There are four classes of memberships from which you may choose. Your choice depends upon the level of support you wish to provide.

GOLD BOOSTER at _(amount)_ or more includes Booster Club Membership, a family plan athletic ticket,* and a special listing on the GOLD BOOSTER page of the high school athletic calendar.

SILVER BOOSTER at _(amount)_ includes Booster Club Membership, a family plan athletic ticket,* and a special listing on the SILVER BOOSTER page of the high school athletic calendar.

BRONZE BOOSTER at _(amount)_ includes Booster Club Membership, a family plan athletic ticket,* and a special listing on the BRONZE BOOSTER page of the high school athletic calendar.

BOOSTER at _(amount)_ includes Booster Club Membership and a family plan athletic ticket.*

*This family plan athletic ticket will admit parents and pre–high school age children to all regularly scheduled home athletic contests at the district high schools.

Two special events sponsored by the Booster Club are scheduled to take place. The first annual Booster Club golf outing is scheduled for _(date)_. The Annual Spring Dinner Dance is also scheduled to take place at the city hotel on _(date)_. Mark these dates on your calendars; you will not want to miss them!

We hope that we can count on your support of the athletic programs and the activities of the Booster Club. Please join us through one of the membership categories available by sending your check made out to ___(name)___ in the enclosed envelope. We need your check no later than _(date)_ so that your name may be included in the special listing on the high school athletic calendar.

Thank you for your support!

Sincerely,

Booster Club President

Booster Club Members

Names	*Names*	*Names*	*Names*
Names	*Names*	*Names*	*Names*
Names	*Names*	*Names*	*Names*
Names	*Names*	*Names*	*Names*

Notice that the letter of invitation also refers to the dance to be held later in the spring of the year. Because such activities are money-making efforts for the booster club, they should be mentioned as often as possible in communications to parents. We have had parents call for tickets after receiving the first letter of the year, particularly if they attended the dance before. Figure 9-9 provides an example of an invitation to include in the mailing. Sufficient copies should be made for inclusion in other mailings throughout the year.

Figure 9-10 offers a sample listing of items donated by the booster club in previous years. It, too, should be included in the letter inviting parents to become boosters. With the exception of one or two sport-specific purchases, it identifies donated items that benefit the entire athletic program. Be sure to avoid listing purchases for just one or two teams, particularly if they are successful and highly publicized. Nothing will discourage donations from the parents of other athletes faster than observing—even casually—that the "favored child" is getting the money as well as the media.

In negotiating the sometimes treacherous waters, you must possess as much political acumen as God-given energy. Both assure the survival of the program as well as your personal survival. "Politics" may be a bad word in some circles today, but it may be more important than many of us think. With it, we experience occasional confusion, double-dealing, and self-serving behavior. Without it, however, we compromise our own survival, so allow politics to guide some of your thinking—not to indulge, but to protect yourself.

Recognition of Special Days

Whether political or plain, old common sense, recognizing coaches and athletes for their contributions and accomplishments is both thoughtful and organizationally wise. From the National Women in Sports Week to National Coaches Day, people are eager to acknowledge the work schools are doing with the nation's youth. Capitalize on these special times of the year to congratulate coaches and to inform the community of the critical jobs they perform.

Figure 9-11 provides a sample letter to share with each coach in the department. It thanks coaches personally for their contributions to the program and invites them to visit the athletic office for refreshments and a token of appreciation. Some schools provide a day-long buffet for coaches; others provide pancake breakfasts; some offer a can of soda and a brownie. No matter how elaborate the cuisine, the primary focus is the message you send to coaches of your genuine appreciation.

The token of appreciation can be simple as well: a key chain with the school's logo, a pen, a clipboard, or, if you want to spend more money, a nylon briefcase or a jacket. The more expensive the gift, of course, the stronger the impression it will make. The point is, the strongest impression is made when you first offer the gift; beyond that, the impression is only a matter of degree.

Organize such moments for your coaches, then be sure to provide a press release comparable to the one in Figure 9-12 to alert the community to the event and to the possibility of acknowledging the valuable work coaches perform for the school and community. Such a sharing of information is appreciated by the community as well as the coaches. Good PR and good personnel relationships are an unbeatable combination.

Figure 9-9
Invitation to Booster Club Function

Annual Dinner Dance

The High School Booster Club
cordially invites you to dance the night away in support of
high school athletics.

An evening of fine dining, dancing and entertainment
is being planned at the city hotel.

This year a buffet is featured.
Music and entertainment by ______(name)______.

Date
Location
City, State

*Cocktails 6:30 P.M. * Lobby Dinner 7:30 P.M. * Ballroom*

Cash Bar Raffle Prizes Live Auction Silent Auction Prize Capsules

Reservations are limited. Please respond early!

---------------------------------- Tear Here ----------------------------------

Annual Booster Club Dinner Dance

Name(s) to be printed on name tag:

____

____

Number of tickets at ____($amount)____ per person: ____________________

Wish to be seated with: ______________________________

Sorry, we cannot attend. However, here is out tax deductible donation in the amount of: __________

Make checks payable to: ______________________________

Figure 9-10
Sample Listing of Donated Items

BOOSTER CLUB PURCHASES and PROGRAMS

Athletic/academic award plaques each year
$500 scholarships for college-bound athletes each year
Pictures of senior athletes and their parents
Championship patches for each member of all-league championship teams
Pocket sport calendars sent to members each season
Lighting at stadium
Raingear for boys' and girls' golf teams
Baseball/softball batting cage for outdoor area
Bab system for gymnastics/diving area
Scoreboards for baseball and soccer/softball
Guide booklet for college-bound student athletes and their parents
Sponsorship of athlete leadership workshop
Communication radios for athletic trainer
Football/soccer/track scoreboard for stadium
Accutron therapy machines for training room
Flooring for weight room
Scoreboard and time display board for pool
Electrical generator for softball pitching machine
Jumping box for vertical jump improvement
Galvanic stimulator for the training room
Timer clock for swimming
Nautilus exercise equipment
VHS systems (camera, recorder, TV) used by all sports
Electronic starter equipment for track and cross country
Scoreboards for the main and lower gyms
Baseball dugouts
Orthatron knee machine for the training room
Whirlpool for the training room
Mettler sonicator (ultrasound equipment) for the training room

Figure 9-11
Coaches Holiday Letter

Athletic Department

Interoffice Memorandum

Date

Dear ____________________,

____(date)____ is National Coaches Day! You play a vital role in the athletic program at the high school. Your hard work, dedication, and leadership in our interscholastic athletic programs have been important components in the success of the athletic department.

We wish to personally express our appreciation for a job well done. On ____(date)____, please come down to the athletic office to share some refreshments to celebrate National Coaches Day, and to receive a token of appreciation for your hard work and efforts.

Sincerely,

Athletic Director

Figure 9-12
Sample Coaches Holiday Press Release

Press Release

National Coaches Day

TO: The Clairfield *Review*, the *News Sun*, the Marshfield *Tribune*

For Immediate Release

(Name, address)

Thursday, October 19, is National Coaches Day, an annual opportunity to acknowledge and thank coaches for the valuable service they perform for our schools and community. The Clairfield High School athletic department will celebrate the day by offering refreshments and a token of the school's appreciation to each coach in the school. We have long acknowledged the dedication of our coaching staff, and the time and effort they expend on behalf of our student athletes. As a school, we try to recognize such contributions as often as possible, but especially on this particular day.

Please join us in our efforts to thank coaches for the tremendous job they do helping our children develop into mature, responsible members of our community. Your expressions of appreciation are the finest and most satisfying tributes they receive for their hard work. Thanks for your help.

Rental of Facilities

Athletic directors sometimes find themselves responsible for coordinating the rental of facilities such as the gymnasium, the pool, the football field, or any of the areas normally within the jurisdiction of the athletic department. This responsibility has significant legal implications, so it is wise to use a contract like the one in Figure 9-13 to protect the rights of everyone involved in the rental agreement.

Notice particularly the Special Conditions and additional stipulations in the contract. All of these provisions guarantee the proper use of the facility, assure proper supervision and protection of valuable equipment, and guard against school district liability for someone else's negligence.

Transportation Policies

School district and personal liability are potentially significant issues when transporting athletes to practice or contests. Figure 9-14 offers a Transportation Policy; you can use it or develop your own to inform coaches and others of proper procedure when transporting athletes. Be sure to discuss the policy with coaches and to guarantee their compliance with it. Don't be afraid to stick to your guns on these issues; the minor inconvenience you may cause a few athletes and their parents is well worth the avoidance of possible injury to athletes or the major litigation that can result from a misguided willingness to bend the rules.

More About Scheduling

Figure 9-15 provides a contract used by the Illinois High School Association for scheduling athletic contests. Use something like it to arrange for contests among schools in your conference or between nonconference schools. You might also use the form in Figure 9-16 if you find you have to reschedule one or more contests. Both forms are simple, yet comprehensive.

Participation Numbers

Maintain annual records of student participation by sport. The building principal or other members of the school's administration may ask for such numbers when determining personnel allocations, and the athletic department will need them when assessing student interest in specific programs. Student participation changes for a variety of reasons. New sports or especially popular coaches may attract numbers away from other sports in similar seasons, or burned-out or unnecessarily demanding coaches may discourage student participation. Whatever the reasons, be aware of them during coaching evaluations or long-range planning sessions within the department.

Numbers may have changed dramatically, for example, with the introduction of a new coach. Whether they went up or down, the numbers reveal something about the popularity of the sport, and can be dramatic evidence of a coach's impact on the program. The numbers may even reveal the need to drop a particular sport from the program. Such a decision, however, must consider a number of other factors that may be affecting the popularity of the sport. Figure 9-17 provides an excellent sample format to use as a starting point.

Figure 9-13
Use/Rental Contract

HIGH SCHOOL
address

This agreement entered into this __________ day of ______________, 19_____, between the Board of Education, *City, State,* and ______________________________ hereinafter provides:
(name and address)

1. For the use of ____
(area/s to be used)

   at the High School on ____
(date/s)

   at ________________ for ____
(time/s) (type of program)

2. For fees to be paid based on CLASS __________ of the attached schedule.

   AREA FEES

   ______________________ (   ) Rehearsals $ ________________

   ______________________ (   ) Performances ________________

   ______________________ ________________

   ______________________ ________________

   SALARIES

   ______________________ ________________

   ______________________ ________________

   ______________________ ________________

   OTHER

   ______________________ ________________

   ______________________ ________________

   ______________________ ________________

3. *OTHER* ____

   ____

Reprinted with permission from Glenbrook South High School.

SPECIAL CONDITIONS

1. All groups using the facilities on weekends will be assigned one custodian or one supervisor to open the doors, to be with the group throughout the performance or rehearsal, and be responsible for locking all doors and turning out all lights. The custodian or supervisor will be paid at an overtime rate, and the total cost will be paid by the using organization.
2. Custodial staff will be paid for one-half hour before a performance in order to allow time to open doors, turn on lights, etc.
3. Whenever custodial staff is called back to work after leaving the building, the renting organization will be charged a minimum of two hours' wages.
4. When more than one custodian is required, as determined by the school staff, the contract will contain the additional cost.
5. In most cases, cleanup after a large event will require additional custodial staff for a limited number of hours. These costs will be billed to the using organization.
6. When, in the opinion of the school staff, a custodian must be on duty for a week night activity, it shall be a contract requirement to be billed to the using organization.
7. Parking attendants and security personnel are available and will be scheduled through the student activities office, as required. The renting organization will be charged the out-of-pocket expenses.
8. *Auditorium*
   (a.) The auditorium supervisor will be on duty at all times during which outside organizations are using the facility.
   (b.) The renting organization will meet with the auditorium supervisor at least 48 hours before use of the auditorium to determine the number of people needed and the services required.
   (c.) The auditorium equipment will be operated only by school district employees. Time sheets for these employees are to be signed each night by the person in charge for the renting organization.
   (d.) The auditorium supervisor and the stage crew shall be paid for one-half hour before each rehearsal and one hour before each performance. Estimated cleanup time is two man hours after each rehearsal and six man hours after each performance.
9. *Pool*
   (a.) The pool will not be used for fund-raising purposes by outside organizations.
   (b.) Whenever the pool is in use, the following district staff members will be present:

1–30 people	1 staff member
31–70 people	2 staff members *or* 1 staff member and 2 guards

10. *Pianos.* The cost for moving the grand piano and the cost for tuning any piano after use will be paid by the organization renting the facility.

The undersigned certifies that the above organization is nonprofit and that funds raised by this rental will not accrue to the benefit of a profit-making organization.

The undersigned further agrees that:

1. The organization shall abide by all rules, regulations, and conditions listed in the APPLICATION FOR USE/RENTAL OF FACILITIES.
2. The organization shall be responsible for the conduct of persons present and for damage, loss, disappearance, or breakage of school property during the use/rental period.

Figure 9-13, continued
Use/Rental Contract

3. The user agrees to save harmless, defend, and indemnify the high school district, the Board of Education and the individual members thereof and its employees against all loss, liability, damage, and expense, including attorneys' fees, incurred by any of the above-named parties on account of any injury to or death of any person or persons while on the premises as a result of user's activities, regardless of whether a claim is made that the district, the board or any of the above named persons were negligent or acted in a wanton and willful manner or with a wanton or willful disregard for the injured party.
4. User shall provide a certificate of insurance to the district certifying that the high school district, the Board of Education, and the individual members thereof and its employees are named insureds in a general liability policy in an insurance company acceptable to the district, insuring the above named persons against claims for bodily injury or death to any person who is on the school property as a result of user's activities, said insurance to cover the above-named as insureds regardless of whether a claim is made that the above-named insureds, or any of them, were guilty of negligence or wanton or willful actions or failure to act.
5. The district may at any time deny or refuse to grant any application or cancel, without liability, any USE/RENTAL CONTRACT whenever the use, in the reasonable judgment of the Board, presents or may present a clear and present danger to persons or property, or may be in violation of or contrary to applicable federal, state, or local law or ordinance.
6. Advertising for the activity shall clearly indicate the name of the sponsoring organization with _______________ High School listed only as the place where the activity will be held.
7. It is understood that whenever regular school staff members are not present, the school district will require a custodian to be on duty during the use/rental. Custodian's hourly wages will be charged to the users as well as the cost for additional cleanup.

____
Signature of Representative

____
Name of Organization

____
Address

____
Date Phone No.

APPROVED:

____
Signature of School Official

____
Date

IMPORTANT: This agreement is not binding unless it has been signed, returned to Athletic Director, _______________ High School, address, City/State, ZIP, and signed by the School Official.

Figure 9-14
Transportation Policy

Transportation Policy Philosophy

The high school athletic department shall provide authorized transportation services for all student athletes and coaches of athletic teams to all away contests.

Transportation Policy Procedures

1. All high school athletic teams will be transported to away contests in the following order:
   —School Bus driven by certified bus driver.
   —Rental vehicle with no more than 15 passengers including the driver.
   —Private vehicle driven by coach or team member's parent.

2. The athletic director shall be responsible for making transportation arrangements for all athletic teams.
   a. The head coach shall submit to the athletic office all departure times for away contests one week prior to the beginning of the season.
   b. School buses shall be used in all possible cases. In the event that school buses are not available, rental vehicles, driven by the adult coach, will be used to transport team members.

3. In the event that a bus or rental vehicle is unavailable, consideration may be given to use of a private vehicle under the following restrictions:
   a. Automobile is driven by adult coach or the individual student athlete's parent. No team member is allowed to be transported by another's parents or another student athlete.
   b. In the event of an accident, the coach or the school district is covered by the district's liability insurance, but only after the coach's personal automobile liability insurance has been expended.

Figure 9-15
Sample Contract for Scheduling Athletic Contests

ILLINOIS HIGH SCHOOL ASSOCIATION

CONTRACT FOR INTERSCHOLASTIC ATHLETIC CONTESTS

PLEASE RETURN WITHIN 10 DAYS

This contract is drawn under the supervision of the Illinois High School Association and must be used in arranging contests between member schools.

This contract is made and subscribed to by the principals and coaches or athletic directors of **Glenbrook South High School** and the school(s) named below for the contest listed:

Mailing date :

Sport :
Level(s) :
Opponent :

Day :
Date :
Time :

Location : **Glenbrook South High School, 4000 W. Lake Ave. Glenview, IL 60025**
Entry Fee :
Comment :

Schools Include :

The By-laws of the Illinois High School Association are part of this contract. The suspension or termination of its membership in the IHSA by either of the contracted parties shall render this contract null and void.

______________	______________	**GLENBROOK SOUTH**
Principal	Athletic Director	School
______________	______________	______________
Principal	Athletic Director	School

**Reprinted with permission from the Illinois High School Association.*

Figure 9-16
Notice of Athletic Schedule Change

DATE ____________________

High School
City, State, ZIP
Telephone Number
Facsimile Number

Addition __________________________ Postponed __________________________

Cancellation __________________________ Rescheduled __________________________

Sport __________________________ Opponent __________________________

Level __________________________

Site __________________________ Change To __________________________

Date __________________________ Change To __________________________

Time __________________________ Change To __________________________

Notes:

Notify:

________Opposing School(s) ________Main Office

________Assignment Chair ________Principal

________Coaches ________Assoc. Principal

________Plant Manager ________Activity Director

________Athletic Director ________Athletic Trainer

________Asst. Athletic Director ________Athletic Secretary

________Ticket Manager ________Asst. Principal

Figure 9-17
Sample Athletic Participation Numbers Record

________ HIGH SCHOOL														
ATHLETE PARTICIPATION NUMBERS														
Sport	**66/67**	**67/68**	**68/69**	**69/70**	**70/71**	**71/72**	**72/73**	**73/74**	**74/75**	**76/77**	**77/78**	**78/79**	**79/80**	**80/81**
B-C. Country	25	36	38	44	42	38	27	20	26	28	29	24	27	55
G-C. Country													15	23
B- Football	170	172	160	170	184	188	178	146	150	170	185	150	162	141
B- Golf	48	49	51	57	61	53	34	45	55	40	36	34	41	37
G- Golf								8	19	17	15	15	17	13
B- Soccer							64	64	70	77	91	89	64	79
G- Swimming							38	45	53	50	58	66	68	56
G- Tennis							28	21	22	29	43	28	34	32
G- Volleyball							22	23	21	28	50	53	53	41
B- Basketball	75	61	61	60	67	78	74	78	76	67	68	60	58	56
G- Basketball							26	32	22	28	40	37	34	32
G- Gymnastics							18	22	32	26	26	32	29	28
B- Swimming	66	87	89	86	88	88	99	86	73	84	75	70	67	68
B- Wrestling	66	83	88	96	92	83	86	62	75	57	50	48	56	50
G- Badminton							24	29	26	33	30	36	25	33
B- Baseball	86	81	96	98	93	94	101	96	102	104	102	80	76	67
B- Gymnastics	42	46	47	68	71	81	85	61	59	46	50	32	16	17
G- Softball							26	40	37	38	52	57	50	40
B- Tennis	31	29	42	43	40	37	28	28	41	36	38	41	34	39
B- Track	56	68	84	86	86	67	82	69	73	79	67	79	91	110
B- Volleyball														
G- Track								28	26	44	50	58	54	64
G- Soccer														
TOTAL	655	712	756	808	824	807	1030	1006	1049	1081	1155	1083	1071	1081

Figure 9-17, continued
Sample Athletic Participation Numbers Record

______ HIGH SCHOOL													
ATHLETE PARTICIPATION NUMBERS													
Sport	**82/83**	**83/84**	**84/85**	**86/87**	**87/88**	**88/89**	**89/90**	**90/91**	**91/92**	**92/93**	**93/94**	**94/95**	**95/96**
B- C. Country	60	74	55	68	73	80	69	80	72	74	53	52	49
G- C. Country	21	22	18	26	20	20	20	30	29	31	43	30	51
B- Football	146	163	156	161	159	155	139	126	123	114	122	117	134
B- Golf	46	41	48	38	45	44	45	33	30	31	36	34	31
G- Golf	22	25	33	21	15	20	18	28	25	27	23	23	19
B- Soccer	89	100	119	97	95	97	106	92	94	90	94	93	87
G- Swimming	61	78	80	82	74	57	74	79	79	68	65	76	80
G- Tennis	24	29	47	33	27	31	31	30	31	46	43	42	28
G- Volleyball	40	40	62	49	49	50	60	52	51	53	54	49	59
B- Basketball	55	50	54	53	50	50	54	52	58	56	61	65	67
G- Basketball	30	41	39	38	39	37	41	49	50	47	50	57	50
G- Gymnastics	31	29	32	42	31	30	37	27	27	27	26	21	21
B- Swimming	72	75	71	83	76	65	45	59	59	57	58	42	39
B- Wrestling	58	65	78	76	61	75	75	55	76	58	67	32	32
G- Badminton	45	42	42	52	42	52	46	53	53	53	72	46	
B- Baseball	75	75	70	72	72	70	72	67	65	65	68	75	
B- Gymnastics	23	33	36	35	46	36	26	32	31	31	36	31	
G- Softball	45	48	44	52	51	49	48	51	53	42	44	44	
B- Tennis	40	44	40	37	36	35	39	34	38	35	36	44	
B- Track	109	97	120	131	122	127	118	134	135	133	105	92	
B- Volleyball						19	24	43	40	44	43	39	
G- Track	46	67	59	63	68	85	95	89	92	100	113	90	
G- Soccer		37	76	53	55	62	67	65	55	57	57	59	
TOTAL	1138	1275	1379	1362	1307	1346	1349	1360	1366	1339	1369	1253	

EVALUATING COMMERCIAL RECRUITERS

The reality of commercial recruiters has become especially sensitive within the past few years. Many young athletes and their families have fallen prey to the promises of varying commercial organizations across the country. A few of these organizations have provided worthwhile services; most have used empty promises to attract hundreds of dollars from dreamy-eyed athletes and their families.

In determining the merits of such organizations, you must first acknowledge their purposes. The primary purpose of any *commercial* organization is to make money. When the organization is more interested in making money, however, than in providing an honest and worthwhile service, it should be avoided. Consider the following points when evaluating the potential service of a commercial recruiter:

- Does the representative express continuing interest in the career and educational goals of the student athlete? Is he or she attempting to match the student's academic program and test scores with the appropriate university?
- Does he or she seek a match between the college and the athlete that is in the best interests of the athlete? Specifically, are the size of the school, geographical location, and proximity to cultural, educational, or recreational opportunities consistent with the student's needs?
- What does the organization promise for its fee? Will the representative be in frequent contact with the athlete and his or her family? Does the organization have a computer data base that consists of at least two thousand colleges and universities? These questions are especially important for the athlete who is unrecruited or only marginally recruited—and they are important for you, as you will often be asked for advice regarding the use of commercial recruiters. You don't want to be the one who advises families to invest hundreds of dollars in an organization that simply takes their money and runs. Meet with the representative(s) of any organization that seeks to work with athletes from your school.

When considering the appropriateness of such organizations, you must also take a realistic look at the extent to which coaches in their own schools help athletes with the college selection and recruitment processes. Some coaches are unwilling, others are unable to provide such assistance. Many high school coaches are intimidated by college coaches and are afraid to pick up the phone to initiate contact with them. Some high school coaches avoid the process entirely for fear of parental complaints or possible litigation if the family is dissatisfied with the end result.

Most coaches are unable to maintain the contacts with college coaches or to keep updated on the changing skill and performance levels of today's crop of college athletes. This lack of knowledge results in a reluctance to offer the kind of help that most families need when considering a sport in college—especially when the time and energy demands of the sport may interfere with the academic and career efforts of the athlete.

At this point, commercial organizations may, in fact, offer a valuable service. The athlete who is marginally recruited but who possesses talent or size potential may benefit from a computer base of two thousand colleges and universities. The more schools that have opportunities to evaluate his or her potential, the more likely the student is to find a school that meets his or her specifications.

In such a circumstance, perhaps the best way to handle the involvement of commercial organizations is to engage them in the preliminary process—assuming that parents are willing to foot the bill—and to have the coach, the counselor, and others in the school assist the student and his or her family with the actual selection process.

Be sure, however, to guard against using the services of commercial organizations to let your coaches off the hook. The good coach accepts responsibility not only for the fundamental skills and strategic needs of athletes but for their personal and educational development, during and *after* the season. Admittedly, this may be too time consuming for the coach who jumps from one sport to another throughout most of the school year. It may also be unreasonable for first- or second-year coaches who have yet to develop a network of college coaches or an understanding of the intricacies of sports participation in major universities.

In such instances, you must provide supervision for young coaches or help the overcommitted coach by developing a process that accommodates the needs of athletes and their parents who need help sorting through the significant number of issues that relate to playing a sport in college—not the least of which involve the athlete's talent levels and his or her educational needs. With an appropriate process in place, commercial organizations will be less influential than many of them currently are, and students and their families will receive the quality of advice and assistance they require and deserve.

ORGANIZING PEP AND VARSITY CLUBS

Pep clubs are the student equivalent of booster clubs. They provide opportunities for students to get involved in the school's athletic program, primarily to promote school spirit and to donate time and energy to organize projects and programs for the athletic department. Pep clubs consist mostly of cheerleaders, members of the pompon squad, and a coterie of students who enjoy the excitement of athletics and a sense of involvement with one or more of the school's teams.

Varsity clubs generally consist of varsity letter winners. Like all coalitions, varsity clubs are synergistic combinations of talent and energy. They possess a great deal of potential power, but that power requires proper supervision. With effective faculty and student leadership varsity clubs can help schools in a variety of ways—the specific responsibilities limited only by the imaginations of the school's athletic department and administration.

We have seen schools use varsity club members to:

- Supervise the grounds at athletic contests.
- Conduct fund-raising efforts within the school and community.
- Deliver speeches about drug abuse at elementary and junior high school assemblies.
- Accompany coaches and athletic directors to presentations at luncheons of community and fraternal organizations.
- Maintain crowd control at school assemblies.
- Represent the athletic department at student council and class executive board meetings.

- Write press releases for local media.
- Supervise the corridors during passing periods in school.

As important as the assistance they provide is, the knowledge and experience they gain from such responsibilities is equally valuable for them. The old dictum that the best way to learn something is to teach it is particularly true for successful athletes who are encouraged to use their influence with younger students. Even the most headstrong and self-willed middle linebacker learns to curb his attitude when he is expected to model consideration and self-control for the rest of the student body.

Use the form in Figure 9-18 to outline the requirements for membership in the varsity club and to promote a worthwhile experience for everyone. With the right coach running the program, the varsity club can become a valuable adjunct within the athletic department.

LET'S WRAP IT UP

This section has covered a lot of ground. Like the other sections in the book, it illustrates the scope of the athletic director's responsibilities. It proves once again that the job of athletic director is not for the weak-willed or burned-out coach looking for a "greased skid" into early retirement. Successful athletic directors must have the patience to push pencils, the discipline to develop workable schedules, the foresight to create comprehensive policies, the interpersonal skills to work with a wide range of divergent personalities, the knowledge and character strength to supervise and evaluate coaches, and the energy to do all this at once!

If just the thought of all this hasn't exhausted you, read on. The next section adds to the list! The athletic department's support staff is one of the most important elements in the program. It warrants a great deal of attention.

Figure 9-18
Varsity Club Membership Requirements

Varsity Club Policy Philosophy

The high school athletic department varsity club shall provide an opportunity for girls and boys who earn their varsity letter to participate in the high school varsity club.

Varsity Club Policy Procedures

1. Membership will be open to all high school girls and boys who earn a varsity letter.
2. The membership will vote yearly on four leadership positions within the club:
   a. President
   b. Vice-President
   c. Secretary
   d. Treasurer
3. The club will meet monthly with the membership to coordinate activities.
4. The club shall be responsible for the following:
   a. Accompaniment of coaches and athletic directors to presentations at luncheons or meetings of community organizations.
   b. Assistance with supervision of crowds during school assemblies.
   c. Assistance with press release information to the local media.
   d. Financial sponsorship and organization for the spring dance held at the high school.
   e. Assistance with developing sportsmanship programs for the high school.
   f. Assistance in developing school spirit programs for the high school.
   g. Working with the school sponsor to complete any other responsibilities assigned by the principal or athletic director.
5. The varsity club will coordinate an awards banquet to honor the outstanding varsity club members and their activities.
6. The varsity club, in conjunction with the sponsor, will develop rules and regulations that govern the activities of the club.
7. Each varsity club member will follow the athlete's creed at all times during their involvement as student-athletes at the high school.

SECTION TEN

Working with the Support Staff

First, a quick story:

Frankie had been the equipment manager of a local high school for more years than any of us could remember. He was a fixture in the locker room, as familiar to every athlete as the school's fight song and the inspirational mottoes on the walls—mottoes that Frankie himself had stenciled above doorways and on empty walls. Frankie's primary job was to organize and distribute PE and athletic equipment, but he also inventoried stock, swept the floors, painted lockers, and not only maintained discipline in the locker room but also, to the surprise of many parents in the community, helped raise their children by promoting a value system that would have been the envy of Billy Graham.

Many of the school's counselors had come to depend on Frankie to identify students with subtle problems; teachers depended on him for occasional interventions with misbehaving students. The deans relied on him more than they knew. Discipline problems in the PE area that might have consumed hours of their time were handled by Frankie well before they required administrative attention. Frankie's understanding of adolescent behavior derived not from textbooks but from day-to-day contact with teenagers and his lifelong commitment to them.

We bumped into him in a local restaurant one afternoon during a meeting to discuss the particulars of this book. As he left, we both smiled, remembering the time a group of students in Frankie's school decided to slam dance to the music concluding their Homecoming pep rally. The story, told by a teacher in the school, indicates that bodies were colliding and ricocheting all over the gym floor.

One of the school's assistant principals was standing on the periphery of the growing chaos demanding, then beseeching, that the students stop. No one was paying attention to him, and the dancing became increasingly violent. Suddenly Frankie emerged from a corner of the gym and walked into the middle of what can be described only as a tangle of bodies. Stepping between students, pushing them in opposite directions, each time thanking them for their cooperation, Frankie stopped the dancing almost as quickly as it had started.

The students simply smiled at Frankie, shouted "See you tomorrow," and left the gym. No one was upset or hurt, least of all the assistant principal, who used the story for years afterward to illustrate the unique relationships support personnel enjoy with the student body and the valuable contributions they make within the total school program.

He realized, as do most good administrators, that every adult in the school contributes in some way to the education of young people. Most of us discovered a long time ago that values and appropriate behavior are more easily learned than taught. The more of us who teach them, therefore, the more likely that students will learn the lessons we feel are so valuable for them.

The family concept that prevails in successful athletic programs embraces everyone in the department, including equipment managers, maintenance personnel, custodians, security personnel, locker room attendants, and groundskeepers. Whether directly or indirectly involved with students, the functions each performs are essential to the successful operation of the program. Such functions also involve taking tickets, maintaining crowd control, announcing contests, and—perhaps most important—providing secretarial services.

Effective athletic directors establish trusting relationships immediately with all support personnel, and establish pipelines with teachers who readily volunteer to help with athletic contests. They, too, are support personnel. Such a relationship need not be warm and personal, but custodians, maintenance personnel, and others must understand by your treatment of them that they are valued and competent members of the department, that their responsibilities are important, and that their input and decision making are essential to the success of the program.

"We're all in this together" is much more than a catch phrase when we consider the dimensions of the responsibility facing us. Consider the fact that some 20 percent of American children live in poverty. Consider as well that, when compared with the top 20 percent of Japan's students, American students perform better on a variety of achievement tests, but that the bottom 20 percent score significantly worse than Japan's bottom 20 percent. The gap in this country separating the most advantaged from the least advantaged seems to be widening. The social context in which many American schools are expected to thrive is characterized by poverty, hostility, and crime.

Schools must combat these issues by closing ranks and using the wide variety of interpersonal skills and insights of everyone in the program, including the knowledge and experience of the support staff within the athletic department. Experienced athletic directors realize that student discipline and values education are outside the official purview of most support personnel; the "Frankies" of this world, however, are invaluable staff members who bring a broad band of "support" to the responsibilities and mutual caring that must characterize every school's athletic family.

Most of them may not have a significant impact on the lives of students, but all of them must perceive their jobs as essential in the department. You and the school's coaches accomplish that when you work closely with support personnel and acknowledge the valuable jobs they perform within the department. Periodic recognition goes a long way toward promoting a sense of pride in workers and a willingness to go the extra mile to do high-quality work.

Figure 10-1 provides a "Welcome Back" memo to distribute to all coaches and support personnel early in the school year. It promotes a family concept and recognizes that teamwork is essential within the department to guarantee a successful program. A memo is, of course, only one way to promote teamwork, but it represents a good start, and it creates an attitude within the department that acknowledges and rewards mutual support.

THE PRIMARY TASKS OF SUPPORT PERSONNEL

The athletic department's support personnel have a primary responsibility for maintenance of the facilities and assistance with the delivery of services within the department. You'll find here a few reproducibles designed to make your job easier as you coordinate their specific responsibilities. The materials and explanations in this section acknowledge the tasks of all support personnel, including teacher helpers, officials, and maintenance and security personnel.

MAINTENANCE PERSONNEL

Because the school's maintenance personnel are supervised outside the athletic department, the athletic director and coaches sometimes have awkward relations with them—particularly when practice facilities require maintenance or repair within a specified time. You must develop positive relations with them and seek to promote their input and involvement in operation of the athletic program. Their involvement results from an understanding and acceptance of the demands of their jobs, as well as an awareness that you and your staff are available to them to discuss specific requests. Such discussions should identify, and offer solutions to, problems that may interfere with the completion of the request, and promote the kind of ongoing dialogue that maintains a sense of teamwork.

Work Requests

The form in Figure 10-2 is a routine request for work to be done by the maintenance department. Figure 10-3 is a sample completed form. Often, coaches and others fail to receive information regarding one or more problems that may be interfering with the completion of a work request. If maintenance personnel understand the reasons for the request, they are quicker to help resolve them. Discuss the use of such a form with the head of the maintenance department. Once the form is accepted within his or her department, it will avoid the kinds of misunderstandings that inevitably result from inadequate information.

Figure 10-1
"Welcome Back" Memo

Athletic Department

To: Athletic Department Family

From: Athletic Director

Date:

WELCOME BACK!!

Let me take this opportunity to welcome each of you back for another highly successful school year. I hope you had a relaxing, restful, and enjoyable summer vacation—no matter how long it lasted! Getting back into the swing of things is always a little difficult, but it's made considerably easier when we find ourselves returning to one of the best athletic departments in the state. Be sure to look around you during these first few weeks back in order to appreciate the magnificent job the grounds crew (use names, if possible) did on the practice and game fields, the maintenance personnel (again, use names) did on the gyms and practice rooms, and everyone did to brighten up the halls and classrooms for the teachers and students.

I want to personally thank everyone who prepared the way for another successful school year. Nothing much of value could happen around here without the help of (use names of personnel) to establish the tone for the rest of us. It's gratifying to know that *everyone* in this department is so competent in the performance of his or her job. I also appreciate our traditional willingness to work together and to provide the mutual help each of us needs to do as a good job. Teamwork is important everywhere in the building, but the athletic department is the most logical place to find it, and we have it in abundance!

I'd like to invite all of you to stop by the athletic department office for some coffee cake and a beverage (time and date) for an official but informal welcome back. That might also be a good time for us to talk a little bit about some upcoming projects that may require a little effort from all of us.

Again, welcome back and remember that my door is always open. We're all in this together, and I want to work closely with each of you. I wish each of you a rewarding, enjoyable, and successful school year.

(Signature)

Figure 10-2
Athletic Maintenance Request

Date: ______________________ **Day:** M T W TH F S S

Area Desired: ______________________ **Request By:** ______________________

Maintenance Request: ____

____

____

____

Comments: ____

____

____

Authorizing Signatures:

______________________ ______________________

Faculty Sponsor **Athletic Director**

Diagram of Request

Copy to Equipment Manager: __________ **Date Completed:** __________

Figure 10-3
Sample Completed Athletic Maintenance Request

Date: ______________________ **Day:** M T W TH F S S

Area Desired: Main Gymnasium

Request By: Badminton Coach

Maintenance Request: The lights above courts 1, 5, 6, and 8 need to be replaced.

Comments: Thank you. High school is hosting a large tournament and needs to have all lights in working order.

Authorizing Signatures:

Badminton Coach — **Faculty Sponsor**

Athletic Director — **Athletic Director**

Diagram of Request

1	2	3	4
5	6	7	8

Copy to Equipment Manager: (date) **Date Completed:** ______________

Sometimes it's also a good idea to submit a general memo outlining the specifics of a particular job to someone in maintenance. Figure 10-4 provides a sample. Notice that the athletic director also asks to be kept informed of the status of the request. Again, this is an important part of the process. Effective two-way communication avoids a whole range of potential misunderstandings.

Checklists

Checklists like the one in Figure 10-5 detail the maintenance needs of areas of the building and serve as reminders for coaches, students, and maintenance personnel. The checklist in Figure 10-5 can be distributed to head swimming coaches to provide a reference to the maintenance needs around the pool, deck, and locker rooms. The coach can then share the list with assistant coaches and athletes in order to help maintain the area.

Ask the head coaches in other sports, perhaps in conjunction with maintenance personnel, to develop similar lists for their areas, using the swimming checklist as a model. The process gives coaches ownership of the checklist and encourages them to work collaboratively with maintenance personnel to determine what is needed to maintain the area.

The completed checklists can be shared with the maintenance department to clarify the expectations of the athletic department. Meet with the head of the maintenance department to ensure understanding between the two departments. Remember—and be sure your coaches remember—that your goal is to obtain the willingness of maintenance personnel to go the extra yard in assuring well-maintained facilities and equipment.

If you recognize the importance of proper maintenance and treat maintenance personnel with the respect they deserve, you create the kind of synergy within the athletic department that assures cooperation and the timely repair and maintenance of facilities and equipment. When you share checklists with the head of maintenance, indicate that you already have given them to coaches to request their assistance, and to help make the job easier for custodians and maintenance personnel.

CROWD CONTROL

A well-coordinated crowd control program is essential if the athletic department expects to provide an entertaining, exciting, and safe environment for students and parents during athletic contests. Exciting and victorious teams promote fan support and encourage attendance at athletic contests. Increased gang activity in many communities, overzealous fans, and smuggled alcohol and drugs can cause disruptive and sometimes violent behavior in the stands and surrounding areas. Schools must be especially vigilant, therefore, to assure a wholesome and safe environment for everyone in attendance. Remember that many athletic programs are dependent on the revenue derived from contests, and as athletic director, *you* must do all in your power to guarantee that safe, wholesome environment.

Figure 10-4
Sample Maintenance Memo

Athletic Department

TO: Maintenance and Grounds Crew

FROM: Athletic Director

RE: Grounds assistance for opening of fall season

DATE:

The following work details need to be completed for the opening of soccer practice on ___(date)___:

1. All goals repaired and assembled with nets.
2. Three game fields lined.
3. Mini field 40 × 40 lined with penalty boxes.
4. Practice Grid Area (East of mini 40 × 40 field and west of varsity field)
5. Two goals placed in right field area of freshman baseball field.

The soccer tournament will be played on August 31, September 1, 2, and 4. Two bleachers need to be set up at each of the west and east fields. This is the same arrangement as last year. Team benches, tables, and chairs will be needed at each field.

Please keep me informed of the status of this request and notify me if there is a problem with any of the above requests.

Thank you in advance.

cc: Maintenance Supervisor

Figure 10-5
Pool Cleanliness Checklist

Date ______________________

Acceptable	Not Acceptable	
_______	_______	Hallway entrance to natatorium lobby
_______	_______	Hallway stairs to Girls locker room
_______	_______	Hallway stairs to Boys locker room
_______	_______	Girls locker room floor (includes towel pickup, floor clean of debris, drains clean of debris, water fountain clean, mirrors clean, waste baskets empty)
_______	_______	Boys locker room floor (includes towel pickup, floor clean of debris, drains clean of debris, water fountain clean, mirrors clean, waste baskets empty)
_______	_______	Girls restroom facilities (sanitary disposal cleaned daily, ample toilet paper, toilet disinfected and cleaned daily, floor area clean of debris)
_______	_______	Boys restroom facilities (urinals and toilets disinfected and cleaned daily, floor area clean of debris)
_______	_______	Girls shower area (drains clean of debris, towels picked up, tile area free of debris
_______	_______	Boys shower area (drains clean of debris, towels picked up, tile area free of debris
_______	_______	North and south spectator stands (swept, free of debris or towels, etc.)
_______	_______	Pool deck (free of debris, drains cleaned, area clean and swept around storage area and under team benches, offices cleaned and trash emptied
_______	_______	Pool (vacuumed, tiles around sides scrubbed, diving boards scrubbed)
_______	_______	Pool weight room (vacuumed, general pickup of debris, towels, etc.)

Several people are involved in a good crowd control program. Faculty members assigned to circulate throughout the stands can be among the most effective deterrents to student misbehavior. To do the job well, persons responsible for crowd control must recognize three distinct tasks, all of which are outlined in the reproducible in Figure 10-6:

Before the Contest. The person responsible for coordinating the activities of faculty volunteers must assure that seating areas for home as well as visiting fans have been appropriately designated. This is not a problem in most schools. Traditional rivalries—the kind most likely to introduce problems—are usually held in gymnasiums or stadiums familiar to everyone in attendance.

Problems arise, however, when students from a school decide to sit in their opponents' stands and sing the praises of the home team. That's why faculty members must circulate in both stands and remain in their assigned areas before, during, and after the contest.

During the Contest. Teachers must be reminded periodically of how to respond to misbehavior; outline and discuss faculty relationships with students. Inappropriate or excessive adult reactions to relatively harmless misbehavior can provoke responses from students that complicate a simple problem. Figure 10-6 addresses this issue, but only briefly. The topic is so important that committee or inservice activities should be devoted to it early in the school year.

After the Contest. Persons responsible for crowd control should refer chronic misbehavior to the appropriate administrator. Faculty members also should not feel responsible for removing students from a contest, or for contacting the police when misbehavior becomes extreme. Teachers without proper administrative training risk litigation for themselves and the school district if they mishandle a dangerous or potentially dangerous situation.

They also risk litigation by wandering from their assigned areas. They should be expected, therefore, to remain in them before, during, and after each contest. *After* the contest is particularly important, given the fact that most incidents occur outside the building or in the parking lot—especially after heated rivalries or close contests.

A Few Additional Considerations

Effective crowd control involves a few additional considerations. The following should be addressed before, during, and after contests at home:

Student knowledge of expectations. Sometime during the pep rally that kicks off the fall season, discuss with the entire student body appropriate behavior at athletic contests. You might also distribute an informative handout like the one in Figure 10-7. It discusses the kinds of behaviors expected of students, as well as of coaches and officials. It is important for all participants to respect one another, and to recognize that winning is subordinate to the need to compete with dignity, and with personal and school pride.

Displays of good sportsmanship are sure signs of maturity and respect. A strong desire to win requires a clear head and a steady hand. Neither is possible without generous doses of self-control—the kind that is developed by teenagers when adults like you and me expect nothing but their best behavior during school activities.

- **Cheerleader , pompon squad, and pep band behavior.** As representatives of the school, cheerleaders and other members of the pep squad must also be on their best behavior. Meet periodically with the cheerleader and pompon sponsors to assure that cheerleaders and others perform at appropriate times, avoid provocative cheers and songs, and promote positive feelings throughout the contest. A written reminder, or a brochure like the Publication of Expectations in Figure 6-22, p. 197, can also be shared with cheerleaders, the pompon squad, and the pep band early in the school year.
- **Provide constant reminders.** Highly visible reminders of such behavior sustain a focus for students, particularly when the reminders also identify consequences for misbehavior. Expulsion from a contest and possible future discipline, for example, can be effective deterrents to the use of alcohol, drugs, and overt misbehavior. Place posters conspicuously in gymnasiums, wrestling rooms, and game fields to remind students of the importance of appropriate behavior as well as the consequences of violations.
- **Supervise the parking area.** Proper supervision in parking areas, particularly after contests, assures an orderly emptying of the lot and avoids potentially serious problems. Student and parent behavior is especially good when local police officers provide such supervision. Police usually know many of the students and parents, and can be friendly, yet firm, as they direct an orderly flow of traffic from the lot. In addition, their mere presence often prevents conflicts. Figure 10-8 provides a memo to the school's security department, requesting police supervision.
- **Assure a wholesome environment.** Take a page out of Disney World's maintenance manual to promote cleanliness and appropriate behavior from visitors to the school. Attractive concession stands and well-maintained grounds are constant reminders to fans to use trash receptacles and to respect the people and property around them.
- **Anticipate problems.** The familiar ounce of prevention also avoids a whole wagon load of headaches for ADs. If you live in a community populated by citizens who spend more time talking to their lawyers than to their next-door neighbors, you're well advised to anticipate as many problems as possible. Be sure, for example, to put officials in locker rooms that are separated from players' and coaches' areas, and to provide an escort for them if circumstances require.

Be sure that the visiting school has provided adequate supervision for its students and parents. Figure 10-9 provides a form that you or the faculty person responsible for supervision during athletic contests can mail to the visiting school to get the names of such supervisors. Such a form assures the visiting school's awareness of the need to help, and having the names of visiting faculty promotes an immediate working relationship with them.

One of the best ways to anticipate problems is to keep everyone busy. If trouble is to develop, it occurs most often in the parking lot or on the grounds of the school building after the contest. It can also occur between the halves of a heated contest. A good way to avoid such troubles is to provide an entertaining and engaging half-time program and to assure that crowd control personnel are especially vigilant during this time.

Figure 10-6
Crowd Control Policy Statement

Any high school having an interscholastic athletic program, before the start of the school, should have a well-planned crowd control program. Personnel who should be included in administering this plan are: administrators, athletic director, coaches, supervisor of cheerleaders, band director, security personnel, the game announcer, and the staff who are working crowd control and tickets.

If the athletic program is to be successfully administered, the athletic director must be concerned with the welfare of the fans and the student body.

Crowd Control

Before the Contest

1. Make sure that the specific seating arrangements are designated for Home team and for Visitors.
2. Make sure that crowd control workers arrive 30 minutes before the contest is scheduled to start. Please obtain crowd control name tags so that you are identified to fans who attend the contest.
3. Crowd control workers are to remain in designated sections of the student and staff seating areas. They are not to congregate with other adults or staff members who are attending the contest.

During the Contest

1. When approaching a problem student or adult, please discuss the problem carefully and ask the individuals to refrain from continuing the inappropriate behavior. If the student or adult refuses and continues the poor behavior, please alert the administrator on duty or the security personnel to have the individual removed from the premises.
2. During half-time, please help security prevent fans from getting on the field or court area, around the players' bench area, or directly into the areas of competition.

After the Contest

Planning for after the contest is probably the most important of the three stages in crowd control. Most incidents occur after the game, when the fans are on their way out of the building or stadium.

1. At the end of the competition, please help security prevent fans from getting on the field or court area, around the player's bench area, or directly into the areas of competition.
2. Assist the security personnel in the orderly exit of all visiting and home team fans.
3. Remain on duty until 15 minutes after the contest is completed, or the administrator on duty informs you that it is acceptable to leave.

Printed with permission from the National Interscholastic Athletic Administrators Association Handbook.

Figure 10-7
Sport a Winning Attitude

The Participant

1. Lives clean and plays hard. Plays for the love of the game.
2. Wins without boasting, loses without excuses, and never quits.
3. Respects officials and accepts their decisions without question.
4. Never forgets that he or she represents the school.

The Coach

1. Inspires in his or her athletes a love for the game and the desire to win.
2. Teaches them that it is better to lose fairly than to win unfairly.
3. Leads players and spectators to respect officials by setting a good example.
4. Is the type of person he or she wants the athletes to be.

The Official

1. Knows the rules.
2. Is fair and firm in all decisions. Calls them as he or she sees them.
3. Treats players and coaches courteously and demands the same treatment.
4. Knows the game is for the athletes, and lets them have the spotlight.

Printed with permission from the Illinois High School Association's Sportsmanship Mission Statement.

Figure 10-8
Request for Police Supervision

Athletic Department

TO: School Security

FROM: Athletic Director

RE: Basketball Game/Dance

DATE:

Please be advised that two weeks from today, our high school will host the final conference basketball game. Upon completion of this game we will move all spectators out of the main gymnasium for readmittance to the dance, which will be held in the field house.

The athletic department will need one city police car in the parking lot to aid school security. We will also need one city uniformed officer to assist the two school security officers at the game and dance. All workers are needed at 6:00 P.M. until midnight. Please find the Assistant Principal in charge of Student Activities upon your arrival to see where he needs assistance.

Thank you in advance for your assistance.

cc: Assistant Principal—Student Activities
Assistant Principal—Dean of Students

Figure 10-9
Security Pass List

Contest ____________________ vs. ____________________

Date____________________

Please list the supervisors who will be in attendance at the above contest. Send or fax this list prior to the contest so that the individuals will be admitted free to the game.

We appreciate any security assistance you can provide our school.

Signed,

Athletic Director

- - - - - - - - - - - - - - - PASS LIST - - - - - - - - - - - - - - -

Principal ____________________

Asst. Principal ____________________

Asst. Principal ____________________

Dean of Students ____________________

School Security ____________________

____

____

Head Coach ____________________

Asst. Coach ____________________

Asst. Coach ____________________

Prior to contests involving traditional rivalries—particularly if both schools are vying for a championship or if one or both of the schools has unusually disruptive students—meet with crowd control personnel to discuss the school's "game plan" for maintaining order. A brief meeting for breakfast or at the end of the school day is sufficient to impress on supervisors the need to direct students to their own stands, watch them carefully during half-time activities, and patrol the grounds and parking lot after the contest.

Finally, organize a room for emergencies. Be sure it contains some kind of first-aid treatment for injuries. Also use it to notify parents or appropriate community agencies of fighting, intoxication, or criminal behavior. Inform everyone responsible for crowd control of the location and use of the room. In addition, ask that the appropriate administrator be notified each time the room is used.

THE ANNOUNCER AND CROWD CONTROL

If the contest involves an announcer, he or she is as important to crowd control as anyone circulating among the fans. A good announcer sets the tone for the kinds of behaviors expected of fans before, during, and after the contest. You can provide the following things to enable announcers to do a good job:

- **A microphone in good working order.** This item may sound obvious, but, in the heat of preparation for the contest, many schools forget to check the condition of audio equipment. Assign someone on the maintenance staff the responsibility of checking the microphone and the PA system prior to each contest.
- **Provide rosters and announcements.** Either encourage the announcer to meet with the coaches before the contest to secure team rosters or have someone get them. Also provide all announcements to be read before or during the contest, such as the one in Figure 10-10. In addition, special announcements may have to be made—the death of someone important to the school and community, or significant national or local events occurring at the time of the contest.
- **Provide information about half-time activities.** Provide descriptions of half-time activities, including a time schedule, and all announcements to be made during the program. If the announcer is expected to narrate the program, provide a script that is carefully coordinated with the program's activities. Figure 10-11 provides a sample time schedule. A poorly coordinated half-time program may provoke more disruptive behavior than cheering and applause.

The announcer must be professional and impartial while announcing contests. Traditional rivalries are already bubbling with potential trouble, and you don't need an announcer who adds heat to the fire. Share the Policy Statement in Figure 10-12 with your announcer(s) early in the school year to assure a professional approach to announcing contests.

Figure 10-10
Pregame Announcements

Athletic Department

THIS ANNOUNCEMENT SHOULD BE READ BEFORE THE SOPHOMORE OR JUNIOR VARSITY GAMES AND AGAIN BEFORE THE VARSITY GAME

ON BEHALF OF THE ADMINISTRATION, FACULTY, STAFF, AND STUDENTS OF OUR HIGH SCHOOL, WE WELCOME YOU AS OUR GUESTS TO THIS INTERSCHOLASTIC CONTEST.

(NAME OF SCHOOL) HIGH SCHOOL AND (NAME OF OPPOSING SCHOOL) ARE PLAYING THIS GAME THROUGH AN AGREEMENT ENTERED INTO BY BOTH SCHOOLS. THE SCHOOLS ARE MEMBERS OF AND HAVE AGREED TO ABIDE BY THE CONSTITUTION AND BYLAWS OF THE ILLINOIS HIGH SCHOOL ASSOCIATION AND THE CENTRAL SUBURBAN LEAGUE TO INSURE THE HIGHEST POSSIBLE STANDARDS OF CONDUCT IN THEIR INTERSCHOLASTIC PROGRAMS.

THE OFFICIALS FOR THIS CONTEST HAVE BEEN ASSIGNED THROUGH APPROVAL BY BOTH SCHOOLS. OFFICIALS FOR TODAY ARE:

____

____

____

WE ASK THAT EVERYONE PRESENT DEMONSTRATE AN ATTITUDE OF GOOD SPORTSMANSHIP THROUGHOUT THE CONTEST, NO MATTER WHAT PERSONAL FEELINGS OF LOYALTY THEY MAY HAVE TOWARD ONE TEAM OR THE OTHER. OBSCENE CHEERS, THE THROWING OF OBJECTS, AND VERBAL INDIGNITIES DIRECTED TOWARD ATHLETES, COACHES, OR OFFICIALS HAVE NO PLACE IN HIGH SCHOOL ATHLETICS. ANY SPECTATOR NOT DISPLAYING APPROPRIATE CONDUCT WILL BE ASKED TO LEAVE THE GAME. YOUR COOPERATION IS EXPECTED AND APPRECIATED.

Read before the Varsity Game:

In a few minutes we will have the starting line-up for each team. At this time we ask that you please rise for the playing of our National Anthem.

Reprinted with permission from the Illinois High School Association.

Figure 10-11
Sample Time Schedule

Athletic Department

Contest________________ **vs.** ________________ **Date** ________________

Time line

5:25 P.M.	Warm-up clock started
5:45 P.M.	Clear court
5:50 P.M.	Announcements
5:52 P.M.	National Anthem
5:55 P.M.	Introduction of players/officials/coaches
6:00 P.M.	Sophomore game
7:00 P.M.	Warm-up clock started
(Or conclusion of game 1)	
7:20 P.M.	Clear court/Announcements
7:22 P.M.	National Anthem
7:25 P.M.	Introduction of players/officials/coaches
7:30 P.M.	Varsity game
Half-time	Ask crowd to remain in stands for pompon and band performance.
7:50 P.M.	Second half begins
End of Game	Announcer remains on microphone until crowd has dispersed: 1. Statistics 2. Assistance with crowd management

Figure 10-12
Policy Statement for Announcers

Any high school having an interscholastic athletic program, before the start of the school, should have a well-planned crowd control program. Personnel who should be included in administering this plan are: administrators, athletic director, coaches, supervisor of cheerleaders, band director, security personnel, the game announcer, and the staff who are working crowd control and tickets.

If the athletic program is to be successfully administered, the athletic director must be concerned with the welfare of the fans and the student body.

Announcer

Before the Contest

1. Please arrive 30 minutes before contest is scheduled to start. Please obtain name tag so that you are identifiable to fans who attend the contest.
2. Obtain microphone from administrator on duty and check if PA is in working order. If a problem arises, please check with a maintenance staff member for assistance.
3. Be sure you have home and visiting team rosters, PA announcements, etc.

During the Contest

1. Be sure you are informed about half-time program.
2. During half-time, please help security by announcing that fans must refrain from getting on the field or court area, around the players' bench area, or directly into the areas of competition.

After the Contest

Planning for after the contest is probably the most important of the three stages in crowd control. Most incidents and encounters occur after the game, when the fans are on their way out of the building or stadium.

1. At the end of the competition, please help security prevent fans from getting on the field or court area, around the player's bench area, or directly into the areas of competition by using the PA system.
2. Assist the security personnel in the orderly exit of all visiting and home team fans by giving directions for leaving the area and reminding them to drive safely.
3. Remain on duty until 15 minutes after the contest is completed, or the administrator on duty informs you that it is acceptable to leave.

Additional Information

1. Be impartial. Do not show favoritism to particular teams or players.
2. Use proper language at all times.
3. Be enthusiastic, but keep calm at all times.
4. Do not anticipate (out loud) plays, first downs, timeouts, touchdowns, etc.
5. Try to be aware of what is going on in the entire stadium/gymnasium so that directions can be given calmly in an emergency. Serious situations can be avoided if the announcer will caution the crowd against coming down to the field/floor, throwing things, or causing other disturbances.
6. Let no one use the microphone besides the announcer. The announcer is responsible for any remarks made into the microphone.
7. Never criticize officials' decisions—directly or indirectly.
8. Read the copy of the rules and regulations governing this contest.

Adapted and printed with permission from the National Interscholastic Athletic Administrators Association Handbook.

TICKET SELLERS/TAKERS AND CROWD CONTROL

Ticket sellers and ticket takers are generally the first people fans see when they arrive at a school athletic contest. For this reason, they should always be adults and, preferably, friendly and well-liked members of the faculty. Such persons make a good initial impression on parents and other members of the community, and they generally command the respect of students, especially those who tend to bend the rules a bit.

Because they have a twofold responsibility—taking tickets and controlling the crowd—they must be constantly alert to any signs of trouble, then either respond personally or refer the situation to the administrator on duty. Ticket sellers should be instructed to continue selling tickets well into the final quarter of any athletic contest to prevent fans from loitering outside the gate, hoping to be admitted free at the start of the second half.

If the contest is heated and students from both schools are permitted to wait outside the gate, problems can occur at any time. Encourage ticket sellers to supervise the entrance to the school and refer suspicious activities to another person responsible for crowd control—probably the administrator on duty. It's a good idea to equip ticket sellers with walkie-talkies to permit them to sell tickets while they supervise the gate. (Walkie-talkies are valuable aids to everyone in crowd control. If possible, supply everyone with a walkie-talkie in order to promote immediate communication with one another and with the administrator on duty. The more quickly everyone responds to potential problems, the less likely they are to become significant.)

Share the Policy Statement in Figure 10-13 with ticket takers early in the school year, or as soon as they are assigned the task. As with all staff responsible for crowd control, they should be in-serviced regarding their responses to student or adult misbehavior during contests. Inappropriate responses to students or adults can transform a relatively simple situation into a major issue involving lawyers, the superintendent of schools, and a host of others who would much prefer being somewhere else.

Finally, provide a Ticket Sales Report Form like the one in Figure 10-14 to a teacher identified as the Ticket Supervisor. Notice that the form distinguishes between adult and student tickets sold, and tallies the total receipts for the day or night. You should write the number at the beginning of each roll on the form before giving the form to the Ticket Supervisor, then simply ask him or her to write in the number of the last ticket sold in each roll. Such a procedure avoids misunderstandings.

WORKING WITH OFFICIALS FOR CONTESTS

First and foremost, officials must be properly licensed. Many states apply sanctions to schools that hire unqualified persons to officiate contests. This is perfectly understandable. Although such persons may be less expensive and more immediately available than qualified officials, they generally are less familiar with the rules of the game and less able to handle situations that can occur during the heat of battle.

Young athletes can experience a range of unnecessary injuries because of poorly officiated contests. Not only do such injuries interfere with the athlete's ability to perform in future contests, but they open the door to lawsuits involving sums of money that stagger the imagination. Always be careful, therefore, to hire only qualified officials and to see that both schools agree on them.

When contracting with officials, assure the following:

- Parking and comfortable accommodations should be provided to each team of officials for every contest during the year.
- Officials should be notified of unusual circumstances, such as lengthened halftimes, playing conditions, pregame activities, or the anticipated intensity of the contest.
- Neither school can be allowed to object to any aspect of officiating or to seek to change an official's decisions once the contest begins.
- Neither team is permitted to demonstrate against an official's decision by shouting or leaving the contest.
- Coaches, however, will have the opportunity after each contest to evaluate officials in order to influence hiring decisions in the future. Use the Official's Evaluation in Figure 10-15.
- Coaches also will have a process available to them to notify the athletic director of situations regarding officials that require immediate attention. The Special Report form in Figure 10-16 will be helpful.

The hiring and evaluating of officials usually is governed by procedures developed and regulated by your school's state association. Be sure to get a copy of such procedures and policy statements to assure compliance with state mandates. Violations, no matter how inadvertent, usually result in sanctions and will threaten your security as an athletic administrator.

A GOOD SECRETARY

A good secretary runs an office and can answer questions about the organization faster than anyone in the executive suite; after all, good secretaries do a great deal of the work. They not only record the activities in the athletic department or type memos and letters, but they make decisions about processes and procedures and have access to significant and, sometimes, sensitive information.

A good secretary is an ally in the day-to-day struggle to run the athletic department effectively and efficiently. For the athletic director, the secretary is a buffer from all that can be handled by someone else; a welcome reminder about appointments and tasks to be completed, some of which are personal; a trusted recipient of confidential information; an organizer, a paragon of patience with a ready smile; a safety net as you walk your job's several tightropes; and a source of both professional and moral support.

The secretary has diverse responsibilities, touches several lives each day, and is the glue that holds the department together—the first face people see when they visit your office and the last face you see when you leave it. Hiring a person to handle such prodigious responsibilities is no easy task. It should be handled carefully. The job description in Figure 10-17 will provide a starting point.

Figure 10-13
Policy Statement for Ticket Takers

Any high school having an interscholastic athletic program, before the start of the school, should have a well-planned crowd control program. Personnel who should be included in administering this plan are: administrators, athletic director, coaches, supervisor of cheerleaders, band director, security personnel, the game announcer, and the staff who are working crowd control and tickets.

If the athletic program is to be successfully administered, the athletic director must be concerned with the welfare of the fans and the student body.

Ticket Takers

Before the Contest

1. Make sure that the signs indicating specific seating arrangements are designated for Home team and visitors.
2. Arrive 45 minutes before the contest is scheduled to start. Please obtain school name tags so that you are identified to fans who attend the contest.
3. Ticket workers are to remain in designated sections of the stadium/gymnasium. They are not to leave area or money/tickets unattended at any time.

During the Contest

1. If there is a problem student or adult, please discuss the problem carefully and ask the individuals to refrain from continuing the inappropriate behavior. If the student or adult refuses and continues the poor behavior, please alert the administrator on duty or the security personnel to have the individual removed form the premises.
2. Tickets should be sold throughout the beginning of the fourth quarter to discourage individuals from loitering outside the gate, hoping to be admitted free during the last half of the contest.

After the Contest (beginning of fourth quarter)

Planning for after the contest is probably the most important of the three stages in crowd control. Most incidents and encounters occur after the game, when the fans are on their way out of the building or stadium.

1. At the beginning of the fourth quarter, please assist maintenance by moving chairs and tables out of the way of the entrance to speed exit of teams, officials, and spectators.
2. Assist the managers by giving them the final money collected from the contest.
3. Remain on duty until 15 minutes after the contest is completed, or the administrator on duty informs you that it is acceptable to leave.

Adapted and printed with permission from the National Interscholastic Athletic Administrators Association Handbook.

Figure 10-14
Ticket Sales Report Form

Contest ______________________ Date ______________________

Beginning Balance $ ____________

First ticket number ________ Last ticket number __________

Number of adult tickets sold	________	@	________	$	________
Number of student tickets sold	________	@	________	$	________
Number of passes sold	________	@	________	$	________
Number of family passes allowed entrance	________				
Number of student passes allowed entrance	________				
	________	=	*Total # Attendance*		*$ Total Cash Received*

____

Less Balance ________

Total Deposit ________

- -

Bookstore Deposit

________ Change

________ Currency

________ Checks

________ Total Deposit

______________________ ______________________

Ticket Manager (Signature) Date Deposited

Figure 10-15
Official's Evaluation

This form is to be signed and filled out by coaching staff for the purpose of official's performance evaluation.

Sport ______________________ Official's Name ______________________

Date of Contest Evaluation

Please rate the above officials on the below scale:

1	Excellent
2	Above Average/Acceptable
3	Average/Needs Improvement
4	Below Average/Unacceptable/Needs Improvement
5	Poor/Unacceptable

_____ Knowledge of Rules

_____ Application of rules during contest

_____ Treats players, coaches, and other officials fairly

_____ Maintains confidence, poise, and dignity during contest

_____ Maintains integrity and abides by rules

_____ Displays sportsmanship on and off court/field

_____ Arrives to contest on time and prepared to perform

Subjective Evaluation: ____

____

____

____

____

Please use back of page if necessary

Date ______________________ Signature ______________________

School ______________________ Address ______________________

Figure 10-16
Special Report Regarding Contest Official's Performance

(This form is to be used if officials fail to perform their responsibilities in accordance with rules and guidelines submitted by the National Federation and the High School Association)

Name of Official ______________________ Date of Contest ______________________

Location of Contest __________________ Opponent ____________________________

Report of Concern:

________________________ ____

Date Signature of Coach

________________________ ____

Date Signature of Athletic Director

cc: Assignment Chair
Official
Athletic Director Files

Figure 10-17
Secretary's Job Description

Title:	Athletic Secretary
Qualifications:	Knowledge of sports Organizational skills Technology skills Ability to work with interruptions
Reports to:	Athletic Director
Performance Responsibilities:	

Assists athletic director in ordering buses for all away contests.

Prepares purchase orders for request of equipment.

Supervises the receipt of equipment and organizes bills for payment.

Provides assistance with contracts and scheduling.

Coordinates deposits of money from entry fees and lost equipment.

Supervises the ordering of awards for athletic contests.

Prepares the programs and invitational sheets for all sports.

Develops rosters for all interscholastic sports.

Responsible for submission of scores to sport liaisons.

Evaluation:

Performance of job will be evaluated annually by the athletic director.

It should be shared with everyone in the department and modified periodically to reflect the changing perceptions and expectations of persons who work with the secretary routinely. Then it should be used by a representative group of coaches and others who will constitute the department's interviewing committee. They will formulate questions and develop a schedule—in conjunction with the AD, of course—to interview candidates for the position.

Prior to the actual interviews, distribute the reproducible in Figure 10-18 to give the committee some sample questions to consider before they meet with each candidate. Many of these questions promote thoughtful responses from candidates and provide insights into their motivation and strength of character.

Following each session, you should meet with the interviewing committee to discuss their impressions of each candidate. Figure 10-19, Interview Feedback, should be shared with them to promote some kind of preliminary input before the meeting. This reproducible requires them to give some thought to their impressions, and it gives you the opportunity to identify a few key elements in their reactions to discuss at greater length. Both reproducibles are taken from Mike's *Department Head's Survival Guide*; they can be modified for use when hiring coaches and others in the athletic program. As athletic directors are indeed department heads, you would undoubtedly find a great many other useful reproducibles in that book as well.

LET'S WRAP IT UP

Once again, we find ourselves emphasizing relationships in this section. We do so for good reason. Very little in education, let alone coaching, is possible without solid working relationships with our colleagues. The athletic department would stumble over a trail of busted equipment and mediocre facilities without the competent intervention of the maintenance department. Smart athletic directors, therefore, establish trusting, if not always warm, working relationships with maintenance and custodial personnel.

"Prudent" and "survivor" are words that describe the athletic director who establishes effective relationships with maintenance personnel and with the person in the building or district office who controls the purse strings. These individuals are critically important if you seek to provide the best possible equipment and facilities for coaches and student athletes.

We have identified several others who also play an important role in the delivery of the athletic department's programs. Faculty members who volunteer time away from home to supervise athletic contests perform an invaluable service for the athletic department. Usually, they are teachers who enjoy sporting events as well as informal associations with students. They also appreciate the few extra dollars that reward their efforts.

Develop a form similar to the one in Figure 10-20 to establish a policy and procedures governing the identification, assignment, and reimbursement of such personnel. Notice that it fails to include the hourly rate; it is likely to change each year or to vary according to geographic location. You also will want to include the teachers' specific reporting and ending times. Such information assures that everyone is on the same page regarding time commitment and reimbursement.

Finally, the voucher in Figure 10-21 will be useful to you as you process and document reimbursement. Notice that it provides copies to the district's financial officer, the athletic department, and the staff worker. The more professionally staff workers are accommodated, the more likely they are to continue offering their time to assist with crowd control and ticket taking. Faculty members who repeat from year to year provide a level of experience that is hard to duplicate.

When we find teachers who relate well with parents, maintain friendly but firm relationships with students, and arrive and depart at the right times, we have found assets to the program. And we all know that assets must be handled carefully if they are expected to pay the kinds of dividends we require to survive in our jobs. It's important, therefore, that we maintain friendly relationships with them and provide levels of reimbursement that compensate (if that's ever possible) for their time away from home.

Well, that brings us full cycle. We started and concluded this section with a discussion of relationships. In fact, much of this book has been devoted to the importance of relationships. Athletic programs, for that matter, entire schools, are a great deal more than programs and procedures. They are groups of people who bring their special needs to school each day and satisfy them through the associations they develop with others in the building, especially with their department heads and principals.

To the extent that we as athletic directors promote the satisfaction of such needs, we improve the quality of services delivered to students and parents, and we provide a wholesome environment for everyone involved in the school's athletic program. Such an environment is the necessary first step in developing a successful and winning program. To that end, we hope this book has been helpful.

Figure 10-18
Sample Interviewing Questions

The kinds of questions we ask each candidate ultimately reveal the kind of information we need to make a hiring decision. Several different elements within the candidate's background must be explored. Following are some sample questions you might think about—or use—before each interview.

Job-focused questions:

What was your biggest achievement in your last job?
What failures did you experience in your previous job?
How did you learn from them?
Of everything you did on your last job, what did you like best? Least?
For what kinds of things did your former employer compliment you?
Criticize you?
How have you adjusted your secretarial style within the past ____ years?
What current topic in your profession do you find most promising? Why?

Personality questions:

MOTIVATION

Why did you decide on secretarial work as a career?
What is your long-term career goal?
What do you seek in this job that you can't find now?

RELATIONSHIPS

What is it you like about your former employer's methods of supervision? Dislike?
What kinds of activities do you most enjoy?
How do you feel about the movement toward collegiality in the work place?

ADAPTABILITY

What do you do differently now that you didn't do five years ago?
What are some of the biggest problems you faced in the last ____ years?
If you had to keep your current job, how would you change it?
How do you plan to improve your performance within the next few years?

STRENGTH OF CHARACTER

What has been your biggest professional disappointment?
How did it change you?
Whom do you routinely seek out when you're having problems?

Figure 10-19
Interview Feedback

Candidate's Name: ______________________________

Committee Members:

____

____

____

____

____

Following are the impressions of the committee regarding the above-named candidate. This feedback includes reference to our perceptions of the candidate's stability, resourcefulness, energy, social and professional skills, goals, job expectations, and "fit" with the rest of the department.

We plan to review each of these feedback documents before making our final recommendations.

Figure 10-20
Sample Athletic Workers Contest Fees

Contests	Contest Payment
Indoor Contest (1 level)—Ticket Takers/Crowd Control	$30.00
Indoor Contest (2 levels)—Ticket Takers/Crowd Control	$35.00
Indoor Contest (1 level)—Table Personnel	$35.00
Indoor Contest (2 levels)—Table Personnel	$40.00
Outdoor Contest (1 level)—Ticket Takers/Crowd Control	$40.00
Outdoor Contest (2 levels)—Ticket Takers/Crowd Control	$45.00
Outdoor Contest (1 level)—Table Personnel	$45.00
Outdoor Contest (2 levels)—Table Personnel	$50.00

Please Note:

All athletic workers will be paid on their regular paychecks on the 15th of the month.

Appropriate deductions will occur on paycheck from wages earned.

Priority job assignments will be based on seniority in working athletic contests.

Figure 10-21
Pay Voucher

School District
_____–_____ School Year

Please check the appropriate sections that apply:

_____	Official	_____	Crowd Control
_____	Table Personnel	_____	Ticket Taker

Sport

_____	Badminton	_____	Basketball	_____	Baseball
_____	Soccer	_____	Track	_____	Wrestling
_____	Swimming	_____	Cross Country	_____	Gymnastics
_____	Tennis	_____	Football	_____	Volleyball
_____	Softball	_____	Golf	_____	Other

Please print information below:

Name	Date of Contest
Address	City, State, ZIP
Social Security Number	Athletic Administrator's Signature

-------------------------- **For Administrative Use Only** --------------------------

_______ $ Fee to be Paid   _______ Date Sent to Payroll

White Copy—Payroll Office
Pink Copy—Athletic Office
Blue Copy—Payee